SUPPLY AND MARKETING CONSTRAINTS
ON LATIN AMERICAN
MANUFACTURING EXPORTS

Edited by
Hugh H. Schwartz

Published by the Inter-American Development Bank
Distributed by The Johns Hopkins University Press

January 1991
Washington, D.C.

The views and opinions expressed in this publication are those of the author and do not necessarily reflect the official positions of the Inter-American Development Bank.

**SUPPLY AND MARKETING CONSTRAINTS
ON LATIN AMERICAN MANUFACTURING EXPORTS**

© Copyright 1991 by the Inter-American Development Bank

Inter-American Development Bank
1300 New York Avenue, N.W.
Washington, D.C. 20577

Distributed by
The Johns Hopkins University Press
701 West 40th Street
Baltimore, Maryland 21211

ISBN: 0-940602-35-0

TABLE OF CONTENTS

PREFACE

Work on this study began in 1981, when Cecilio J. Morales, then manager of the Economic and Social Development Department of the Inter-American Development Bank, requested a study of Latin American manufacturing exports that would go beyond the basic data and the most common concerns being expressed at that time. Although the delay in completion of the effort has been unfortunate, it is much clearer now than it was in the early 1980s, that shifts in demand side factors are not enough to elicit the large and sustained increases in Latin American manufacturing exports that have been so fervently sought.

Initial drafts of the chapters were submitted during the period 1981–85, and all were revised in 1989 in an effort to take account of the important comments by two anonymous reviewers. Chapter I also benefitted from observations by Máximo Jeria, Elio Londero, Montague Lord, Raymond Magloire, René Monserrat, Uziel Nogueira, Clifford Pratten, Simón Teitel and Francisco Thoumi. Jorge Ruíz Lara and John Elac were the supervisors closest to the study and provided assistance and encouragement in various ways. Willem Daniels made many suggestions to help improve the presentation, and José Núñez del Arco and Paul Raimondi rendered truly invaluable editorial assistance. Sonia Berríos Carroll typed the initial drafts, and the expanded chore in 1989–90 was undertaken by María Teresa Coleman and Amada Fernandez.

Hugh H. Schwartz

INTRODUCTION

Hugh H. Schwartz,
Inter-American Development Bank*

The debt crisis currently occupies center stage in much of the analysis of the Latin American economies, and rightly so. One of the effects of the crisis has been to underscore a reality that was already clear before August 1982—namely, that the foreign exchange earnings that the region has been generating do not reach the level needed to import the goods and services essential for the level of development sought by Latin America. Moreover, the foreign exchange gap is now less likely than before the crisis to be filled by large increases in foreign investments, or by borrowing from abroad as in the 1970s (even if there were a political disposition for the latter solution, which, in most of the countries, there is not). In part, as a response to the debt crisis, the countries of Latin America have turned increasingly to exporting manufactured goods as a way of tapping a major new source of foreign exchange earnings. In this they were clearly influenced by the remarkable export-led growth of a number of East Asian economies, whose success they wished to emulate.[1]

The region's exports of industrial products, which had grown appreciably in the 1970s, have indeed risen further since 1984 in those

---

[1]On the latter, see Bela Balassa, "Exports and Economic Growth: Further Evidence," *Journal of Development Economics*, vol. 5, no. 2 (June 1978), pp. 181–190; and Gershon Feder, "On Exports and Economic Growth," *Journal of Development Economics*, vol. 12, nos. 1–2 (February–April 1983), pp. 59–74. Howard Pack notes in a recent survey article that exports are viewed as generating a greater growth of production as a result of: a) greater capacity utilization in industries in which the minimum economic scale of plant is large relative to the domestic market; b) greater horizontal specialization as each firm concentrates on a narrower range of products; c) increased familiarity with new technologies; d) greater learning by doing insofar as exports permit greater output; and e) increased stimulation (and pressure) to achieve internationally competitive prices and quality. Pack, "Industrialization and Trade," in Hollis Chenery and T.N. Srinivasan eds., *Handbook of Development Economics*, vol. I, (Amsterdam: North Holland, 1988), p. 349.
*Currently, Visiting Professor CEIPOS, University of the Republic, Montevideo, Uruguay.

countries in which a more outward-oriented strategy has been emphasized. Nevertheless, these exports remain small in relation both to world
trade in manufactures and to the total output of manufacturing industry
in the region. Mexico and Brazil are becoming exceptions (even though
their new export strength derives as much from weakness in the domestic
market as from increased competitiveness). Accordingly, some of the
best explanations of the growth of Latin American manufacturing exports have dealt with industries in those two countries—with the assembly industry in Mexico and the automotive and steel industries in
Brazil, in particular. The present volume touches on both countries'
successes. Chapter I deals with the assembly industries in the context
of the trend toward international specialization at the component level,
and Appendix A gives a brief account of the export successes of both
Brazil and Mexico in the 1970s and 1980s.

The main objective of this book, however, is the analysis of supply
and marketing constraints on Latin American manufacturing exports.
The analysis addresses basic factors not always taken into account when
considering exports, especially when short-run solutions are emphasized.
The study is directed primarily toward those in government who for-
mulate and implement policies, and it attempts to provide guidelines to
help them to deal with the issues directly or to specify more fully what
is needed from outside specialists. The study should prove useful also
to trade association officials and to producers who seek to influence
policy, as well as to students of Latin American industrialization generally.

Chapter I discusses the major considerations at issue. Chapter II
deals with economies of scale and exports of manufactures. Chapter III
offers a case study of the contribution of learning to the development
of manufacturing exports in Brazil and makes reference also to comparable developments in Argentina. Chapter IV provides a case study
of the importance of marketing in developing Peruvian exports of manufactures and describes the full range of microeconomic and macroeconomic considerations that helped shape the initially successful but
ultimately somewhat disappointing outcome.

Much has been written about the problems Latin America faces in
attempting to increase exports of manufactures. This literature has emphasized demand side constraints, taking note, in particular, of the close
correlation between the growth of Latin American manufactures exports
and the growth of income in the OECD.[2] In the early 1980s, the growth
of Latin American manufactures exports slackened, coinciding with

---

[2]See, for example, Inter-American Development Bank, *Economic and Social Progress in
Latin America*, 1982 Report (Washington, 1982), Chapters 1 and 5.

recession among Latin America's major trading partners—attributable initially to the oil price shock and subsequently to the adoption of deflationary policies in those countries. These factors did reduce the demand for Latin American manufactures abroad (and ultimately within the region itself), *nevertheless they did not have nearly as adverse an effect on OECD demand for manufactures from East Asia*—a point we shall come back to later. The continuing decline of certain traditional industries such as garments and shoes in the advanced industrial nations fostered an increasing protectionism there that threatened to limit even further the growth of markets for Latin American production; this protectionist cloud has in fact continued, despite economic recovery in the United States and in Europe in the second half of the 1980s.

Latin America has negligible influence on these demand side factors—only very limited weight in mitigating foreign protectionism and a very minor and indirect effect on the growth of national income abroad. But there are other non-demand-related reasons that the region's exports of manufactures have been disappointing. One that has been given a great deal of attention has been the Latin American countries' own role in discouraging sales of their manufactures abroad: 1) by erecting protective barriers and overvaluing the local currency, thereby providing greater incentives for sales in the local market than in foreign markets; 2) by not providing compensating export promotion measures (though GATT regulations regarding some of those measures may have understandably contributed to the reticence); and 3) by not assuring that exporters and potential exporters had access to internationally priced primary and intermediate goods.[3] When the price signals were finally altered and the disincentives to produce exports were finally reduced, few local Latin American manufacturers found themselves in a position to take advantage of the new export opportunities. The technology and scale of their facilities, their product mix and marketing capability, and, indeed, the level of efficiency of their everyday manufacturing operations were often simply not up to international competition. Moreover, given the long history of regional anti-export bias, industrialists aware of political realities could hardly be expected to believe that sudden changes in price signals were likely to herald a permanent trend; there-

---

[3]For an analysis of the importance of these factors and related means of implementing an even-handed policy toward exports, see Yung Whee Rhee, *A Framework for Export Policy and Administration: Lessons from the East Asian Experience*, Industry and Finance Series, vol. 10 (Washington: The World Bank, 1984). Rhee documents the East Asian tendency toward a "neutral status" development strategy, which enables exporters to compete with foreign competitors in world markets on an equal footing, and the noticeable but less strong tendency toward "extended neutral status," which would assure equal incentives between export and import substitution forms. For the full study, see Rhee, *Instruments for Export Policy and Administration: Lessons from the East Asian Experience*, World Bank Staff Working Paper no. 725 (Washington, March 1985).

fore only a limited revamping of plant and equipment or market reo-
rientation could be anticipated.

Latin American governments' need to "get the prices right" has
received a great deal of attention in the literature. There has also been
some discussion of the need to provide export financing comparable to
that offered by competing countries (notably the countries of East Asia),
and limited acknowledgment has been made of the degree to which the
complexity and pronounced discretionality of many Latin American
administrative procedures relating to exporting (and to importing essential raw materials and components to manufacture those exports)
have discouraged some potential exporters. Beyond that, there have
been forceful but often rather general observations on the failure of
Latin American governments to take a more active and effective role
in developing their countries' export potential, in stimulating the organization of export trading companies, and in otherwise encouraging
producers and traders to respond more energetically to export opportunities abroad. Several other factors, not often mentioned by Latin
Americans but cited by foreign authors comparing Latin American and
East Asian growth experiences, are the region's more controlled labor
and capital markets,[4] its lack of "fundamental policy reforms" that would
facilitate a shift of entrepreneurs from inward-oriented to export-oriented
growth,[5] and its rapid inflation (which may or may not be a serious
constraint, considering Brazil's export success over the past two decades
and, the moderate attention that price stability has received in Korea).

Yet in contrast to the statements of only a few years ago, an increasing number of students of the Asian experience are now uncertain
as to whether the Asian countries' changes in relative prices and even
the other factors mentioned are quite enough to explain the economic
successes of those countries. One author contends that if we are truly
to understand Asia's export growth we must focus on the transformation
process—i.e., on the technological change, managerial experience, and
social and organizational relations within the factories which determined
productivity gains—and on the high level of subcontracting and the
leadership role of the state.[6] Another author cites a need to explore
more systematically the growth of skills as a necessary factor in facili-

---

[4]Bela Balassa, "The Lessons of East Asian Development: An Overview," *Economic
Development and Cultural Change*, vol. 36, no. 3 Supplement (April 1988), p. S282; and
Gary S. Fields, "Employment, Income Distribution and Economic Growth in Seven Open
Economies," *Economic Journal*, vol. 94 (March 1984), pp. 74–83.

[5]Ching-yuan Lin, "East Asian and Latin America As Contrasting Models," *Economic
Development and Cultural Change*, vol. 36, no. 3 Supplement (April 1988), pp. S153–
S198.

[6]Martin Fransman, "International Competitiveness, Technical Change and the State: The
Machine Tool Industry in Taiwan and Japan," *World Development*, vol. 14, nos. 11–12
(Nov.–Dec. 1986), pp. 1394, 1389–90.

tating the export-led expansion of the East Asian newly industrialized countries (NICs).[7] Yet another suggests the usefulness of examining cultural factors in explaining that region's economic development,[8] an observation often expressed informally among economists analyzing Latin America but not usually taken into account in the models they use to recommend policy changes. Two other analysts insist that the question still to be answered satisfactorily in explaining recent East Asian growth is the following: What, precisely, were the factors that enabled those countries to expand their supply *so greatly* in response to the favorable incentives and expanding world markets?[9]

Finally, a major study on Korea that became available in mid-1989 contends that in this arguably most spectacular example of East Asian growth, the leadership role of the state was the critical factor, with the state intervening to distort relative prices deliberately in its efforts to stimulate economic activity.[10] The state intervened to "get the relative prices wrong," the 1989 Amsden study maintains—particularly the exchange rate and the price of long-term credit, the latter of which is characterized as "wildly wrong." The state did something else: it exercised considerable discipline over private firms, penalizing poor economic performance and rewarding favorable results, evaluating economic performance in terms of production and operations management (rather than financial indicators), and especially in terms of success in meeting export targets (Amsden suggests that some exports probably were not profitable but were conditions for important producer subsidies, direct and indirect, received in producing for the domestic market). The primary factor that made the Korean success possible, that explained the dramatic increases in exports amid often appreciating exchange rates, was high productivity—facilitated by the government's concern with the economic performance of enterprises, by the strong educational base that Korea built in a very short period, and by the greatly increased rates of saving and investment that government policy had helped stimulate.[11] Amsden lists as the direct means to the high

---

[7]Howard Pack, "Industrialization and Trade," especially p. 339.

[8]Vernon Ruttan, "Cultural Endowments and Economic Development: What Can We Learn from Anthropology?" *Economic Development and Cultural Change*, vol. 36, no. 3, Supplement (April 1988), pp. S247–S271.

[9]Chung H. Lee and Seiji Naya, "Trade in East Asian Development with Comparative Reference to East Asian Experience," *Economic Development and Cultural Change*, vol. 36, no. 3. Supplement (April 1988), pp. S149–S150.

[10]Alice Amsden, *Asia's Next Giant: South Korea and Late Industrialization* (New York: Oxford University Press, 1989).

[11]An article by Cristian Moran points to the importance of domestic capacity and suggests that adjustment programs designed to encourage exports should promote domestic investment, improve the quality of infrastructure (particularly in transportation and communications), and provide other services essential for exports: "A Structural Model for

(footnote continued)

productivity: 1) Korean producers' imports of foreign technology; 2) their scale of output sufficient to minimize unit costs; and 3) their use of technical assistance to learn how to use the imported technology efficiently.[12]

The present analysis takes supply side elements of industrial economics that have been overlooked in the traditional focus on the demand side and incorporates them into the analysis of manufacturing exports. Lack of attention to supply side factors is unfortunate. The importance of being able to produce large quantities of internationally marketable products at low cost on a continuing basis must be recognized, not only in order to take advantage of doors now open but also to lessen the likelihood that doors now open will be closed. This effort entails maintaining or increasing the margin of comparative advantage, and in this way developing consumer interest groups in the countries to which exports have been initiated. Although most analyses of manufacturing exports from Latin America note the importance of GDP growth in the OECD countries and of the exchange rates in Latin America, there has probably never been a sustained growth of manufacturing exports anywhere in the world based solely on rapid growth of the world economy (or of the principal target economies) or on currency valuations that gave producers the incentive to produce for overseas markets. Rather, major gains in productivity have been essential to all of the recent major expansions in manufacturing exports. This importance of productivity is noted in several of the studies on Asia cited earlier and in Chapters I and III of the present study.

Although no one has actually come out and denied the importance of supply side factors in explaining the level of exports, most discussions of how to increase manufacturing exports have thus far had relatively little to say about supply factors despite the fact that the Latin American countries are in such a good position to influence them. The object of the present study is to examine some of these relatively overlooked elements. The focus is on the limits to Latin America's ability to compete internationally in manufactures as a result of basic considerations of production costs and producer level shortcomings in marketing, including, in the case of the latter, the failure to provide the supply side feedback essential for successful exporting over the course of time.

Developing Countries' Manufactured Exports," *The World Bank Economic Review*, vol. 2, no. 3, September 1988, especially p. 333 (with respect to domestic capacity, see also Appendix B on price elasticity estimates).

[12]Also contributing were: (1) the tendency of firms to hire engineers rather than administrators and to use many at the shop floor level; (2) the tendency to maintain a lean operation; and (3) the prevalence of motivated workers—motivated not by traditional organizing rights and benefits (which, in fact, they did not enjoy) but by the opportunity for on-the-job learning (including formal schooling required by the government) and by sharply increasing remuneration.

CHAPTER I

FACTORS AFFECTING THE SUPPLY OF MANUFACTURING EXPORTS: AN OVERVIEW

Hugh H. Schwartz,
Inter-American Development Bank

Introduction

Many factors help determine Latin America's supply of manufacturing exports. Topography, location and economic infrastructure play a role, as do the local availability and relative prices of various inputs. National economic policy exercises multiple influences, and, in particular, shapes the basic incentives necessary for orienting production beyond the domestic economy, while marketing capability determines the extent to which producers take advantage of opportunities abroad. Nonetheless, probably the key supply-side elements for obtaining sustained increases in manufacturing exports are: (a) selection of appropriate technology and investment in production facilities which provide a potential for economies of scale and scope; (b) mastery of production processes and use of best-practice techniques; (c) appropriate international specialization—increasingly at the component rather than product level; and (d) ongoing technological learning, including the adaptation and subsequent modification of products and production processes. All four elements are greatly influenced by the signals of national economic policy, but much also depends upon the particular patterns of managerial decision-making and entrepreneurial response.

This chapter provides an overview of the factors affecting the supply and marketing of manufacturing exports from Latin America and summarizes the case studies presented in Chapters II through IV.[1]

---

[1]The differences between *cultural and behavioral patterns* in East Asia and Latin America are often assumed to be of importance in explaining the difference in recent economic trends in the two areas (see Ruttan, *op. cit.* concerning East Asia), but they will not be dealt with in this analysis. Some behavioral factors of a psychological nature appear to be of consequence in explaining export behavior, and are dealt with briefly in conjunction with factors already listed.

Topography, Location and Economic Infrastructure

Topography, location and economic infrastructure can be quite important for countries seeking to emphasize exports. Clearly the recent increase in the industrial exports of Mexico to the United States—in finished products as well as assembly components—is attributable in part to proximity, as is the assembly industry activity of the Caribbean Basin. For Latin America as a whole, problems of topography, location and economic infrastructure appear to have represented no more than a mild constraint on the development of manufacturing exports, except possibly in Bolivia and Paraguay (location), Colombia (topography), and the Caribbean nations for products other than assembly industry components (location—or rather, the small-nation, island character of the countries), although economic infrastructure may have been moderately limiting in many countries.

The physical isolation of some countries or their distance from large international markets limits their ability to compete in those foreign markets—though not necessarily in others which are closer. Thus, Paraguay is at a disadvantage in competing in Europe or the United States, but not necessarily in Argentina and Brazil, and certainly not in the neighboring Argentine Provinces of Chaco and Formosa or the Brazilian State of Paraná. However, comparative advantages and thus the gains from trade are likely to be smaller if trade is limited largely to such nearby markets. The degree to which topographical barriers inhibit export trade depends upon their nature and location, and the degree to which (and the cost at which) infrastructure is constructed to overcome those barriers.

Even in the absence of major barriers, the building of economic infrastructure—the construction of roads, the dredging of rivers and coastal harbors, and the establishment of public power plants, gas and water works and communications networks—can be a key factor in facilitating industrial competitiveness. This is perhaps most evident with respect to electric power generation, in which the economies of scale can be a crucial factor regarding the ability of even moderately energy intensive products to compete internationally.

The Availability and Relative Prices of Production Inputs

Agricultural and Mineral Raw Materials

Difficulties which affect primary-sector production or marketing limit the availability of domestic raw material inputs needed for the manufacture of many exportables. This, in turn, limits the ability to obtain the foreign exchange needed to import raw materials, parts and machinery required to produce many other exports. The problem, sometimes aggravated by price controls, probably has been more important for some of the smaller, least industrialized countries, though it has been a concern in most of the countries of the region at one time or another.

The Relative Prices of the Factors of Production

Differences in the relative prices of inputs affect the comparative advantage of particular manufactures. While the traditional focus has been on the contribution of inexpensive labor to labor-intensive manufacturing exports, and to policies which have tended to alter the relative price of that factor of production, changes in the relative price of other inputs may have been another source of difficulty. The extraordinary increase in the relative price of energy was a worldwide problem for a relatively energy-intensive sector such as manufacturing for several years beginning late 1973, and then again in the 1979–80 period. Its impact was particularly sharp for Brazil, Central America, Panama and the Caribbean. Since then, energy conservation has been greatly increased, technological changes have reduced energy intensity in some industries, and, in the last few years, energy prices have declined relative to those of other inputs, but the pre-1973 assumptions about inexpensive energy and the stability of energy prices no longer prevail, with adverse implications for some countries and certain industrial exports.

Human Resources

Human resource limitations that might affect Latin America's capacity to export manufactures include lack of a "critical mass" of skilled workers, engineers or scientists; an imbalance between skilled workers and professionals; lack of foremen and supervisory personnel; and a scarcity of capable managers, particularly those with experience in handling large-scale operations.[2] These factors affect all manufacturing, but in each category the comparative situation of a country helps determine its competitive strength relative to that of other nations. To the extent that some Latin American countries have overvalued currencies which are politically difficult to set aright, it might be possible to offset (or reduce) any wage-cost disadvantage of that tendency by increasing em-

---

[2]Some distinction must be made between those situations in which there is a scarcity of such persons in the country despite efforts to attract them from abroad and train them at home, those situations in which there is a scarcity of such persons of local citizenship but little effort has been made to attract others from abroad, and those situations in which the scarcity is due in part to the emigration of many skilled persons from the country— for any of various reasons.

phasis on human resource development (particularly as an alternative to the more commonly used export subsidies, which are more likely to lead to countervailing duties).

There are no studies that provide even rough estimates of the significance of major human resource factors in explaining the ability of individual industries to export. Yet certain differences in human resources would seem to lead to major differences in the ability to export manufactures, while others are of negligible consequence, either because products are exported that are less dependent on human resources or because the deficiencies can ordinarily be alleviated quickly by short courses, by on-the-job or evening programs, or by attracting those with the necessary skills from other countries.

The human resource endowment of a country reflects both public and private sector decisions, but public sector expenditure is not always critical to achieve or correct certain human resource deficiencies. Training the needed specialists in the enterprises themselves or contracting specialists from abroad may raise costs over what they would be if specialists were available locally in considerable numbers and had been trained at government expense. However, there also may be added benefits (due to the specificity of the training, which may, in turn, offset part of the risk that those receiving the training will leave their position before their employers are compensated for their added costs). In any event, the costs ordinarily would be smaller, relative to the benefits obtained by an enterprise, than in the case of electric power, road construction or other physical infrastructure.

National Economic Policy

A wide range of national economic policies have tended to limit the growth of industrial exports from Latin America. First and foremost (apart from a general anti-export bias, where that has existed) have been the various constraints on importing raw materials, intermediate goods or capital goods which are required to develop internationally competitive output. This problem has plagued many countries of the region, particularly those which have most emphasized import-substituting industrialization.[3] Second, there have been difficulties in the basic fi-

---

[3]Marcelo Diamand, an Argentine industrialist and economist, identifies foreign exchange problems as the key (and chronic) bottleneck for industrial production and, along the lines of the two gap analysts of the 1960s and early 1970s, for economic development as a whole. He defines a bottleneck as the insufficiency of an item not very significant in terms of its own value but essential for the carrying out of an activity of a much greater value. Marcelo Diamand, "Towards a Change in the Economic Paradigm Through the Experience of Developing Countries," *Journal of Development Economics*, vol. 5, no. 1

(*footnote continued*)

nancing of industries likely to develop manufacturing exports, and even in financing manufacturing exports. This has been a general problem, seriously affecting all countries, with the possible exception of Mexico (and, until recently, Venezuela). Third, relatively little has been done to advance project identification—to help identify product lines that warrant more detailed appraisal, particularly in the smaller and industrially less advanced countries where such assistance could have been most used. Fourth, there have been a number of other government policies that have been widespread throughout the region, though of varying impact on manufacturing exports—and this often adverse effect on exports extends also to the manner in which those policies have been implemented. Among the most prominent of the policies have been those which relate to employment and labor relations, government purchasing policies and price controls, while the chief concerns with respect to implementation have related to the bureaucratic procedures affecting production and trade. Finally, in many countries the large number of regulations affecting manufacturing for export and the lack of continuity of policies and policy implementation have led to major fluctuations in the net incentives to export, increased difficulty in ascertaining those net incentives, and created uncertainty greater than in other regions of the world concerning the likely trajectory of those incentives.

Constraints on Importing Essential Inputs

Protectionist restrictions and, more recently, the lack of foreign exchange with which to import raw materials, intermediate goods, and capital goods inputs have often been cited as leading constraints on industrial development and, perforce, on the development of internationally competitive manufacturing exports. Only a few comments on this point are made here, in part because of the widespread acknowledgment of the phenomenon, but primarily because alleviation of the problem now seems to lie primarily with macroeconomic policy more than with the microeconomic detail emphasized in this analysis.

Examples of difficulties in importing inputs due to limited foreign

---

(March 1978), pp. 20, 26, 30, and *Doctrinas Económicas, Desarrollo e Independencia* (Buenos Aires; Paidos, 1973), pp. 20, 28, 33, 34, 55. A broader view of the bottlenecks concept can be found in Hugh H. Schwartz, *Bottlenecks to Latin American Industrial Development* (Washington, D.C.: Inter-American Development Bank, 1983), and "Industrialization Bottlenecks and the Development of Industrial Technology," *Technovation*, vol. 3 (Fall 1985), where it is maintained that bottlenecks to industrial development are those impediments to a smoothly functioning process of industrialization that are costly to overcome, cannot be easily or rapidly (i. e., inexpensively) circumvented and do not generate a rapid or strong corrective response. The lack of such a response may be due to the nature of the impediment itself or to a limited capacity to adapt, which may in turn be rooted in institutional arrangements or behavioral characteristics.

exchange earnings were noted for several countries, even during the period before the debt crisis, in the report, *Bottlenecks to Latin American Industrial Development*, just cited.

In some cases, the protectionist limitations on imports referred to above clearly lowered export potential, and in others, they may well have done so. The significance of such restrictions was greater for exports than for overall industrial output inasmuch as the domestic markets were generally protected, but it is difficult—and increasingly less accepted in the international community—to provide the compensation needed to place exports on a competitive footing. The importance of these protectionist limitations on imports varies considerably from country to country and from industry to industry. There are undoubtedly many cases in which the use of local inputs (or inputs from within common market or free trade groups) has raised the cost of the finished product to a level 3 to 10 percent or more above that of international competition. This has led to an exaggerated notion of Latin American industrial inefficiency, as Daniel Schydlowsky has long pointed out.[4]

Until the onset of the debt crisis in the second half of 1982, producer difficulties in importing needed inputs were attributable to protection more than to balance of payments problems, and because the former were more likely to lead to expected (and the latter, to unexpected) difficulties in importing key inputs, producers were better able to prepare themselves in advance for the dominant form of import constraint— and even to mount lobbying efforts to change the situation.

Since the latter half of 1982, however, it has been payments pressures that have most constrained imports, and although that kind of constraint is now more predictable than before, the extent of the constraint has been so great that perhaps only Brazil, among all the countries of the region, has been able to succeed to any notable degree in substituting for formerly imported inputs at costs approximating international levels (even though not in the information technology industry). The added cost due to the use of inputs that are protected or that have become difficult to import because of balance of payments problems can be quantified, and the dissemination of this information may be enough in some cases to focus attention on the conditions under which the inputs in question are produced and to foster some measure of cost reduction accordingly. This possibility might be increased, moreover, if such calculations were coupled with estimates of the additional domestic sales and the potential for penetration of foreign markets which the cost-facilitated price reductions might lead to. These types of quantitative exercises are not yet common practice, but they may prove as cost-

---

[4]Schydlowsky, "Short-Run Employment in Semi-industrialized Economies," *Economic Development and Cultural Change*, vol. 19 (April 1971), pp. 391–413.

effective in stimulating exports as the estimation of effective rates of protection or domestic resource costs analyses, and perhaps even more so.

Financing Industrial Production and Exports

Although the favorable rates of growth achieved in Latin America in the 1960s and 1970s seem to suggest that financing was not as serious a problem for industrial development as many economists writing in the 1950s and 1960s had anticipated, the way in which financing needs were resolved appears to have had an adverse impact on the evolution of industry. Equity investments were discouraged by capital market controls. Credit markets were distorted by usury laws that left real interest rates low and even negative in many countries through much of the 1960s and 1970s, leading to credit rationing. Short-term credit with rollover arrangements became the dominant form of loan availability in many countries of the region. A few activities were especially favored with long-term loans, but many of these involved government enterprises for which the economic rate of profitability was not always a principal concern and for which exports were rarely an objective.

Problems were accentuated in several countries in the late 1970s as increasingly overvalued exchange rates in combination with more open capital markets led to sharply higher domestic real rates of interest in local currencies. Dollarized local loans became more common, and many firms turned increasingly to foreign credit markets. Both those using foreign and those using domestic credit markets, were hit hard, however. First came the international repercussions of the dramatic tightening of U.S. credit policy in the 1979–80 period. Then, though average international interest rates declined in 1981, Latin American credit ratings plummeted with the onset of the debt crisis in the second half of 1982, and the real rates that regional borrowers had to pay rose again. The difficulty of obtaining new funding intensified, even for export projects. On top of this, as devaluations became more pronounced (at times leading to the undervaluation of currencies in some countries) the balance of Latin America's loans outstanding from foreign lenders rose extraordinarily in terms of local currencies, further weakening Latin American industrial enterprises.

There are three components of the financial constraint affecting the export of Latin American manufactures: export financing itself (including pre-export and post-shipment financing), the general financing of working capital, and the financing of industrial investment. Export financing itself is not a serious problem in the larger countries of the region (nor in a few of the others, as far as pre-shipment financing is concerned), thanks to the establishment of substantial government programs to supplement commercial arrangements from domestic institutions and some foreign sources.[5] Such foreign as well as domestic financing of manufacturing exports has long been common for traditional agricultural exports with only limited manufacturing value added. Pre-export financing, or the financing of working capital (and even fixed capital, in some cases) to underwrite production for which export contracts have been made, is common only in the larger countries, however. General financing of fixed assets conditioned upon export performance (or at least promises to export certain target levels), is of consequence for only a few categories of manufacturing exports in Mexico and Brazil, notably the automobile industry.

The main financing obstacle to exports arises from the basic nature of industrial financing in Latin America. Equity markets are so weak that most entrepreneurs have solely their family and friends to turn to for shareholder support. Only a small volume of long-term credits is available, and that has often been rationed, using non-market criteria because frequently this credit is subsidized (though such subsidization became less common and quantitatively less significant in the 1980s). Medium-term funds are somewhat more available, from banks and investment companies, but the allocation of these funds, too, has sometimes been subject to other-than-strictly-economic criteria. The scarcity of long-term and even medium-term sources of financing means that there is a bias against projects whose economic and financial justification requires longer gestation periods.

This leads to financial signals that undoubtedly cause entrepreneurs to underinvest in some product lines in which the country might have a comparative advantage potential, and it results in the development of facilities without as good a potential for yielding minimum unit costs as would be the case if financing were no more of a constraint than in a more advanced industrial economy. Even if the productive facilities were equal and endowments as well as technology were identical, differences in the cost of working capital could change comparative advantage.[6] This general problem is aggravated by what has been referred to as the need for financial compatibility, the need for enterprises to have financial structures compatible with the capital market structure of a country and the monetary policies of the government.[7] The situation can become particularly acute in periods of increasing inflation, when the type of

[5]Even so, export financing is much more limited in Latin America than in the countries of East Asia. See Yung Whee Rhee, *Trade Financing for Developing Countries*, draft, Washington; The World Bank, February 1989.
[6]Kenneth Kletzer and Pranib Bardhan, "Credit Market Patterns of International Trade," *Journal of Development Economics*, vol. 27 (1987), p. 69.
[7]Francisco Thoumi, "Financial and Real Sector Interaction in the Economy," draft, Washington, 1983.

financing obtained can be the key to enterprise profitability because even enterprises whose projects have a satisfactory rate of economic return can be forced into bankruptcy due to difficulties in meeting payments or in arranging for refinancing.

Decisions by foreign creditors to reduce trade credits to individual Latin American countries predate the current debt crisis, and a portion of the curtailed credits would have been used to finance imported inputs for manufactures to be exported. Such reductions accompanied fears of individual country debt crisis in some cases and fears of political instability in others. When the cutbacks occurred, there were inevitably even larger cutbacks in the medium-term credits from abroad as well. The result was adverse both for short-term exports and for building the longer-term basis of future exports. Short- and medium-term foreign credits were replaced primarily by short-term domestic credits, and the level of the external cutbacks was rarely fully counterbalanced by increases in domestic funding.

Moreover, the tendency toward increased domestic budget deficits in many of the countries of the region meant that an increased proportion of available domestic credits went to finance government debt and were not available for the financing of the industrial sector, because of either credit allocation decisions or the "crowding out" effect which raised interest rates. Efforts such as the IDB Industrial Reactivation Program helped alleviate the problem in the 1983–85 period, as have some World Bank Structural and Sectorial Adjustment Programs in the mid- and late 1980s, but they have not been able to fill the huge financing gap that has developed.

The effect of all of this, in addition to the general recessionary trend in most countries of the region in the 1980s, has been to reduce greatly the level of industrial investment, thereby leaving without funding some projects that might have developed exports and lowering the elasticity of supply response of those lines of output that continued to be exported. The exports forgone as a consequence of the unavailability or higher costs of financing undoubtedly are large and may be almost of the order of magnitude of those exports that actually were realized.

Lack of Government Assistance in Project Identification

The lack of analyses designed to identify sector and subsector projects may be even more serious for industrial development generally than for the development of industrial exports, but it has serious consequences for the latter as well. One might imagine that products with favorable prospects for export would have looked so attractive financially as to enjoy smooth sailing. Yet in Mexico, the countries of the Caribbean, Uruguay, and elsewhere, there have been major, at times feverish, and not always successful efforts first to uncover activities with emerging comparative advantage.

Analyses of revealed comparative advantage, domestic resource cost and effective rates of protection have figured prominently among the techniques most employed by economists and government officials to identify product lines presumed to be worth emphasizing and encouraging. These concepts were not developed for the purpose of identifying future areas for resource allocation, however, and there are major limitations to their use for that purpose over and above the obvious ones of not being able to take account of sectoral and inter-industry interdependencies and not being able to provide much guidance on shifts already underway in many relevant supply and demand side elements.[8]

A number of methodological approaches have been used to help detect projects that offer promise in economic terms.[9] An analysis of domestic resource costs provides only point-in-time indicators of efficiency but has become more widely employed and can serve as a useful starting point for identifying product lines and even projects that are good candidates for detailed cost-benefit appraisals. This is true *only* if consideration is also given to half a dozen categories of adjustments and their varying impact on the initial ranking of products. Products related to those already manufactured, other products manufactured by similar techniques, and at least a few products that represent entirely new undertakings also should be taken into account if there is to be meaningful identification of areas of competitive strength.

The analysis of the initial group of products must be revised to take at least some account of the potential for each product afforded by the following:

(i) Increased capacity utilization;
(ii) Improved operational efficiency; ·
(iii) Economies of scale through increased product specialization;
(iv) Economies of scale as a consequence of larger plants, multiplant operation, and economies of scale in distribution;

---

[8]For a strong (but apparently minority) view on the lack of a relation between measures such as the effective rates of protection and domestic resource costs on the one hand, and the industrial activities with the best growth potential, on the other, see J. Bhagwati and T. N. Srinivasan, "Trade Policy and Development," in R. Dornbusch and J. A. Frenkel eds., *International Economic Policy* (Baltimore: Johns Hopkins Press, 1979).

[9]For a discussion of the advantages and disadvantages of alternative approaches to sector studies aimed at project identification, ranging from analytically simple exercises to process analysis studies and semi-input-output studies, see Schwartz, "Industrial Project Identification in an Integration Context," pp. 126–144 in José Núñez del Arco, Eduardo Margain and Rachelle Cherol eds., *The Economic Integration Process of Latin America in the 1980s* (Washington: Inter-American Development Bank, 1984); and Arie Kuyvenhoven, "New Industrial Planning Techniques; Macro, Sectoral and Project Linkages," in UNIDO, *Industry and Development*, no. 5 (1980), pp. 18–40.

(v) Use of more appropriate (in the sense of more efficient) production technology; and

(vi) Benefits of externalities, such as those provided by learning, and the costs of others, such as environmental pollution.

Consideration of new products must include the same factors. The end result would be a new product ranking that might have little in common with the initial point-in-time analysis. Moreover, because so many elements would be based on very rough estimation, the reordering might be in terms of, say, three to five groups of descending competitive strength (rather than individually, in declining order, as in the point-of-time evaluations).

Small increments in operational efficiency may entail negligible added costs, and there need not be any measurable costs to achieving at least an initial level of benefits from learning. Similarly, small increments in capacity utilization may not entail much in the way of additional costs and may not entail any increase in fixed costs. For the most part, however, to take account of the adjustments listed—to increase specialization and scale of operation, to consider the use of alternative technologies (with, perhaps, some adaptation), to substantially increase producers, capacity utilization or operational efficiency—all would require significant additional costs including some (often major) additions to fixed costs in order to achieve the added benefits, as do the learning curve experience and the elimination of problems of environmental pollution.

Even such a preliminary ranking of activities requires consideration of the net effect of decisions involving additional expenditure—and attention may have to be given to some industry interdependencies as well. Moreover, what is involved is the *process* of industrialization, and that process may be affected by physical, institutional, and behavioral factors. If these factors approach the bottleneck stage, attention to means of alleviating or bypassing bottlenecks also would have to be taken into account.[10] Thus, serious project identification depends as much upon engineering data as on the record of past economic performance, and it may depend even more upon interdisciplinary information about ongoing processes. Efforts to ignore this and concentrate on data from the past (data that reflect only realized market transactions) at the expense of information on constraints to industrial development, cannot be expected to be very helpful in characterizing the probable relative profitability of industrial activities in the future, even if consideration is

---

[10]See Schwartz, "Industrialization Bottlenecks and the Development of Industrial Technology," *op. cit.*, pp. 300–303, and Schwartz, "The Potential Role of Behavioral Analysis in the Promotion of Private Enterprise in Developing Countries," *Columbia Journal of World Business*, vol. XXIII, no. 1 (Spring 1988), pp. 53–56.

limited to product lines in which technological change is not a major factor (which, of course, it should not be).

Although there is not much professional agreement on the methodology of sector studies aimed at project identification, the approach just outlined is considered further in Appendix C.

Other Impacts of Government Policy and Policy Implementation

A number of generic aspects of government activity can help foster the growth of manufacturing exports, while their absence can inhibit that growth. To begin with, it is useful to have a political leadership committed to growth and cognizant of the contribution that exports can make to meeting that objective, directly or indirectly.[11] Second, it is desirable for the relevant government bureaucracies to have a sense of mission—a demeanor sometimes made difficult by low levels of remuneration and serious exceptions to what could be termed a merit system. Third, it is important that any tradition of gratuities that may exist not interfere with success by the most efficient producers. The fourth is perhaps the most serious hurdle of all in Latin America: pervasive and often heavy-handed bureaucratic regulation. This regulation tends to hit foreign trade more than domestic commerce and is often more of a problem for exports than for imports, particularly since exports usually incorporate imported inputs as well.

No one has estimated the degree to which bureaucratic red tape leads to delays, higher costs and even to decisions not to attempt to export—but these results undoubtedly are common in many Latin American countries. It is noteworthy that the East Asian "superexporters" have given as much attention to the improvement of official regulations as to macroeconomic policy changes.[12] Finally, it is necessary to recognize that there is much that we do not understand about what makes for competitiveness—which should serve as a caution to excessive intervention and regulation by even the best-intentioned policy makers. At the same time, particularly favorable producer response to incentives is often associated with what can be characterized as strong entrepreneurship—which is an argument for establishing the general conditions that enable entrepreneurship to thrive.

Employment regulation can raise costs and make a country's products less competitive internationally (particularly the more labor-intensive products), and appears to be a problem in many Latin American

---

[11]According to W. Arthur Lewis, "the engine of growth should be technological change, with international trade serving as a lubricating oil and not as a fuel." Lewis, *The Evolution of the International Economic Order* (Princeton, N.J.: Princeton University Press, 1978), cited in Pack, "Industrialization and Trade," p. 371.

[12]See Rhee, *A Framework for Export Policy and Administration, op. cit.*

countries. What may most inhibit production for exports, however, are regulations that limit temporary work and, in so doing, constrain the ability of manufacturers to take advantage of temporary markets or markets whose longevity cannot be well gauged. The countries that may be most disadvantaged by this are those with an underdeveloped assembly industry potential. In such cases, only a small group of workers benefit, but sizable employment gains may be forgone elsewhere in the economy and there is a cost to the country as a whole as a consequence of its being somewhat less able to earn foreign exchange and reap the benefits of trade. This understanding has led, in recent years, to the introduction of major changes in the labor laws of several countries in the region, particularly for "temporary workers" or for workers generally in export-oriented free zones.

Lack of restraint of market power can lead to situations in which domestic producers have to pay more for domestic inputs than foreign buyers of those same inputs (see also discussion of economies of scale). This may not be a frequent problem nor one of great magnitude but it does tend to raise the costs of some local production that would enter the international market, and it can occasionally be important (as seems to have been the case, for example, in the early 1970s for Colombian garment producers who exported in competition with foreign producers, but sometimes paid more than foreign producers for Colombian textiles).[13]

Government purchases are important for some industries, and an absence of government purchasing plans may inhibit exports insofar as it discourages long-run enterprise planning and the establishment of a sufficiently large and efficient production base in individual industries. This would be true for machinery and heavy capital goods, and for other industries requiring a relatively long lead time. It probably is more serious in discouraging production generally than in discouraging exports, however. A regular source of demand (that a government could provide) may be a necessary condition in a small-to-medium size market, but it is hardly sufficient and cannot be expected to lead to exports in most cases.

Signals from government edicts or from policy implementation that change, offset each other, or simply are not sufficiently clear are a general problem constraining productive activity. Occasionally they affect exports in particular, as when there are both incentives and disincentives to export a particular product, some of which change over the course of time. A few economists have attempted to estimate net in-

---

[13]See David Morawetz, *Why the Emperor's New Clothes Are Not Made in Colombia* (Oxford: Oxford University Press, 1981).

centives,[14] but some of the incentive to export doubtless is lost when signals are mixed, changeable or somewhat inscrutable rather than consistent and clear.

Traditional Economic Considerations: Choice of Technique/ Appropriate Production Process, and Economies of Scale/Cost Minimization

This section considers two issues often mentioned in conjunction with industrialization in developing countries. The first of these is the question of choice of technique and the appropriate production process. The second is economies of scale and related issues of cost minimization. Failure to select the most appropriate production process from those available may be of importance in the manufacture of a moderate number of products—in auxiliary if not always in core production processes—and in the export of those products by the lower-income countries, especially to other low- to middle-income countries. The second concern, economies of scale/cost minimization, appears to have broader implications for Latin American manufacturing exports. Many Latin American manufacturers are not in a position to minimize costs because their facilities are smaller than necessary to achieve optimum economies of scale, and because even the potential of those facilities is not realized due to the tendency towards capacity underutilization and short production runs.

The search for production process alternatives has always received a certain measure of attention, particularly from industrial engineers seeking to achieve some technical objective, cope with the unavailability of certain raw materials, or reduce costs. But the options they take into consideration tend to be restricted to those derived from their own personal experience, along with perhaps the best publicized examples of the professional group with which they have worked most closely. In some cases this means that a wide range of processes actually in use somewhere in the world are *not* taken into account—not even if changes in the local situation lead to a major shift in the prevailing relative prices.[15] The failure to select the most appropriate technology, or to

---

[14]See especially William Tyler, "Trade Policies and Industrial Incentives in Brazil, 1980–81," manuscript, Instituto de Planejamento Econômico e Social, Rio de Janeiro, August 1981, revised subsequently as "Effective Incentives for Domestic Market Sales and Exports: A View of Anti-Export Bias and Commercial Policy in Brazil, 1980–81," *The Journal of Development Economics*, vol. 18, nos. 2–3 (August 1985), pp. 219–242.

[15]Limitations in the selection of the most appropriate production processes also may arise from an inability or an unwillingness to pay as much as is demanded by a foreign licensor. This may be due to a purchaser's reticence, the exercise of control by a government regulatory board, or a foreign company's unwillingness to "unpackage" the technology and license only those components of the production process that are really sought.

come even reasonably close to it in some industries characterized by large numbers of stop-and-go operations such as metalworking and woodworking, is an obstacle to efficient industrialization in Latin America that may be of consequence to those countries in the lower-to-middle per capita income range.

Choice of Technique/Appropriate Production Process

Studies of production technique alternatives show that, to a significant degree, differences in relative factor prices determine the appropriateness of production technology in discrete-process (batch type) and semi-process industries, and that they also play a role in ancillary continuous-process activities.[16] Among the most striking conclusions of the study by Pack on the subject is that the size of investment required to construct a plant large enough to attain maximum economies of scale is typically half as great if use is made of an appropriate technology such as a (slightly) adapted version of the process employed in more advanced industrial economies (in some non-process industries, investments can be even more sharply reduced).

Pack has also shown that the more appropriate technology, while increasing the financial profitability of an undertaking, also can raise employment opportunities by a factor of two, three, and even five in various non-process industries. In those industries, the investment required per job created can be a fifth or less of that needed when the more capital-intensive technique is used. The often cited need of more skilled workers in the more labor-intensive process does not always hold, and where it is true, there are often extraordinarily favorable benefit-cost ratios for the required training expenditures.

Pack has shown that if the wages of a developing country are very low and production techniques used are as capital-intensive as in advanced industrial countries, then simply by responding to market prices, it would be possible to increase manufacturing value added by more than 70 percent, non-wage income by 50 percent and employment and wage income by 300 percent (these are gross benefits before subtracting the opportunity cost of labor in its current employment). Most Latin American countries have higher wage levels and do not employ technology as capital-intensive as assumed in the study cited, but there appears to be some opportunity in many countries of the region to increase value

---

[16]See Howard Pack, *Macroeconomic Implications of Factor Substitution in Industrial Processes*. World Bank Staff Working Paper no. 377 (Washington; World Bank, 1980), revised as "Aggregate Implications of Factor Substitution in Industrial Processes," *Journal of Development Economics*, vol. 11 (1982), pp. 1–37. In most cases the appropriate technology is a combination of what Pack maintains are compatible processes from a number of plants.

added, profits and employment and to reduce prices to consumers simply by selecting more appropriate production techniques.[17]

Insofar as the use of a simpler or "more appropriate" technology modifies product characteristics, it also will affect export potential: in lower-income markets, added sales are likely to result from a lowered price, but in middle-to higher-income markets, such as those to which Latin America has been orienting most of its new manufacturing exports, any change in quality that is assessed as a lowering of standards is likely, for many product lines, to result in reduced sales even at the lower price. The overall impact will vary according to the products involved and the markets to which exports are oriented.

Traditional Cost Minimization Concerns

(i) *Economies of Scale*
In the survey "Industrialization and Trade," prepared for the *Handbook of Development Economics*, Howard Pack notes that "the role of scale economies in the industrial development process has not been the focus of sustained analysis in recent years despite robust evidence that the minimum efficient scale of plant is quite large [Pratten (1971)]."[18] This section is addressed to that subject. The most usual reference is to the economies of scale that are facilitated by turning to international trade, but the focus here is primarily on the degree to which Latin American failures to exploit economies of scale or scope may have limited the growth of manufacturing exports from the region. The section draws heavily on the study prepared by Clifford Pratten for the volume and on a chapter by William Cline for another publication of the Inter-American Development Bank.[19]

Economies of scale refers to the more than proportionate increase in output that accompanies proportionate increases in inputs for at least some range of production in the case of virtually all products. Average unit costs decline, reflecting economies of scale in a single plant, in multiplant operations, in marketing and distribution, and product design and in research and development (R&D) generally.

---

[17]For a discussion of the reasons why manufacturers might not exploit the gains available and of steps that might be taken to lead to the selection of more appropriate technologies, see Schwartz, *Bottlenecks to Latin American Industrial Development*, pp. 36–38.

[18]Hollis Chenery and T. N. Srinivasan eds., vol. 1 (Amsterdam; North Holland, 1988), p. 343. Several exceptions are noted, however.

[19]Clifford F. Pratten, "Economies of Scale and Latin American Exports," Ch. II in this volume, and William R. Cline, "Economies of Scale and Economic Integration in Latin America," in Eduardo R. Conesa and José Núñez del Arco eds., *Terms of Trade and the Optimum Tariff in Latin America* (Washington: Institute for Latin American Integration and Inter-American Development Bank, 1984), pp. 233–277.

Some evidence has been marshaled on each of these areas, but the most seriously regarded group of empirical studies deals with economies of scale at the plant level and is based on "engineering" estimates including estimates by managers, engineers, accountants and sometimes industrial economists. Such estimates of individual activities are regarded as preferable to those based on census data, but engineering estimates do nevertheless involve the use of judgments. Moreover, in the last analysis, they are estimates of *hypothetical* operations, some of which might not be borne out in practice.

The studies confirm the prevalence of an L-shaped curve for most industries, with average costs dropping sharply as the scale of facility increases, and then leveling off. The range in which the latter takes place (where a further doubling of scale would reduce unit value added by less than 5 percent, for example) has been referred to as minimum efficient size (MES) and minimum optimum size (MOS), and estimates have been made relating the MOS to consumption in a number of countries. In theory, a firm could construct an MOS facility and plan to export what was not sold in the home market, but in practice most manufacturers insist upon having the experience (and, if possible, the protected experience) of producing for the local market before they are willing to face international competition and the uncertainty arising from economic trends and policies over which they have no control and little influence.[20] A producer has (even) less influence over economic trends and trade policies in other countries than at home, but an international broadening of the market may provide greater stability as many major shifts in some countries are offset by those in others, or their impact on the overall market is reduced by the presence of market segments that are less volatile.

Two problems arise in applying available MOS data to Latin America. First, most of the data in the studies referred to reflect the technologies of the late 1960s and early 1970s. A great deal of technological change has taken place since then, increasing the size of the MOSs in many cases and reducing it in others, such as in some phases of automobile production. Second, shifts have taken place in relative prices,

---

[20]Some domestic entrepreneurs with small home markets do invest in MOS facilities with the express purpose of producing primarily for export (particularly in the case of textiles and processed agricultural commodities), some foreign investors do so if permitted, and other domestic manufacturers may respond to incentives such as subsidized credits and protection to construct larger-than-national-market size facilities even if the incentives are only for a limited "learning" period (as, e. g., in Korea). In any event, it has been contended that an orientation to export may be the key to the specialization needed to realize full economies of scale and that only the plants that employ "best practice" production runs are those that export. Howard Pack, *Productivity, Technology, and Industrial Development. A Case Study in Textiles.* (New York: Oxford University Press, 1987), pp. 44, 98.

with certain forms of capital becoming more expensive relative to labor than previously. Third, in developing regions such as Latin America, capital is more expensive relative to labor than in the more advanced industrial countries in which those calculations were made (particularly imported capital). This is probably even truer now than in the late 1960s and early 1970s in both financial and economic terms, due in considerable part to the elimination of much of the earlier subsidization of capital.

The international shift in relative prices may have had its greatest impact in accelerating the case against older, less energy-efficient plants and in favor of newer facilities. Beyond that, however, the shift in relative prices may have offset some of the tendency of technological change to increase the size of MOS in certain industries. The difference in relative factor prices in Latin America would reinforce that tendency, at least for those industries for which capital-labor substitution is feasible. The engineering estimates of the late 1960s and early 1970s may thus provide a plausible first approximation for many industries in Latin America, other than those that are energy-intensive.

In a study undertaken six years ago, William Cline cited data from the late 1960s to early 1970s indicating that for the 20 product lines that he considered,[21] the domestic market was large enough to absorb the full output of an MOS plant in most of the product lines (only) in the larger countries, approximately half of the product lines in the medium-sized countries, but only two or three product lines in such small markets as Bolivia, Haiti and Honduras. This was used as an argument for Latin American economic integration, but if the list of products were extended from 20 to 200 or 2,000, there would be many more product lines in which the inability to capture economies of scale because of the size of the domestic market would not be a constraint on the development of internationally competitive industrial exports. This would make an extraordinary difference in foreign exchange earnings potential—assuming no more than current levels of difficulty of access to foreign markets.[22] Among such product lines it is likely that there would be some

[21]Beer, cigarettes, cotton fabrics, gasoline, shoes, cement, steel, refrigerators, batteries, flour, newsprint, sulfuric acid, synthetic rubber, cellulose, detergents, tires, electric motors, autos, aircraft, and bicycles.

[22]Unfortunately, some domestic manufacturers who are potentially competitive internationally but who use inputs produced by local monopolies or oligopolies which have attained the requisite MOS may see their drives to export adversely affected if local market power is exercised and the inputs are sold for much higher prices locally than internationally (the predicament of the garment producers of Colombia in the 1970s). In any event, a firm in a very small country with an MOS production facility may find it more profitable to exploit its market power in the domestic economy rather than enter international competition, where average unit revenues would certainly be lower. Exports from underutilized capacity should contribute to profits as long as the marginal costs are below the export prices, but several facts may inhibit enterprises from making such exports

(footnote continued)

in which the advantage of having domestic demand large enough to accommodate the output of an MOS facility is currently offset by having two or more plants producing the product in question. The protected learning experience of those enterprises might nevertheless have provided them with enough production experience to enable them to take advantage of export opportunities. In some cases the opportunities for export may be clear enough actually to trigger production with an MOS facility.

In some product lines, especially in medium-sized to larger countries, the most serious impediment to the establishment of an MOS facility that might look toward export markets after a break-in period of two to five years might lie in the requirement that a person managing the size facility necessarily be of local citizenship, even if no qualified individuals are available. Also, in some relatively raw-material-intensive industries it might not be easy to find experienced and able managers willing to live in the remote locales that are often most advantageous for low-cost production.

Cline's analysis helps underscore the degree to which lack of economies of scale can constrain opportunities for industrial exports. The extraordinary growth of manufacturing exports from East Asia is characterized by a great deal of attention to long production runs and other economies of scale, but it began in activities with relatively small MOS such as clothing. Small-MOS activities still account for a large share of East Asian manufacturing exports from countries other than Japan and possibly Korea. Much of Latin America's recent growth in manufacturing exports also has been in relatively low MOS activities, but in addition there has been remarkable growth in activities characterized by intermediate and large MOS. Some of this growth reflects serious recession at home, variable cost pricing, and even subsidized exports rather than production in MOS facilities. However, an increasing amount of it would seem to suggest that in the larger countries of the region domestic consumption can absorb all or most of the output of MOS facilities and either that the companies have achieved average unit costs low enough to make export activity highly profitable *or that they are required to export in order to be able to import or to qualify for favorable credit or fiscal treatment.*

There is a "survivor" argument worth noting. In Latin America, perhaps even more than in East Asia, manufacturing exports are dominated by large firms—apparently even more so today than a decade

---

a major thrust of their activity. A major marketing effort may be required that entails both a kind of investment expenditure and often, in a closely held business, unaccustomed trust in an "outsider." Also, new import restrictions abroad or erratic domestic incentives to produce for export cause uncertainties that may lead to a decision against making the necessary investment in marketing.

ago.[23] Some of this is a reflection of public policies that favor large enterprises—or industries dominated by large enterprises result from bureaucratic difficulties which are relatively more onerous for smaller firms. But part of it may also reflect the importance of economies of scale in the manufacture and marketing of the particular products exported. The domination of manufacturing exports by large companies may even indicate that Latin America has not exploited low MOS activities as well as Asia. In part, this reflects the fact that less attention has been paid in Latin America than in Asia to trading companies, to operational efficiency in smaller enterprises, and to other factors referred to elsewhere in this chapter. Finally, one prominent international economist has noted that a number of concerns and heterodox views about those concerns have been tied together by the contention that dynamic economies of scale can play a crucial role in international specialization.[24]

(ii) *Short Production Runs and Low Capacity Utilization*
Just as they tend to discourage the construction of MOS plants, the small size of many domestic economies, combined with producer reluctance to target a large proportion of output toward the international market often give rise to short production runs and a low level of production specialization.[25] On the other hand, long production runs tend

---

[23]Many economists have observed that, except for a few countries (notably Taiwan), exports of manufactures are dominated by large firms and that the ratio of exports to output is higher for large firms than for small. See Albert Berry, "Firm (or Plant) Size in the Analysis of Trade," a paper prepared for the WIDER Conference on the New Trade Theories and Industrialization in the Developing Countries, Revised Version (November 1988), pp. 5, 7, 31–32, and 49, citing several studies to that effect. Substantiation of the importance of larger enterprises in exports from Colombia during the period 1975–83 can be found in Juan A Pinto S. and Juan I. Arango F., *La Pequeña y Mediana Industria en Colombia. Situación y Perspectivas* (Bogotá: Universidad Externado de Colombia, 1986). Of course, the exports of larger firms include indirect exports from smaller subcontractors, and that phenomenon has been growing in several countries in the region. Also, in the case of the Caribbean Basin countries, the rise of the assembly industries has led to more exports from medium, if not large, enterprises. In Mexico, large firms appear to be gaining in importance, except for assembly exports, particularly because of the recent rise of automobile components produced by major foreign companies. In Brazil, large companies also predominate, especially because of the importance of such capital-intensive activities as steel, transportation products, and chemicals. Even in such resource-based activities as orange juice, export success has been attributable to large facilities with major economies of scale (for an indication that the role of small enterprises in Taiwan's export successes may have been exaggerated, see Amsden, *Asia's Next Giant*, pp. 161–164).
[24]Paul Krugman, "The Narrow Moving Band, the Dutch Disease, and the Competitive Consequences of Mrs. Thatcher. Notes on Trade in the Presence of Dynamic Scale Economies," *Journal of Development Economics*, vol. 27, nos. 1–2 (October 1987), pp. 41–55, esp. 53.
[25]Government policies often accentuate the tendency towards short production runs, as when protection takes the form of comprehensive restrictions on imports; occasionally
(footnote continued)

to generate major economies of scale, however—although certain recent innovations, such as those reducing die set-up times, have decreased the differences. In the case of some individual industries, estimates of economies of scale and of the optimal length of production runs can be found in technical publications, along with estimates of the increase in average unit costs of producing at 75, 50 or 33 percent of the optimal scale and the minimum optimal production run.

The author has interviewed several hundred primarily medium-sized producers for IDB socioeconomic studies over the past decade. The results suggest that many enterprises, in making production and investment decisions, are not aware of the magnitude of the cost advantage of larger scale or longer production runs, primarily because they do not consider data on production and investment for levels of output significantly larger than those they are accustomed to (the domestic market or a portion thereof). Moreover, such supply-side information is rarely found in economic analyses and public-policy expositions dealing with industrial production and the possibilities of manufacturing exports. The extent to which such knowledge might overcome the reluctance to invest in larger-scale facilities and to attempt the longer runs with a view toward venturing into foreign markets is a matter of speculation, but publicly available data along such lines might well repay the expense of its preparation.

Some manufacturers utilize their equipment virtually full-time with a series of short production runs (though not without some loss of efficiency), as in the case of certain stamping, forging and other metalworking establishments. In some cases, this is an example of economies of scope for the equipment in question. But, more often, production runs that are too short to take advantage of economies of scale reflect underspecialization or low utilization of productive capacity.

A great deal has been written about underutilized capacity in Latin American manufacturing. Estimates of such capacity have been prepared in many countries, although unfortunately there are many definitions of what is meant by full capacity. Economists have argued about the phenomenon, but all tend to attribute much of the underutilization of capacity to rational producer response to price signals resulting in large measure from prevailing public policies. There has been considerable discussion of the consequences of the phenomenon and of ways to take advantage of underutilized capacity in order to alleviate both employment and balance of trade problems by producing manufactures for export.[26]

---

[26]See especially the writings of Daniel Schydlowsky in the 1970s and 1980s, beginning with Schydlowsky, "La política de empleo a corto plazo en las economías semi-indus-
(footnote continued)

Much of the latter argument provides an economic justification for exporting in the short run at prices that do not cover replacement costs—underscoring the ability to generate exports without new investment. A substantial portion of the initial wave of Brazilian manufacturing exports in the late 1960s to early 1970s was of this type, as was the further surge of Brazilian exports in 1984 and apparently again in the 1987–88 period (though a number of the exports initiated in that way became much more cost-competitive in ensuing years). Much of the dramatic increase in Mexican exports beginning in 1984, as well as the surge in certain Argentine exports in 1988, reflected the same sort of fuller utilization of capacity, again in response to prices that did not cover full costs, but that helped enterprise profitability while contributing to employment and improving the balance of payments. Some Colombian exports have been of this type as well as much of the increase of Peruvian exports in the 1976–81 period, described in Chapter IV. There is a slight difference, however, in that an important component of those Peruvian industrial exports—textiles, in particular—would not have been possible without the sizable modernizing investments undertaken just prior to the period in question.

The ability of the region's smaller economies to capitalize on underutilized capacity in the same manner has been another matter. The initially somewhat disappointing experience of Costa Rica is instructive in this respect. During the late 1970s, Costa Rica began to experience increasing economic difficulties. Although many of these were of domestic origin, in the late 1960s to early 1970s there was also a slowdown in the growth of Costa Rica's manufacturing exports to other Central American countries, attributable to the payments problems within the Central American Common Market, the political turmoil in the isthmus, and the overvaluation of the Costa Rican currency (which increased 20 to 25 percent during 1979–80). In December 1980, a series of devaluations was initiated that increased the real effective exchange rate during 1981, and although much of the change was eroded in 1982, the real effective exchange rate nevertheless remained well above the 1970 level through 1985 and improved further after that time (there was also international pressure for trade liberalization, which also would have favored exports, but little was accomplished in that respect). Even so, in 1980–81 foreign and domestic economists and businessmen anticipated major increases in manufacturing exports within six to twelve months.

That expectation was based on three factors. First, capacity utili-

trializadas," *Económica* (La Plata, 1968), and Schydlowsky, "Short Run Employment in Semi-industrialized Economies," *Economic Development and Cultural Change*, vol. 19 (April 1971), pp. 391–413.

zation was low—only 40 percent in the first half of 1981—and declining. Second, there were new incentives to use that capacity to produce for export markets outside Central America, as a result of the devaluation, the Tax Credit Certificate (Certificado de Abono Tributario or CAT), and the expansion of credits for export financing (at preferential, negative real rates) just when credits for domestic activity became more difficult to obtain. In addition, the incentive schemes for the assembly industry were amplified at a time when Costa Rica's formerly high real wage rates were declining and when U.S.-owned operations in politically more volatile countries were looking for new locations, as were textile plants in Asia affected by U.S. quotas under the Multi-Fiber Agreements. As a result, many new assembly firms were established in Costa Rica at that time (other major export incentives were added—notably exemption from income taxes on profits earned from exports—but not until 1984 and 1985). Third, there was a new emphasis on international marketing which the Government of Costa Rica and the U.S. Agency for International Development encouraged by means ranging from training and subsidized visits abroad to studies identifying products which were produced in Costa Rica (or which could easily be produced there), and for which the United States already had come to rely on imports. In a related development, Costa Rica became eligible for the Caribbean Basin Initiative of the United States. BANEX Trading, the offshoot of a successful private bank, estimated that the mix of factors would lead to additional exports of $50–$60 million outside Central America within a year or so, and without any further investment.

Total exports of manufactures from Costa Rica declined 25 percent from 1980 to 1984 because of the increased difficulties of selling in Central America, but manufacturing exports other than foodstuffs to the United States increased from $58 million in 1980 to $123 million in 1984, or at a compound rate of 14 percent in constant dollar terms. Although this was a remarkable performance, considering that 1982 and 1983 were years of international recession, it was less than the rate of increase of Mexico, Brazil, and, in particular, several Asian countries in the same years. It also fell short of the expectations of many Costa Rican firms, most of which were unsuccessful in their attempts to export even in such a relatively favorable year for international trade as 1981. Those that succeeded (other than the assembly industries) were primarily enterprises that had reacted to the increasing difficulties of exporting to Central America and had begun to reorganize their product mix and/or production processes even before the 1980–81 devaluations. Those firms had made some improvements in productivity or had undertaken some additional investments despite their very large underutilized capacity.

There were four reasons for the limited nature of the initial Costa

Rican success, and these are highly relevant to the general advocacy of producing for export from underutilized capacity.

First, the tradition of Costa Rica's trade and exchange rate policies had been strongly biased against exports, particularly for exports beyond Central America. Then, just when producers needed clear indications that the new incentives were going to remain in place, there were such fluctuations in the exchange rate in 1981—the year in which incentives to export reached their peak, with the real effective exchange rate rising fully 200 percent—that perception of the trend line of incentives appears to have lagged badly for some producers, and for others there even may have been doubts about its permanence. Although most analyses cite monetary and fiscal factors for the relative lack of producer response in 1981, this problem of producer perception and the other problems noted below appear to have inhibited some production and thus to have contributed to the sharp inflation of 1982, which, by year-end, had eliminated most of the recently created exchange rate incentive to export. The initiation of export contracts and other measures again raised the incentives to export as of 1984. These measures, along with the more flexible exchange rates beginning in the 1985–86 period, must have finally convinced producers that the years of anti-export bias were over.

Second, manufacturing exports did not increase as rapidly as had been anticipated because there had been unrealistic assessments of the potential for taking advantage of underutilized capacity. Some of the capacity was not suited to producing exports, particularly for advanced industrial economies—in some cases because the scale was too small and in others because the technology was not recent enough. At the very least, equipment modification or the introduction of new auxiliary equipment would have been required, along with major improvements in the productivity of existing facilities and in improved product design engineering. Indeed, those were just the sort of activities undertaken by the handful of firms that did succeed in increasing exports substantially. By 1984, the Industrial Trade Association was proposing expanded programs of industrial extension services in order to assist small and medium-sized enterprises, and by 1985 plans were being drawn up for cooperative activities with the government.

Third, it was becoming increasingly clear that marketing efforts would have to be much more substantial and better conceived than those that most firms had attempted. If a trading company meant to succeed, it was going to have to be more specialized, and it would need sales staff able to explain clearly to producers why products were not selling.

Fourth, manufacturing exports were disappointing at first also because of constraints arising from a number of underlying problems, such as the cumbersome customs procedures for handling exports (and the imported inputs required), the limitations of economic infrastructure (especially port services and other transportation), and the lack of skills in certain export-related activities.

Private and public sector officials took note of the problems and began to correct them. The incentives to export were increased substantially, by tax measures in the 1984–85 period and also by further devaluations beginning in 1985. In addition, the Industrial Trade Association and the public sector have shown concern for product and process adjustment; in some cases this has provided a critical stimulus to individual enterprises. The result has been an increase in nontraditional exports to destinations beyond Central America, averaging nearly 40 percent annually in the 1986–87 period, and over 30 percent in 1988.[27]

Many of the factors that prevailed in Costa Rica also apply in other small countries. In addition, in all countries small and medium-sized firms accustomed to protection appear to need special measures of assistance from their government or industrial trade associations before they will respond to export incentives.

Developing countries that utilize capacity more fully and that export from small or less-than-optimal technology plants at less than full replacement costs are sometimes only attempting to stave off economic and sociopolitical collapse. Nevertheless, there is an increasing international tendency for such variable cost exports to be categorized as dumping and treated accordingly. For this reason, it may make sense to consider investments that would upgrade production processes and transform existing facilities to MOS. Fuller utilization of existing capacity to produce for export markets should still be undertaken in those cases in which plant scale is less than MOS but sufficiently large to make costs internationally competitive or in which successes growing out of familiarity with an international market environment stimulate new investments in plants of MOS large enough to attain internationally competitive costs within a short time (before other countries apply antidumping measures).

Mastery of Production Processes/Use of Best Practice Techniques

One of the most striking aspects of industrial productivity in Latin America is the large divergence between the high operational efficiency evidenced in many of the region's internationally competitive activities and

---

[27]For a more upbeat account of Costa Rican exports of manufactures, covering the longer period 1965–87 (but also noting certain problems that have impeded growth), see Forrest D. Colburn and Ivan Saballos Patino, "El impulso a las ventas no tradicionales de Costa Rica," *Comercio Exterior* (Mexico), vol. 38, no. 11 (Nov. 1988), pp. 1027–1032.

the low levels of efficiency in many other activities that produce exclusively for the home market under heavy protection. Physical output per worker in the latter is often much lower than in more industrialized countries even with comparable equipment. Yet analyses of Latin American assembly industry operations, U.S. multinationals operating abroad and data on certain successful Latin American-owned industries all show that physical output per worker in these facilities sometimes equals and, in a few cases, exceeds leading international standards. Such Latin American enterprises are well represented in the group of exports, and it is likely that more widespread attention to operational efficiency would increase opportunities for export in a number of product lines.

Two examples of this potential are suggested by experiences in Colombia, on the one hand, and a contrast between experiences in Brazil and Uruguay, on the other. Admittedly, Colombia probably would not have achieved its significant exports of metal products in the 1970s without export incentives and (in the latter part of the decade) a slowdown in the rate of growth of GDP, but even those stimuli would not have been enough to bring about exports of most fabricated metal products in the 1960s, given the high costs, uneven quality, and small production runs of most metalworking plants in the country at that time. Little of the comparative advantage of this group of industries revealed in the late 1970s can be attributed to major increases in investment, accelerated technological know-how, or changes in product mix.[28] The key factor making increased exports possible may have been an improvement in operational and distributional efficiency. If so, more attention should be given to measures to increase x-efficiency for this reason and also because of the externalities that, through the effects on that large proportion of output consumed domestically, provide the economy as a whole with even greater benefits. Low levels of x-efficiency also may provide an important part of the explanation as to why even devaluations involving substantial reordering of relative prices often do not succeed in generating much supply response from exportable lines of output.

A hypothesis concerning improvements in operational efficiency as a potential means of facilitating exports might receive some support if improvement in production and distribution efficiency in the metalworking industries of Colombia between 1970 and the late 1970s were documented—or rather, if some of the critical information had been recorded throughout the period and a study had been prepared using that data. Even so, the potential value of such an effort justifies outlining

---

[28]See, e.g., Luis Alberto Zulueta, Juan Luis Londoño de la C. and Jose Dario Uribe E., "The Colombian Capital Goods Sector and its Technological Development," working Paper presented to the International Labor Organization, Geneva, 1982.

the kinds of considerations necessary to ascertain the role of changes in x-efficiency in facilitating or impeding industrial exports in other situations, which is done in Appendix D.

Another example of the importance of operational efficiency may be provided by developments in Latin American shoe exports during the 1970s. Footwear was a sector in which both Brazilian and Uruguayan manufacturing exports achieved major successes in the 1970s. The product was based on the processing of local raw materials and was relatively labor-intensive. Labor costs were by then much lower than those of major producers in Europe and the United States. Strong international demand helped a great deal, particularly in the early 1970s. Uruguayan devaluations and export subsidies furnished new incentives to produce for foreign markets and, indeed, to invest in new capacity to produce for those markets, and this in fact occurred in both countries. The subsequent rise in the price of leather, the levying of some antidumping duties by the United States, the reduced incentive to produce for foreign markets that accompanied the 1978–81 appreciation of the Uruguayan and Brazilian currencies, and the onset of international recession by late 1981, all caused some difficulties for Brazilian and Uruguayan shoe exports, especially the latter. Much sharper cutbacks were registered in Uruguayan exports and in overall shoe production despite the fact that Uruguayan producers had lower raw materials costs, while their labor costs had declined almost to the level of those in Brazil.

Although overvaluation did become much more of a problem in Uruguay than in Brazil, some of the explanation for the extraordinary difference in shoe-export performance appears to lie with supply-side factors—differences in the scale of operations and lengths of production runs between typical Brazilian and Uruguayan plants (some of the latter were well below the one-third MOS example of the textbook comparisons on economies of scale), differences in the degree to which product lines were adapted to changing demand abroad, and differences in operational efficiency between the typical Brazilian and Uruguayan facilities. The first two factors have been cited on a number of occasions, but the last may be every bit as important. The first step toward documenting the role of improved operational efficiency in facilitating the export of Brazilian shoes can be found in a Brazilian MBA thesis which indicates that in Brazil, the shoe companies which achieved the greatest increases in exports had done much more to improve operational efficiency than those with lesser rates of increase.[29]

---

[29]João Gomes Neto, "Mucanças Tecnológicas e Desempenho das Empresas Brasileiras Productoras e Exportadoras de Calçados," MBA Thesis, Faculty of Business Administration, Federal University of Rio de Janeiro, May 1982.

Recent studies of the Uruguayan leather and shoe industry maintain that productivity improvements in those sectors were relatively minor during the export boom. When the incentives to export dropped sharply in the late 1970s, the only footwear manufacturer to continue to look to exports for profits was one that had been undertaking major, sustained efforts to increase productivity. Indeed, judging its comparative advantage to lie in the most leather-intensive products, it shifted out of shoe production entirely and into the manufacture of boots. Recognizing, moreover, that there were economies of scale that could not be obtained in producing for a market as small as that of Uruguay (even in footwear), the firm decided to produce 100 percent for export, reaffirming the decision in the midst of the international recession of the 1982–83 period and continuing that market focus in the 1986–88 period of local recovery. This success and that of a few firms in other leather products, amidst the general collapse and bankruptcy of so many Uruguayan leather goods producers, are developments that should be carefully documented and publicized. They suggest that a long-run commitment to producing for export markets may be financially advantageous at the enterprise level even if national incentives fluctuate dramatically, as long as the product is one which would ordinarily enjoy a comparative advantage, and strong anti-export biases do not prevail.

Empirical support for the importance of x-efficiency in developing countries can be found in a recent survey by Roger Frantz,[30] and, in particular, in a detailed base study by Howard Pack.[31] Pack indicates that a firm's productivity may be affected by conditions determined at the national and industry levels, the managerial capacities of the firm, and by the task-level productivity of individual workers. His detailed analysis of textile mills in Kenya and the Philippines concludes that task level deficiencies are minor relative to those that result from shortcomings in managerial capacity, production engineering, and the decisions reflecting choices relative to best practice. This reinforces the argument of Fransman that organizational and managerial experience and organizational relations within the factory were the main determinants of productivity gains in Taiwan and Japan.[32] Impressed by findings of substantial variations in productivity, even within firms with similar equipment in the same country, Pack attributes a major part of the explanation to the absence of knowledge about technical factors or the adoption of

---

[30]Roger, Frantz, *X-Efficiency: Theory, Evidence and Applications* (Boston, Kluwner Academic, 1988).
[31]Howard Pack, *Productivity, Technology and Industrial Development.*
[32]Martin Fransman, "International Competitiveness, Technical Change and the State: The Machine Tool Industry in Taiwan and Japan," *World Development,* vol. 14, nos. 11/12, (Nov.–Dec. 1986) p. 1394.

economically inappropriate behavior, even in cases when simple procedures previously brought to management's attention would have led to a different course of action. He concludes that many firms lack the organizational capacity to apply readily available information.[33]

An Emerging Tendency in International Specialization: Specialization at the Component Level

The output of assembly industries involving international subcontracting (also referred to as production sharing and complementary intraindustry trade) has, together with trade in fully manufactured parts and components, been among the most rapidly growing categories of exports from developing countries over the last twenty years. This participation of international subcontracting and sourcing reflects the growing internationalization in the process of manufacturing individual goods, a logical extension of the tendency of producers in the more advanced industrial economies to specialize in fewer stages of production, extending what manufacturers had long referred to as the "make or buy" decision.[34] Although international subcontracting largely reflects new undertakings, much international sourcing involving more integrated manufacturing processes originates from industries which were initiated to service local developing-country markets. Subcontracting develops varying degrees of backward (and forward) linkages in the local economy, and the existing productive base of international sourcing is sometimes modified to accommodate the demands from abroad. As a result, the

---

[33]What Pack refers to as "a lack of organizational capacity" may overlap with what the author of this chapter has referred to as problems in economic perception and judgment which lead to a similar failure to use readily available information. See Schwartz, "Perception, Judgment and Motivation in Manufacturing Enterprise: Findings and Preliminary Hypotheses from in-depth Interviews," *Journal of Economic Behavior and Organization*, vol. 8, no. 4, December 1987, pp. 543–566.

[34]Evidence on the increase in the relative importance of international sourcing can be found in United Nations Industrial Development Organization, *Industry in a Changing World* (New York: United Nations, 1983), Ch. 7, esp. p. 218. Nearly a third of the trade of developing countries with each other is intra-industry trade, and the share is still higher for LDC trade with advanced industrial nations, except for Latin America. Oli Havrylyshyn and Engin Civan, "Intra-Industry Trade among Developing Countries," *Journal of Development Economics*, vol. 18 (1985), p. 266. Some of the recent increase in intra-industry trade reflects an increase in intra-firm trade by multinational corporations. See Gerald K. Helleiner, *Intra-Firm Trade and the Developing Countries* (New York: St. Martin's Press, 1981). This appears to be of much more importance for Latin America than for Asia, and it accounts for a particularly large share of Mexico's exports of manufactures. Aside from assembly industry exports, it may very well be, as Helleiner suggests, that "contrary to the usual assumptions that intra-firm trade should be highly responsive to price changes, intra-firm trade could be highly price-inelastic in the short run and highly elastic only in the longer run" (Helleiner, *op. cit.*, p. 92).

dividing line between the two can be somewhat blurred. Both continue to offer highly favorable prospects for Latin American exports, with neither dependent any longer on the special incentives so often associated with these activities.

Production sharing—national or international—is justified financially whenever it is less expensive for an enterprise to purchase certain components (or services) from others than to undertake the production or service itself[35] (it is justified in economic terms when the same is true in terms of shadow prices). Large differences in labor costs are the principal explanation of the cost differential leading to much of the current international subcontracting. Most subcontracting arrangements persist even as the wage gap between developing and more advanced countries declines. The reasons for this are that basic labor productivity tends to rise somewhat, additional skills are developed, a higher level of economic infrastructure has been built up, and the wage gap—and thus the profitability—was so great to begin with.

But even this source of cost differential has not yet been fully exploited. To date the portion of the production process undertaken in the low-wage country has consisted for the most part of assembly operations. International production sharing is fostered by the fact that the nature of the assembly process is ordinarily rather labor-intensive, creating an incentive to carry it out in an area where unskilled labor is inexpensive. That is only the beginning of what can be obtained from production sharing based on wage differentials, however. In industries in which manufacture through to the final goods stage is characterized by many production discontinuities, alternative production processes using different factor proportions can be used to manufacture some of the components. Not only do different relative prices establish different production processes as the low-cost choices, but also when the geographic options for producing the complete product include several different sets of relative prices, the lowest-cost package of processes is likely to include some processes that are low-cost in one locale and some that are low-cost in others. This type of production sharing based on wage differentials may be even more important than that currently being exploited. If production sharing were to occur only when there were *large* wage differences, however, the phenomenon would not attain anything approaching its full economic potential. Production sharing

---

[35]Certain international production sharing results are a consequence of forced market sharing, as in the case of decisions by developing countries to turn to import substituting industrialization (ISI) when they are able to produce only a portion of the final product locally. In some of these cases the final ISI product is eventually produced at a cost comparable to that of the formerly exporting nations, especially when the option of continued international production sharing is kept open and a portion of the components can continue to be imported.

within the industrialized countries has increased in such countries as the United States and Japan and may be even more important today than in earlier times when wage differences within those nations were much greater.

Various other factors justifying "buy rather than make" even within the confines of a national market provide additional reasons for international subcontracting. Prominent among these are economies of scale, both those resulting from larger facilities and those resulting from longer production runs. Small metalworking shops producing long runs of a few items sometimes obtain economies of scale that the metalworking sections of very large factories cannot. This is attributable to a number of factors. The larger facilities have a relatively small demand for the components that the smaller establishments produce. In addition, they lack the long runs, and, in some cases, the specialized equipment of their small enterprise counterparts. As long as the quality of the product is assured and inexpensive, reliable transportation is available, production sharing is advantageous whether the dependent firms are 10 or 10,000 miles away.[36]

Still other factors can lead to the kind of comparative advantage that fosters production sharing: special skill availability, long experience with a particular production process, or a lower density of industrial facilities where pollution has become a serious threat or special environmental regulations are in force. A country can foster competitive advantage in certain production processes by emphasizing training in certain skills even if its unskilled labor cost advantage is relatively small. Long experience in managing a small number of processes also may lead to a learning-curve gain in production and control activities that will offset other advantages inherent in larger, single-location operations. The question of which processes to emphasize (and thus, which components to produce) so as to foster the greatest competitive advantage

---

[36]Yung Rhee and Larry Westphal have demonstrated that significant gains can be realized fron international subcontracting and servicing arrangements (which they refer to as complementary intraindustry trade), thanks to factor substitution possibilities and economies at the processing level that stem from the joint impact of specialization and economies of scale. However, their work understates the gains from trade (as they note), first, because it focuses on specialization at the component level whereas specialization at the process level offers the greatest gains and, second, because their analysis does not take account of dynamic externalities from the process of production and trade such as learning-by-doing and the transfer of technology. Yung Whee Rhee and Larry E. Westphal, "Microanalytical Aspects of Complementary Intraindustry Specialization," paper presented at the UNCTAD Seminar on North-South Complementary Intra-Industry Trade, Mexico City, August 18–22, 1980. Their paper also shows that there is no easy way to categorize the pattern of specialization between countries, because "production technology does not admit of simple characterizations that preclude such things as factor-intensity reversals, nonhomotheticity, and scale economies." *op. cit.*, p. 28. It is possible, however, that shifting the emphasis from components to process specialization would reduce the range of indeterminacy as to comparative advantage.

is not an easy one, but the fact that the question is raised at all indicates how broad the scope for production sharing may be.

The mix of production-sharing activities may expand, requiring new skills. The initial production-sharing activities, dependent on low wages and requiring less in terms of skill (perhaps also requiring a high degree of employment flexibility for their maximum success), may or may not continue to exist in a given country, depending on trends in population, education, and per capita income. If wages rise significantly vis-a-vis other countries, then some of the low-skill, low-wage component of the subcontracted activities may indeed prove to be footloose,[37] but the *overall* level of international subcontracting could rise for the reasons indicated, especially if more skills are developed in the country.[38]

The growing importance of international subcontracting and sourcing raises a question as to whether it may not be preferable to analyze trade in terms of comparative advantage in individual production processes rather than in products. The notion that most industrial products are efficiently produced in certain countries and not in others may have to be modified to allow for the fact that countries that do not have a comparative advantage in some final products may have a comparative advantage in several components of those products. It is not just a matter of defining products more narrowly (and including a larger number of components as products). Countries may have a comparative advantage in a particular production process that would manifest itself in an ability to produce low-cost components in not one, but a number of industries. The implications are likely to be more palatable both for newly industrializing countries lacking the technological sophistication to undertake efficiently all processes required for a wide range of products and for industrially mature nations viewed as needing to abandon entire product lines.[39]

---

[37]A further explanation of the wide geographical spread of assembly operations on the part of large multinational corporations is risk diversification. See Kenneth Flamm, "The Volatility of Offshore Investment," *The Journal of Development Economics*, vol. 16, no. 3 (December 1984), pp. 231–248.

[38]It would certainly be a mistake to rely primarily on those private entrepreneurs active in the basically low-skill, low-wage activities to develop the kinds of skills that would most contribute to the alternative types of production sharing. Thus the discussion as to whether existing assembly operations are raising the level of skills seems irrelevant. Moreover, any cost-benefit appraisal of international subcontracting in developing countries should focus more on the probable costs and the attainable benefits of those production sharing possibilities that apply to the period ahead than on costs and benefits of past or existing arrangements, particularly if the latter are characterized by features that, while adverse in character, are also avoidable.

[39]The more products—or the more processes—that should be taken into account, the more likely it is that it will be more costly to determine where comparative advantage lies. In marginal cases, it may not be worthwhile to turn to a given production process if it is first necessary to do all the calculations to prove its comparative advantage status.

If more international manufacturing is based on process speciali-zation, technological advances may be somewhat more likely to relate to processes (rather than products). Such advances will thus strengthen any existing comparative advantage in production processes and benefit countries by lowering risk and perhaps bringing them better rates of return as they become strong comparative-advantage producers of com-ponents rather than somewhat less strong producers of a smaller number of final goods. Any international tendency to emphasize the production of all components of a product in one or a few countries may increase the likelihood of technological developments which are oriented toward products rather than processes, and may thereby reduce the number and increase the continuity of production processes used to produce a given final good. This would increase the incentive for the vertical in-tegration of production processes at one or more locations and would reduce the financial and economic advantage of international (and per-haps even national) production sharing. Economic analyses have long been oriented overwhelmingly toward products rather than processes, which places many single-stage process-oriented production facilities at a disadvantage insofar as they are less able to benefit from what eco-nomics can offer. Perhaps this will begin to change now that develop-ments in international manufacturing are confirming the arguments in favor of process-oriented production sharing.

The share of advanced industrial country imports of manufactures originating in developing countries nearly doubled during the 1970s but was still only 3.5 percent of the apparent consumption of manufactured goods in those countries, with the share only slightly higher in the early 1980s.[40] Of that total, assembly industry imports have been most im-portant for the United States, where, by the early 1980s they rose to nearly a sixth of the total U.S. imports of manufactures other than processed foodstuffs and basic metals (more than a quarter of those from developing countries), becoming the mainstay of industries as tra-ditional as certain lines of apparel and sporting goods, and as modern as semi-conductors. Since then, the share and the value of assembly imports have risen further, with Latin America (principally Mexico) accounting for the lion's share.

---

[40]This paragraph and the two that follow are based on Joseph Grunwald and Kenneth S. Flamm, Global Factory. *Foreign Assembly in International Trade* (Washington: The Brookings Institution, 1984). The share of advanced country imports of manufactures from developing countries rose from 1.73 percent in 1970 to 3.44 percent in 1979, according to Vasilis Panoutsopoulos, "Differences Between the East Asian and Latin American Export Performance in Industrial Country Markets in the 1970s," paper presented at the International Economics Studies Group Conference at the Isle of Thorns, University of Sussex, September 18–20, 1981, Table 12.

Latin America accounts for nearly half of manufacturing value added in the developing countries but for less than a third of the total share of developing country exports of manufactures to advanced industrial economies. However, the proportion is much higher for international subcontracting and international sourcing of components (approximately 50 percent). The more favorable position of the Latin American countries in this trade appears to be attributable primarily to the inclination of many small to medium-sized U.S. enterprises to favor locations relatively close to home. Developing-country firms have played a substantial, though not majority role in the international sourcing of components. On the other hand, the assembly industry has been dominated by foreign enterprises (though joint ventures are not uncommon), leading to concerns within the developing countries about the quality of employment, the limited transfer of technology, the contribution to the balance of payments in border industry situations when the currency is overvalued, and the allegedly footloose nature of such often lightly capitalized activities—the last of these complaints notwithstanding the tendency of assembly industry production in the lower-wage, lower-cost country to hold its own during the more general cutbacks of economic recessions.

Meanwhile, concerns also have been expressed in the advanced industrial countries about the export of jobs and possibly adverse effects on the balance of payments. The current strength and bright prospects of international contracting appear to be due to the following: efforts of the advanced industrial countries to restructure the production of various traditional industries with a view to survival (since the appreciation of the yen in the mid-to late 1980s, Japanese companies also have come to rely more on offshore assembly operations); the rapid pace of technological change and the increasing tendency toward customization in the electronics fields, which limit the amount of automation possible; and style changes notably in the field of apparel. The first of these factors provides the major thrust for more conventional international sourcing as a factor in the growth of Latin American manufacturing exports.

Although low wages are not the only possible explanation of international subcontracting, they certainly have been the dominant factor for that emanating from developing countries, and the combination of low wages and low transport cost explains almost all of that coming from Latin America. Other factors (such as specialization leading to longer production runs and to larger-scale operations and such as increased backward linkages thanks to the development of reliable suppliers) have begun to take on more importance in Asia, where radio and TV assembly has led to indigenous production, semiconductor assembly and the development of related plastics companies and machine shops, while apparel assembly has been almost entirely replaced by fully integrated clothing production for export. These types of developments have not been as common in Latin America.

Technological Learning and Adaptation

Basic Considerations

Difficulties in lowering the production costs or improving the quality of exportable products can often be caused by limitations in the capacity for product or process adaptation. These limitations in adaptation should be considered in terms of the overall subject of technological learning and technological development.

Only a limited understanding of industrial technology is needed for initial state agroindustrial processing aimed at local markets, especially if those markets are either very isolated or highly protected.[41] A better understanding and utilization of technology, along with some updating based on technological change, are required for success in more competitive markets. Eventually, as a capability is developed for handling simple technology well, for progressing to more advanced (and usually imported) technology, and for adapting the latter to the demands of local markets (and perhaps to the constraints of local supply), there is a build-up toward what Dahlman and Westphal have referred to as technological mastery, which they define as operational command over technological knowledge; this may require some creation as well as adaptation of technology.[42]

The overall process might be conceived as falling into four stages. The first stage involves operations using simple technology. The second stage brings more sophisticated technologies into play and may involve higher levels of efficiency, thus requiring the ability: (a) to increase normal operational efficiency (x-efficiency); (b) to prepare preinvestment and more detailed feasibility studies and develop investment capability; (c) to provide for basic and detail engineering; and (d) to ensure that plant personnel are trained to execute a smooth startup and maintain subsequent operations at something close to technical potential. The third stage requires a solid grasp of basic and detail engineering;

---

[41]Industrial technology refers to physical process and to information of both a technical and organizational nature which is required to manufacture industrial products.

[42]Carl Dahlman and Larry Westphal, "Technological Effort in Industrial Development— An Interpretative Survey of Recent Research," in Francis Stewart and Jeffrey James, eds., *The Economics of New Technology in Developing Countries*, (Colorado Springs: Westview Press, 1982), pp. 105–137; and Carl J. Dahlman, Bruce Ross-Larson and Larry E. Westphal, "Managing Technological Development: Lessons from the Newly Industrializing Countries," *World Development*, vol. 15, no. 6 (June 1987) pp. 759–775.

typically, numerous minor (and occasionally some major) adaptations take place, troubleshooting ability grows, and unforeseen bottlenecks are dealt with competently. In the fourth stage, the quest for competitiveness leads to more formalized centers for adaptation and even technological creation—in public and private institutes and on occasion research divisions within leading enterprises.

Progress through these stages is often uneven, with some industries or product lines advancing more rapidly than others. The rate of advance tends to be spurred by: (1) increases and upgrading in formal training in engineering, business administration, vocational programs, etc.; (2) incorporation of skilled personnel and administrators from foreign countries—in domestic as well as foreign-controlled enterprises; (3) learning by doing; (4) careful monitoring; and (5) government policies which foster technological and industrial development. The broader and more complex the industrial base, the greater the need to achieve international competitiveness. The more that the shift to a broader and more complex base is the result of government decisions rather than of market forces, the more difficult the task becomes, though this can be offset to a degree if there is a willingness to turn the new activities over to foreign control (and the foreigners adapt sufficiently to local market demands and production inputs), or if domestic investors are committed from the outset to export within a limited number of years or to compete freely with imports within a given period of time.

The key in all this is the character and quality of the experience. The major body of evidence on this point can be found in two groups of studies. The first, the Regional Program of Research on Scientific and Technical Development in Latin America, was sponsored by the Inter-American Development Bank (IDB), the Economic Commission for Latin America, the United Nations Development Program and the International Development Research Centre of Canada and was directed by Jorge Katz.[43] Simon Teitel, who conceived this program together with Cecilio J. Morales and Enrique Iglesias (then Secretary General of the Economic Commission for Latin America), has prepared

---

[43]See especially the following papers of the Inter-American Development Bank/Economic Commission for Latin America/United Nations Development Program/International Development Research Centre (IDB/ECLA/UNDP/IDRC) Program: Jorge Katz, "Technological Change, Economic Development and Intra- and Extra Regional Relations in Latin America," Working Paper no. 3, Buenos Aires, 1978; Katz, "Domestic Technology Generation in LDCs: A Review of Research Findings," Working Paper no. 35, Buenos Aires, November 1980, and Katz, "Cambio Tecnológico en la Industria Metalmecánica Latinoamericana," Working Paper no. 51, Buenos Aires, July 1982. See also: Katz "Domestic Technological Innovation and Dynamic Comparative Advantage," *Journal of Development Economics* 16 (1984), pp. 13–38; and Katz "Technological Innovation, Industrial Organization and Comparative Advantage of Latin American Metalworking Industries," in M. Fransman and K. King, eds., *Technological Capability in the Third World* (New York: St. Martins Press, 1984).

several analyses of the findings,[44] on which the present exposition draws heavily, though taking a somewhat different perspective. The second group of studies, organized primarily by the World Bank but including some participation by the IDB, provides much of the evidence underlying the articles by Dahlman, Ross-Larson and Westphal cited in this section.

In advanced industrialized countries, technological change is centered on the creation of new products and processes and on cost reduction, reflecting some mixture of the pull of scientific and engineering breakthroughs and the push of economic and financial incentives. While the same is also true in principle in developing countries, the creation of new products and processes, which are much fewer in number than in the advanced industrial economies, has a much smaller impact. Here the push of incentives is the dominant factor. What probably helps foster more technological change (or a different type of technological change) than expected by economists is the fact that the prevailing financial incentives reflect differences in the opportunity costs confronting businessmen which are often greater than or different from economic opportunity costs.

Technological change in the industrial sector of Latin America "seems to be," as Teitel has put it, "an involuntary by-product of the manufacturing output, as well as the result of deliberate decisions to set up laboratories and research institutes by private firms and in the public sector." It involves employing different materials, reducing plant size to the dimensions of smaller markets (as Philips of Holland has been doing since the 1960s), diversifying product mix, adapting product design, using simpler and lower capacity machinery, and stretching the capacity of existing equipment. It also involves cost reduction, but this refers to financial costs, which are often less likely to coincide with economic costs than in advanced industrial countries.

Some of these technological changes facilitate manufacturing exports, but not all. Exports of manufactures may begin in the first of the four stages referred to earlier, and a wider range of such exports becomes possible as an industry advances through the remaining three stages.[45] The advance may be uneven, however, with the share of exports accounted for by manufactures declining before it ultimately increases.

---

[44]See Simon Teitel, "Technology Creation in Semi-Industrialized Economies," *The Journal of Development Economics* 16 (1984), pp. 39–61; "Towards an Understanding of Technical Change in Semi-Industrialized Countries," *Research Policy* 10 (1981), pp. 128–147; and "Creation of Technology within Latin America," *Annals of the American Academy of Political Social Science* 458, (November 1981), pp. 136–150.

[45]Westphal attributes a great deal of Korea's increased exports in the 1960s and 1970s to "mastery of well-established and convetional methods embodied in equipment readily available from foreign suppliers." Larry E. Westphal, Yung W. Rhee and Gary Purcell,

(footnote continued)

One of the principal themes of the articles by Simon Teitel is how difficult it still is to generalize about the nature of technological change in terms of the firm size or market structure that most stimulates it, the skilled resources that are most essential, the effectiveness of protection and of the policies specifically designed to promote technological development.

As manufacturers establish their competitiveness in foreign markets, they often begin to establish manufacturing operations overseas. In some cases this reflects market phenomena and the changing comparative advantages of countries; in other cases it takes place because protectionism prevents or limits exports into those countries.

As manufacturing exports become more sophisticated, the need arises for exports of disembodied products—that is, exports of services related to those products. As international competitiveness is firmly established, and the product or productive facilities come to reflect special adaptation, the export of plant components and even of entire plants becomes feasible, along with management contracts. Such exports of disembodied technology tend to increase as the domestic addition to the technology becomes more significant, with technical services and technology licenses also entering into the picture.

Manufacturing exports from Latin America have increased appreciably, as have the technological sophistication of the products and Latin America's contribution to the technology. Simple products other than processed agricultural and mineral resources, or more complex products in early stages of development have been exported first to lower-income, neighbors (often within preferential trade arrangements), but further product development and cost improvement have led to worldwide sales in many cases. A good portion of the latter admittedly reflects the activity of foreign firms, and much of that, in turn, reflects intra-firm arrangements. However, there are also many exports that do not fit either category, particularly in the case of agroindustries where a wide range of production is based on mature and relatively stable technologies. Local firms also have begun to make headway in the export of some relatively sophisticated products, exemplified in Brazil by machine tools from the private sector and small passenger planes and tanks from government enterprises.

Korean Industrial Competence: Where It Came From, World Bank Staff Working Paper 469 (Washington, D.C., 1981). On the other hand, technological advances have been more important for many of the country's manufacturing exports in the 1980s. Conversely, the inability of Argentina's machine tool industry to remain internationally competitive after the mid-1970s is probably explained by a failure to keep technologically abreast as much (or almost as much) as by adverse macroeconomic policies (and political developments). While the broader factors and the increased uncertainty contributed to lower investment in industry generally, the new technological lag in machine tools appears to have been appreciably greater than in many other branches of manufacturing.

Technological Learning

It is against this background that Morris Teubal considers (in Chapter III) the role of technological learning in explaining the exports of manufactures and, in particular, capital goods from Brazil. Teubal notes that learning is a critical variable for the development of infant industries and for the emergence of dynamic comparative advantage and that it is of special significance for products that are not homogeneous. In considering government policy, attention is given not to the measures most directly affecting exports such as exchange rate policy and export subsidies, but to instruments such as subsidies for broad increases in output and protection of the domestic market, both of which may have an indirect affect on exports via learning.

Teubal's approach is to identify relevant learning processes by examining thirteen cases of technologically sophisticated firms and by concentrating on a small number of variables—in particular, the indirect contribution or spin-offs of early activities or products to other activities or products developed subsequently. Products manufactured by the firms he examined include boilers, furnaces, turbines, equipment for the beverage, food processing, steel, cement and petroleum industries, mixers for the pharmaceutical, petrochemical and nuclear power industries, automotive and aircraft pistons, automotive elevators, motors, overhead cranes, hydroelectric power project components and mining equipment. Also examined were a trading company specializing in certain lines of equipment and an engineering consulting firm.

The learning process relates to plant operation, project execution, product design and R&D. Distinctions must be made between basic learning for manufacturing, gradual mastery of an increasing range of manufacturing processes, and the acquisition of design capability. Design capability enables the firm to specify the equipment required for specific manufacturing processes and requires deeper knowledge of materials and a thorough understanding of the use to which the product will be put. Design capability is broken down further into detail design capability and basic design capability. Basic learning for manufacturing may permit minor adaptation. Design capability assures the latter and adds to the possibility of major adaptations.

Capital goods were chosen for study by Teubal because of their impressive development in Brazil. He indicates that the array of goods being produced and exported provides prima facie evidence of intensive technological learning and identifiable adaptation. Capital goods, broadly defined to include transportation equipment, have become the most important component of exports of relatively sophisticated technological products. The constant money value of Brazilian exports, trebled between 1970 and 1979 and the share of what Brazil terms industrialized products rose more than twofold. Exports of relatively sophisticated products rose threefold, and capital goods exports increased fourfold, from 3.4 to 14.7 percent of the total. This represented a growth from $87 million in 1970, or only 2.2 percent of manufacturing output, to $800 million in 1979 (in constant 1970 dollars), or 9 percent of output.

One would expect such a rise in capital goods exports to be associated with an increase in the profitability of exports relative to local sales, but two studies are cited to suggest that the incentives did not increase over the period so that the explanation for the export growth seems to lie with increased productivity or competitiveness. An excess-capacity explanation has not been tested, but Teubal contends that its significance would be limited insofar as exports of capital goods depend less on price and more on quality, product specifications, and firm reputation. At the same time, the local demand for capital goods increased during much of the period. The importance of skill acquisition and technological learning is suggested by the increasing range of commodities produced and exported and by case studies of thirteen firms.

The export performance of the capital goods sector has been greatly influenced, Teubal contends, by government measures affecting the overall profitability of the firms rather than by changes in the profitability of exports and local sales.[46] Some measures, such as the increase in government purchases of locally produced capital goods, greatly augmented local demand for the output of domestic producers. Tariffs, low interest loans, tax exemptions for the purchase of domestic capital goods, and, particularly, non-tariff barriers also supported purchases from local sources. In some years as much as two-thirds of the total Brazilian demand for capital goods was supplied locally; exports should thus be regarded as a spin-off. The acceleration of exports after 1973 reflects the accumulation of physical capital, technological knowledge, experience and skills during the import-substitution and infant industry stages, and the reduction in domestic demand (but the local market and exports should be regarded as complementary in the long run). The Brazilian experience suggests that export promotion need not be geared to exports in the short run if exporting is appreciably more difficult than supplying the local market (due to product quality or firm reputation requirements, or to servicing or supply replacement needs) or if the supply of goods to the local market has spin-off effects benefiting exports, such as the acquisition of experience and enhancement of reputation.

Findings concerning the technological learning of each of the firms are then presented. Emphasis is given to what Teubal terms the indirect or dynamic effects of economic activity within the firm. Spin-offs from early products were detected in each of the cases; in twelve cases, sig-

---

[46]See Appendix A for different conclusions with respect to automobile exports.

nificant technological learning was involved, and in one case, the only spin-off was enhanced reputation. Eleven indigenous spin-off mechanisms were detected and classified under three headings as follows:

Learning related to manufacturing: (1) accumulation of manufacturing capabilities; (2) operating experience; (3) experience derived from the use of similar equipment; and (4) improvement of quality-control procedures.

Learning related to design: (5) development of a mechanical design capability; (6) development of a process design capability; and (7) development of a total project management capability.

Other mechanisms: (8) enhanced firm reputation; (9) improved ability to plan and execute investments; (10) increased knowledge of markets; and (11) development of a network of suppliers.

A natural sequence of events in successful capital goods firms seems to be one in which the acquisition of manufacturing capabilities is followed by the acquisition of design capabilities in a narrower set of products, with quality control perhaps providing the linkage. Full development of a design capability may be jeopardized by any reduction in local demand, presumably because of the level of fixed costs.

From some of the examples, Teubal maintains, there emerges an important distinction between simple learning and what he first called qualitative learning and now refers to as product learning. Simple learning enables the firm to produce equipment at lower cost and, sometimes by introducing relatively minor technological improvements, to exploit segments of its market more fully. Product learning enables the firm to shift to new but in some respects technologically related types of equipment that are more difficult to produce or that require a design capability as well. This shift enables the firm to better exploit certain existing submarkets related to its area of expertise and thus, in turn, to unearth further opportunities for exports. Exports also were facilitated by the spin-off that came from learning how to assemble turnkey projects to supply the local market.

Teubal puts forward a strong argument that a group of firms producing capital goods, favored by government measures reducing their risk of foreign competition and increasing their profitability on sales to all markets, experienced substantial increases in their technological learning and that learning was the key factor boosting their ability to export. That argument casts some doubt on the oft-heralded proposition that an open economy is essential to keep entrepreneurs cost-competitive and technologically up-to-date, and it tends to support the thesis that exports may be fostered by altering general factors of cost and quality as well as by changing the relative profitability of sales for foreign and domestic markets.

At the same time, however, in order to evaluate properly the overall system that produced these results, it would be necessary to know what proportion of firms favored in the same way had similarly favorable learning and export experiences. Beyond that, it would be necessary to know whether the policies which led to net benefits for some groups of firms penalized others and, if so, whether the latter experienced setbacks in technological learning, growth, and ability to export as a consequence.

In order to orient future policy, guidelines should be drawn up so as to minimize these dangers. These guidelines might include greater selectivity as to which activities receive the favored treatment. Because "picking winners" is such a hazardous undertaking, however, emphasis might better be given to making access to favored circumstances subject to a number of conditions—initially and over the period of time the favor is extended—and strictly limiting the duration for granting such benefits.

Teubal has since documented the importance of learning and technological development for the evolution of Israel's exports of particularly "sophisticated" manufactures. In addition, Teubal has provided an epilogue in which he considers evidence of the effects of production for the domestic market in facilitating exports in another country (Denmark), summarizes the economic argument for initial protection followed by subsequent exports in Japan and other countries with large domestic markets, and discusses the extended economic infrastructure necessary to promote exports—particularly of capital goods—and to facilitate a more sustained economic development.

There is even more evidence available on Korea. Westphal, Rhee and Purcell indicate that, although initially the mastery of production processes was sufficient to permit exports of wigs, plywood, and garments, greater design and production engineering capability and the ability to modify technology became important for international competitiveness in technologically more sophisticated industries such as electronics, machinery, and automobiles, which Korea emphasized in the 1970s and 1980s. Amsden has shown this for Taiwan as well as Korea, and Westphal, Kim and Dahlman have documented it for Korea.[47]

Among the Latin American countries, more exports have come from multinational companies than in the case of the East Asian economies, and thus the barriers to keeping technologically up-to-date would have been smaller (except insofar as market assignments might have intervened). Nonetheless, a notable example of the contribution of tech-

---

[47]On Korea, see Amsden, *op. cit.* (which emphasizes learning more than technological innovation) and Amsden, "A Technological Perspective on the General Machinery Industry in the Republic of Korea," Working Paper, Harvard Business School, Boston, Mass., 1984. See also Larry E. Westphal, Linsu Kim and Carl J. Dahlman, "Reflections on the Republic of Korea's Acquisition of Technological Capability," in Nathan Rosenberg and Claudio Frischtak eds., *International Technology Transfer: Concepts, Measures and Comparisons* (New York: Praeger, 1985), pp. 167–221.

nological development to the emergence of industrial exports—and even to the export of technology—comes from the Brazilian steel company, Usiminas.[48] The beginning of that success was attributed not to heavy investment but to suddenly reduced access to investment. This suggests that adversities may trigger an improvement in productivity not only by reducing slack (a la Cyert and March),[49] but also by stimulating technological modification and innovation.[50] This refers primarily to the doubling of productivity by Usiminas during a six-year period during which investment funds were not available to the company.

The cost consciousness and the more cost-effective process of research and experimentation continued as capital expansion became more available. That process was marked by worldwide searches for technology, constant efforts to modify what was adopted and careful monitoring of R&D results. Although they acknowledge that many firms fail to achieve best-practice levels of productivity, Bell, Ross-Larson and Westphal maintain that one of the major reasons why many infant industries falter (and fail to achieve a potential for international competitiveness) is that they neglect the needed technological efforts.[51] The authors recommend government policies to offset externalities that lead firms to underinvest in technological capability, including in-firm training.

In a recent paper, Claudio Frischtak maintains that Brazil achieved a notable record of growth and diversification of manufactures exports in areas of increased skill-intensity and technological sophistication during the period 1965–80, but that this was not maintained during the period 1980–86. Industrial exports became more dependent on natural resource- and labor-intensive products. In considerable measure, he argues, this happened because both the rate of expenditure on R&D and the general rate of investment in new equipment declined.[52]

---

[48]The basic study was undertaken by Carl Dahlman for the IDB/ECLA/UNDP/IDRC Research Project referred to above. For a concise summary, see Dahlman, Ross-Larson and Westphal, "Managing Technological Development," pp. 759–762.

[49]Richard M. Cyert and James G. March, *A Behavioral Theory of the Firm*, (Englewood Cliffs, N.J.: Prentice Hall, Inc., 1963).

[50]See Martin Bell, Bruce Ross-Larson and Larry E. Westphal, "Assessing the Performance of Infant Industries," *Journal of Development Economics*, vol. 16, nos. 1–2 (Sept.–Oct. 1984), pp. 101–128.

[51]Bell, Ross-Larson and Westphal, op. cit., pp. 36–37. A somewhat different note is struck by Alice Amsden, who notes that trade between developing countries tends to be comprised of manufactures that are skills- and learning-intensive, yet developing countries are missing an opportunity insofar as they are underexporting to each other. Amsden, "The Direction of Trade—Past and Present—and the ''Learning Effects'' of Exports to Different Directions," *Journal of Development Economics*, vol. 23 (1986), pp. 249–74.

[52]Claudio R. Frischtak, "Trade and Structural Change in Brazil and the Newly Industrializing Latin American Economies," in Randall B. Purcell ed., *The Newly Industrializing Countries in the World Economy: Challenges for U.S. Policy*, Policy Study by the
(footnote continued)

Marketing and Feedback to Production

Basic Considerations

The key to increasing foreign buyers' interest in many Latin American manufactures may not be marketing in the strictest sense. Donald Keesing has noted, in perhaps the first major overview of the marketing of manufacturing exports from developing countries,[53] that finished consumer goods are one of the major categories of manufacturing exports from developing countries and constitute one of the areas of greatest growth in the period since 1970. Clothing and shoes have been the leading product lines, but the consumer goods category also includes toys, sporting goods, radios, watches, luggage, handbags and wallets, floor coverings, and many other items. The major impetus for the augmented flow of these exports originated with, and continues to come from, periodic visits of major buyers (representing department stores, discount houses, chains of boutiques, or simply import-export houses) to developing country producers. That is not entirely surprising given the high cost and risk in product design by the buyer. Except possibly in the case of boutiques, the search is unabashedly for low-cost producers or for producers who can readily learn to adopt certain efficient production techniques and to adapt to the changes in style that characterize the product in question. It is such manufactures that foreign buyers seek out, and particularly, centers of such producers. Some buyers simply seek low-cost product delivery in the short run. Others work extensively with local producers, providing technical assistance in various areas of industrial engineering and operational efficiency so as to help contribute to achieving the quality, flexibility and cost goals they seek. This plant-level technical assistance tends to continue for years and in some cases

---

Curry Foundation (Boulder, Co.: Lynne Rienner Publishers, 1989), pp. 159–185. A country with Brazil's resource and human endowments might not be worse off with temporary booms in technologically less sophisticated exports, however, as long as there are some skill-intensive growth areas—as indeed there seem to be, most notably in aviation products but also in other areas. This development does not always evoke a favorable evaluation of analysts, however. See e.g., the criticism (on largely static economic grounds) of the increasing proportion of Brazilian exports of automotive products in the 1980s that are human-capital-intensive in Fischer, Nunnenkamp et. al., op. cit. The latter study explores at a relatively disaggregated level the factors underlying a phenomenon noted in several other studies: that more and more of Brazil's industrial exports were capital-intensive (see Appendix A).
[53]Donald B. Keesing, "Exporting Manufactured Consumer Goods from Developing to Developed Economies," manuscript (Washington, D.C.: The World Bank, 1982). A summary of this can be found in Keesing, "Linking up to Distant Markets: South to North Exports of Manufactures Consumer Goods," American Economic Review, vol. 73 (May 1983), pp. 338–342.

provides a valuable means for producers to keep technologically up-to-date in certain lines of manufacture.[54]

The initiation and continuance of some exports depend upon the full panoply of marketing techniques. Even for those exports, however, it is becoming increasingly clear that major increases in sales depend upon attention to the underlying consideration of supply and productive efficiency. The Morawetz study on Colombian clothing exports mentions a number of problems attributable to inefficient production setups.[55] The Keesing marketing study refers to still others and alludes to the importance of several facets of economies of scale. But nowhere does the "back to production basics" theme emerge more clearly than in some of the studies of the project analyzing Latin American manufacturing exports of the Postgraduate Program in Business Administration of the Federal University of Rio de Janeiro. This project, which has produced several dozen studies,[56] outlines the dimensions of Brazilian manufacturing exports, notes the marginal nature of exports for most Brazilian firms,[57] and analyzes the effectiveness of various marketing mechanisms for most product lines, taking particular note of the more favorable export experience of enterprises that have emphasized quality control and production process modification. The already mentioned 1982 MBA thesis, prepared in conjunction with the program and based on detailed field work on the shoe industry indicates that the enterprises that achieved the best export results were much quicker than the others to increase their capacity (in part to take better advantage of economies of scale), vary their production layout and modify their cutting, assembly and finishing operations.[58]

For international sourcing in the component assembly industry, low cost production is, of course, the one overriding concern. This is not to deny a role for traditional aspects of distribution and marketing (especially in the case of plants owned by entrepreneurs from the local countries and certainly in full-fledged consumer goods manufacturing)

---

[54]The contribution of buyers to the technological development of some product lines and production processes is discussed in Westphal, Rhee and Purcell, *Korean Industrial Competence.*

[55]David Morawetz, *Why The Emperor's New Clothes are Not Made in Colombia* (Oxford: Oxford University Press, 1981).

[56]All of these have been circulated as separate reports by the Program (COPPEAD), and some have been published in Brazilian journals, notably the *Revista de Administração* of the University of São Paulo. The principal authors have been Angela Schmidt, Paulo Fernando Fleury da Silva e Souza and Kleber Fossati Figueiredo.

[57]For evidence suggesting that Brazilian exports in the 1970s were not of a marginal nature—or at least that they reflected a statistically significant growth—see Simon Teitel and Francisco Thoumi, "From Import Substitution to Exports: The Manufacturing Exports Experience of Argentina and Brazil," *Economic Development and Cultural Change*, vol. 34, no. 3, April, 1986, pp. 455–490.

[58]Gomes Neto, *op. cit.*

aimed at increasing profit and reducing the risk that accompanies the usual initial commercial ties with either one or two countries and comparably few companies. In the case of assembly products, however, marketing receives attention from the initial purchasers rather than the sellers. As LDC brand-name consumer goods make their appearance and exports of consumer durables and even producer equipment become a reality, added importance is assumed by distribution considerations and economies of scale, the seller's international marketing capability, and the feedback of the marketing experience on the products manufactured and the processes used in their manufacture. One basic concern is the supply-side element reflected in the economics of distribution to foreign markets. Equally important, of course, are the comprehensive aspects of marketing; providing sufficient information about products to prospective foreign purchasers and doing whatever else helps to carve out a niche in markets abroad. The latter is essential to success in exporting manufactures from Latin America, but important elements of what is required for successful marketing of the region's manufactures are not really conveyed by most of the references to the subject.

These references typically stress analyses of product markets abroad (with emphasis on trends in product and country markets) and active export promotion at home. The latter usually involves government trade offices and services in cities of major export potential in the form of computerized rosters of domestic manufacturers and timely information on foreign export opportunities. The measures ordinarily stressed also include private and public attendance at major trade fairs, sales trips abroad, the use of permanent foreign representatives and extended networks for overseas sales and services, export (and perhaps pre-export) financing, and measures to promote trading companies and consortia that might harness the potential of small and medium-sized companies.[59]

All of these measures are likely to help, although detailed enumerations of what can be done often fail to indicate where the marginal

---

[59]In a recent account of export marketing in Korea, Hong Kong, Singapore and Taiwan, Keesing categorizes the activities of the export promotion agencies in those countries as: (i) trade-related information services; (ii) trade promotion (trade fairs, etc.); (iii) market analyses and market development; and (iv) assistance to firms in product design, packaging, actual marketing and training. However, he maintains, "Even in [those countries], no instance has been found in which official export promotion has succeeded in expanding manufactured exports in the face of policies only in transition toward being satisfactory for manufactures exports." For developing economies still in transition toward those suitable policies, he emphasizes training and concentration of efforts on a reduced core of services needed in the early development of export industries (not including trade fairs, e.g.), and argues for making those services available only to a select group of promising firms. Donald B. Keesing, *The Four Successful Exceptions. Official Export Promotion of Support for Export-Marketing in Korea, Hong Kong, Singapore, and Taiwan, China.* UNDP-World Bank Trade Expansion Program. Occasional Paper 2 (Washington, D.C.: World Bank Trade Policy Division, Sept. 1988), pp. 8, 19, 33–35.

returns are likely to be greatest. Indeed, that depends to a considerable degree on the particular products in question and the conditions governing their supply. Moreover, the critical element in successful overseas marketing is often a heavy involvement abroad by key members of the exporting enterprise or at least by export-promoting organizations comprised of individuals highly knowledgeable about specific products.[60] What is also required, in some cases, is effective use of the marketing experience to modify the products manufactured and sometimes the processes used in their manufacture.

The Peruvian Experience

Shane Hunt has examined the task of awakening foreign buyers to Latin American manufactures, with particular reference to Peru. His study, which appears as Chapter IV of the present volume, identifies the obstacles of Peruvian export development in several manufactures not traditionally marketed abroad and recommends measures by which those obstacles might be overcome.

He first reviews Peruvian industrial exports in the 1970s, noting that the "nontraditional" exports became significant only after 1976, when there was a coincidence of several factors: a strongly devalued real exchange rate, increased export subsidies, and a depressed local market. Nontraditional exports rose from 8.3 percent of total exports in 1975 to 21.3 percent in 1980, from $107 million to $783 million. Among the leading nontraditional manufacturing exports were canned and frozen fish, alpaca and cotton products, copper and zinc shapes and alloys, lead oxides, copper sulfates, fishing boats, pumps—all of which are based on or related to the development of Peru's natural resources—and ISI products such as clothing, refrigerators, soaps and detergents and kitchen stoves. The latter exports benefited from economies of scale made possible by the factories' large size relative to the domestic market. Nevertheless, the potential economies of scale were not fully exploited, operational efficiency was not encouraged by the highly protected environment, and further inefficiency resulted from the need of producers to pay high duties on imported inputs or to purchase inefficient locally produced inputs.

Hunt cites the relative price of exports and the low level of domestic demand as the principal factors conditioning an expansion of Peru's industrial exports, but he also takes special note of product quality and

---

[60]See Berry, *op. cit.*, pp. 54–55, citing Donald B. Keesing and Sanjaya Lal, "Marketing Manufactures Exports from Developing Countries: Information Links, Buyers, Orders and Institutional Support," paper prepared for the WIDER Conference on the New Trade Theories and Industrialization in the Developing Countries, Helsinki, Finland, August 1988.

marketing capability. Canned fish, pumps and motors are examined in depth with particular reference to: the original impetus to exporting them, the importing country, the quality of the product and the potential for product and process improvement, and prevailing marketing patterns.

The export of canned fish (pilchards) appears to have resulted in part from a reallocation of resources following the partial disappearance of anchovies from Peru's waters and the resulting decline of fishmeal production by the late 1970s. But, more importantly, the export of pilchards has depended on the ability of Peruvian producers to respond to the demands of various markets. Peruvian exporters themselves played a major role in marketing grated pilchard to Brazil, but importer-wholesalers have become the principal marketing strategist. In the United States, marketing efforts have involved pricing as much as 50 percent below that of canned tuna, and advertising campaigns directed toward final consumers and supermarkets. Importers also have played a major marketing role in South Africa, primarily because Peruvian producers were unfamiliar with the local product variation, *tipo-tall*. In this case, the marketing experience led to a product variation that is more capital intensive and required a substantial modification of production technology.

U.S. and South African importers worked to improve product quality, indicating a preference for dealing with plants that were clean and orderly. They also attempted to control for the size of fish, time out of water, use of ice on boats, cooking time before filleting, time delay in cooking, filleting and canning, and time in the retort where fish are cooked again for sterilization after sealing. Some importer-wholesalers had inspectors stationed in the plants during the entire process. They based rejections on improper procedures as well as on such observed conditions of the final product as texture, odor, taste, tightness of pack, adequacy of sauce, net weight, and external appearance of the can.

Hunt observes that learning by doing, in this case, took the form of learning by exporting. The organization of production was improved, leading to improved quality (this also might be considered a process change insofar as it tended to reduce costs). A second type of learning related to marketing is also noted, in which a producer gradually sheds his passivity in marketing to become both participant in and evaluator of the marketing process.

Despite years of experience, Hunt conjectures that only the Brazilian market seems secure for Peruvian pilchards. This lack of relatively secure markets is attributed to swings in real exchange rates that adversely affect price-cost margins, the high cost of key production inputs such as locally produced tinplate, a declining world price of tuna, and underinvestment in marketing.

Major attention also is given to exports of pumps, motors and transformers, large heavy duty products purchased by mines, factories and electric power companies. The experience of two producers of motors is considered. One is a partially owned subsidiary of a major multinational that, having established a sales representative in Peru in the 1930s and a repair shop in the 1950s, began manufacturing in 1962 and exporting in 1967; this firm exported nearly half of its output in the Peruvian depression year of 1976, but that figure declined to 20 percent in 1982. The second firm is a wholly owned Peruvian company that began producing in 1950 (initially under foreign license, but subsequently on the basis of basis of Peruvian patents) and then began exporting in 1970; it exports 12 to 15 percent of its output, all to the Andean Group.

Both electric motors and transformers are standardized products, but they also incorporate design features representing local technological adaptation. The foreign subsidiary continues to receive technical assistance from the parent company. The locally owned company has its own program for designing special-purpose motors (to offer added protection or unusual voltages for fish factories or mining camps, etc.) but it avoids substantial overseas repair problems by exporting only its simplest, most trouble-free product lines. The exports of the multinational include large transformers that do incur servicing problems, however. The difficulties of these companies in competing beyond the protected Andean Market appear to stem partially from production of the end products themselves and partially from their local suppliers. In both cases, lack of economies of scale may be a problem. The locally owned company has a weak position even in its best foreign market, Colombia, where the Peruvian products account for 5 to 10 percent of the market, and despite a good reputation for servicing, the Peruvian products are regarded as unattractive and not reliable enough, with sales generally at discounts of 30 to 35 percent below Siemens, the market leader.

Pumps accounted for one of the largest lines of manufacturing exports in the late 1970s, and retained most of its export markets in the 1980s. All of this was attributable to the activity of a single firm, which achieved moderate gains in exporting water pumps to the Andean market, and worldwide success in the export of solids pumps. This remarkable story of innovation and product quality, which began as a response to the needs of the local fish industry, is perhaps all-too-singular, and is left to Chapter IV.

Hunt concludes that only a few Peruvian manufacturing exporters have strengthened their market positions, with most continuing as marginal and even endangered suppliers. Most of the products in question are related to Peruvian natural resources in that either they use local natural resources as inputs or they were originally or still are used in the production of other natural-resource-based products. Their cost advantage is thus limited to the saving of some transport costs and the attainment of economies of scale from having a larger market or, in a few cases, the opportunity to develop superior product design as a result of proximity to the customer. In some cases the same natural resource base exists in other nearby countries. The overvaluation of the exchange rate and incomplete adjustment of the export subsidy to allow for different degrees of industrial value added have limited the scope for Peruvian exports of manufactures farther down the competitive scale.

Hunt emphasizes the problem of deteriorating price-cost margins due to declines in the real effective exchange rate and to the imposition of protective (sometimes countervailing) measures by foreign governments. Major emphasis also is placed on the improvement of product quality and on marketing. He gives only limited attention to the factors related to cost reduction discussed in chapters 1 through 3.

Product quality is characterized as having an objective and a subjective side. Hunt observes that very few Peruvian manufacturing exports were identified as having introduced quality improvements under the pressure of export competition. This might seem to conflict with the studies of Morawetz and Keesing, who found substantial pressure for quality improvements and who differentiated between successful and unsuccessful export experiences according to the effectiveness of the exporter's response to those pressures. Hunt states, however, that those authors focused on product lines in which quality is important and that, since developing countries have substantial cost advantage in production, importer-wholesalers themselves find it worthwhile to make a substantial effort to push LDC exporters into quality improvement. He maintains that many of the products exported from Peru are so standardized as to present little difficulty in satisfying quality requirements (e.g., cotton gray goods, alpaca yarn, industrial chemicals). In canned fish, where the quality demands of leading importers have at times gone unsatisfied, a market can always be found for a second-quality product. In the case of batteries, where the Peruvian brand Pila Chola is widely perceived to be of inferior quality, substantial price discounts are necessary for it to survive in any market.

The major emphasis with respect to products such as those exported by Peru is assigned to marketing. Hunt classifies marketing systems according to the type of relationship between exporter and importer, and he notes that the still-primitive stage of marketing development for some Peruvian products is the result of the essentially undifferentiated nature of the products and Peruvian exporters' general lack of familiarity with the quality standards and marketing requirements in specific foreign markets. This is then related to "stay at home" and "go abroad" marketing strategies outlined elsewhere by Hunt and other authors.

A satisfactory price-cost relationship is a most important factor for manufactures such as those exported by Peru, Hunt insists. For this he assigns importance to a stable real exchange rate and tariff policy. In addition, there are a number of steps that local governments can take when the product lines and the stage of marketing development are known to appeal strongly to importer-wholesaler firms searching the Third World for low-cost production sources: attract those importer-wholesalers to their countries, publicize information among local producers on the quality and design standards required for successful exporting, and investigate complaints about nonperformance both by foreign importer-wholesalers and local exporters. In the case of other products and of local exporters in a somewhat more advanced marketing stage, governments might provide guidance on how to choose a good distributor and how to evaluate the distributor's performance. Hunt does not offer any recommendations regarding cost reduction.

Conclusions and Recommendations

No one ever contended that the export of manufactures from Latin America was a matter of demand alone. Many have commented on the importance of marketing and quality control, and on the need to expand output greatly in order to take advantage of many opportunities abroad. But those observations often have been brief and overly general, with analysis focused almost exclusively on such matters as the determinants of foreign demand, protectionism, and Latin America's own tilting of demand incentives toward the domestic market and away from foreign markets by overvaluation, protection and lack of compensating export incentives. These commentaries pay lip service to the importance of economies of scale in production and distribution, but they provide little notion of the real difference in costs that a doubling of the dimensions might make for some of the industries of Latin America. The commentaries offer even less insight on operational efficiency and on the degree of international competitiveness to which a given closing of the x-efficiency gap might lead. They do not expound on the magnitude of the cost reduction, quality improvement, and capacity for product adaptation that increased production mastery and technological learning might make possible. They provide little guidance on alternative means of accomplishing these various ends and on the likely payback for such improvements and others in the area of marketing. The amount that individual Latin American industries stand to gain by emphasizing one or another of these factors certainly varies, as it does for the same industry from country to country, but the relevant data that would permit a good assessment in advance often are unavailable.

This chapter and those that follow underscore the importance of these supply-side and marketing constraints, and they point to, or imply, a number of measures that might feasibly be undertaken by countries of Latin America and, indeed by the producers of the region to help alleviate supply-side and other constraints on the export manufactures. To begin with, given the available data and the prevailing policies, there is a certain amount that individual enterprises can do and already should be doing to reduce costs, to increase their capacity for technological adaptation, to exploit subcontracting more effectively and to become more directly involved in marketing abroad. Enterprises are likely to accomplish more along these lines if their trade associations promote the objectives more actively—as is common practice with industrial trade associations in the advanced industrial countries. Beyond that, producers are likely to make increased efforts if they are made aware of more data on economies of scale and comparative operational efficiency. Trade associations could help in this, although the efforts of research institutes and government agencies with international funding are likely to be required as well. At present, governments, international agencies, and private research institutes provide almost no information of this type. Moreover, there do not seem to be any supply-side-oriented analyses underway even remotely comparable in scope with the UNCTAD study of non-tariff barriers, or with the various public and private studies of the impact of trade liberalization on overall economic performance in the Southern Cone of South America.

However much this added information would help, a truly major response from manufacturers can be expected only if government policies point the way. These policies must provide unequivocal incentives for industry to be more efficient and to pay more attention to quality, to improve its skill at technological adaptation, and to become more directly and actively involved in international marketing. A wide variety of tax, credit, trade, technical assistance, technological development and even antimonopoly measures could be instituted to achieve such purposes. These could offset or reverse misleading economic signals and help overcome problems caused by years of such erroneous signals. Some measures would involve changing only the form of government support and many would not require increases in the level of expenditure; some, indeed, would lead to reductions in expenditures. Most of the measures should be aimed at stimulating local producers, but consideration also might be given to efforts to attract and involve new foreign entities—not only to invest and produce for export but also to become involved locally in intermediary activities that assist local producers indirectly (see, for example, Shane Hunt's proposals on marketing in Chapter IV). The project identification studies suggested in this overview chapter and Appendix C could be expected to have both direct consequences in terms of new investments, and important indirect effects such as providing data that would enable entrepreneurs to fill in gaps in their own information. The latter would help improve in-house project identification searches and prefeasibility studies and would encourage producers to rely on such studies for information and for suggesting alternative means by which governments, trade associations and the enterprises themselves might deal with the problem areas.

The present chapter outlines many of the major considerations relating to the supply of industrial exportables from Latin America. The chapters that follow provide case studies intended to stimulate further analysis of factors related to the region's capacity for supplying internationally competitive exports of manufactures. It is hoped that the case studies also will encourage officials in government institutions and industrial trade associations to work for measures that will help trigger a new long-term upward trend in exports of manufactures based as much on the direct reduction of product costs and improvement of product quality as on the correction of domestic price signals and the improvement and continuity of macroeconomic policies that contribute indirectly to those same ends. Locally induced cost and quality improvements were probably the most important factors underlying the international competitive success of Japanese autos and electronic products, of Korean textiles, ships and steel, of clothing from several, once less industrialized East Asian countries, and of many other of the major export efforts of recent years. These increases in exports were often achieved without the decreases in real wages often urged upon Latin America in recent years by prominent economists and international institutions to attain a similar objective. Moreover, the East Asian export-led economic expansions helped to stimulate substantial increases in wage levels without any slowdown in the pace of sales abroad. Is there any reasons to believe that it is likely to be different for manufacturing exports from Latin America? Is there any reason to believe that the region will be able to increase exports of manufactures *substantially* on a *sustained* basis without dedicating much more attention to supply-side factors than has been done thus far?[61] Clearly, productivity projects—to utilize available technology more efficiently, to emphasize technological development, and to foster best-practice utilization of new or adapted technologies—are among the keys to any major expansion of Latin American manufacturing exports in the future.

As critical as the broader macroeconomic issues have been and continue to be, even the best designed short-term programs can only

---

[61]According to Amsden, *op. cit.*, Korean export successes accrued despite greatly overvalued exchange rates and high domestic protection; they were made possible only by extraordinary increases in the productivity of plant operations.

provide a platform for the resumption of economic growth. That growth potential can easily be undermined, as it has so often been in the past, if more initiatives are not taken to assist in achieving long-term objectives, and if more use is not made of micro- as well as macroeconomic measures to help achieve those objectives. More must be done to assure the growth of competitive industries, to facilitate strong producer response to incentives, and, in particular, to provide the incentive to export which is indispensable to the overall economic development of the region.

CHAPTER II

ECONOMIES OF SCALE
AND LATIN AMERICAN EXPORTS

Clifford F. Pratten
Cambridge University

Introduction

This study considers the role economies of scale may have had in the growth of manufacturing exports from Latin America, and the possible significance of economies of scale for the growth of exports in the future. To that end, economies of scale are first defined and their significance for the economies of less developed countries outlined. Estimates of economies of scale are summarized and Latin American exports are compared to exports of the European Economic Community (EEC) and East Asian countries. Estimates of the economies of scale are examined to establish any pattern which would account for, or affect, past and future Latin American export performance. The paper is based on the author's study of economies of scale in developed countries and a survey of the literature.

No attempt is made in this paper to provide a complete summary of the literature on economies of scale. The following sources are recommended for readers requiring more information about them:

- Canada, Royal Commission on Corporate Concentration, *Report of the Canadian Royal Commission on Corporate Concentration.* Chapter 3 (Ottawa, 1977: Supply and Services Canada).
- F. M. Scherer et al., *The Economies of Multi-Plant Operation: An International Comparison Study* (Cambridge, Mass.: Harvard University Press, 1975). and *Industrial Market Structure and Economic Performance* (Chicago: Rand McNally and Co, 1980).
- *A Review of Monopolies and Mergers Policy*, Presented to Parliament by the Secretary of State for Prices and Consumer Protection. Cmnd, 7198. (London: H.M.S.O. 1978), Annex C.
- C. F. Pratten, *Economies of Scale in Manufacturing Industry*, (Cambridge, U.K.: Cambridge University Press, 1971).

Definition and Sources of Economies of Scale

Dimensions of Scale

Adam Smith's cogent description of the effects of the division of labor in the manufacture of pins is the origin of the analysis of economies of scale. But in spite of its long history there are still some misconceptions and ambiguities about the term economies of scale. It is often associated with the reductions in the average unit costs of production attributable to increases in the scale of plants and factories. In reality there are many interrelated dimensions of scale to which economies relate, and the size of plants and factories is not necessarily the most important.

The main dimensions of scale can be found in three major areas:

Efficiency of production

- Rate of production of particular components and products per unit of time;
- Duration of production runs, i.e., the period during which a distinct component or product is made or processed before switching to the production of another item (the size of batches being determined by the duration of production runs and the rate of production);
- Extent of standardization of components and products;
- Total capacity of plants and factories.[1]

Selling and distribution costs

- Sales to each customer;
- Geographic concentration of customers;
- Size of consignments to customers.

Financial costs and the ability to take risks and absorb setbacks

- The size of firms.[2]

---

[1]Examples of other dimensions of scale which affect the efficiency of production are: the output of a group of components or products made with the same equipment (generally referred to as economies of scope); the capacity of plant, machines and production lines within plants; the overall size of a complex of plants at one site, and the extent of vertical integration (i.e., the sequence of operations and stages of production performed at plants and by firms).

[2]Examples of other dimensions of scale which may affect costs and competitiveness are the scale of an industry in a country (which may, for example, affect the costs of supplier industries) and the scale of a national economy, which influences the total output of products made in a country.

Scale economies are reductions in costs attributable to different positions along dimensions of scale. In the same way that there are scale economies attributable to the size of plants, scale economies may relate to the size of batches, the size of a firm or industry, and so on.

The Sources of Economies of Scale[3]

These include:

(i) *Indivisibilities*: There are many costs which are at least partly independent of scale over certain ranges of output, i.e., costs which are wholly or partly indivisible with respect to output. The following are examples:

Type of cost:	Partly or wholly indivisible with respect to:
Initial development and design costs.	Output of a product.
First copy costs of books, newspapers, etc.	Number of copies produced.
Obtaining tenders and studying sources of supply.	Size of orders placed.
Items of capital equipment, e.g., gauges in units of chemical plant, presses used for stamping metal parts and cranes.	Total output for which equipment is required.
Office records for a batch of a product	Size of batch.

As the relevant dimensions of scale are increased, indivisible costs can be spread over a larger throughput and the cost per unit is thereby reduced.

(ii) *Economies of increased dimensions.* For many types of capital equipment both initial and operating costs increase less rapidly than capacity.

(iii) *Economies of specialization.* The larger the output of a product, plant or firm, the greater will be the opportunities for, and advantages of, specialization of both the labor force and the capital equipment.

(iv) *Economies of massed resources.* These may result from the operation of the law of large numbers. For example, a firm using several identical machines will have to stock proportionately fewer spare parts than a firm with only one, because the firm with several machines can assume that all of its machines are unlikely to develop the same fault at the same time. A large company's ability to spread risk may enable it to take more or greater risks.

---

[3]This subsection and the one that follows summarize material in Pratten, *Economies of Scale in Manufacturing Industry, op. cit.*

(v) *Superior techniques or organization of production.* Increased scale may make it possible to use more efficient techniques or methods of organizing production; for example, as scale is increased automatic machinery may be used instead of manually operated machinery.

(vi) *Learning effects.* Learning may be included as a component of technical progress rather than an economy of scale. It relates to movements along some of the dimensions of scale. It is a source of economies attributable to both the rate of production and the duration of production runs.

(vii) *Economies through control of markets.* A vertically integrated concern may be able to achieve economies by evening out the flow of output.

Sources of Diseconomies of Scale

Increases in unit costs may occur as scale is increased for two groups of reasons: the supply of a factor of production is fixed or the cost of a factor increases as demand for the factor rises (examples of factor limitation: the labor supply in an area available to a firm and the space available at one site for a factory), or the efficiency with which a factor of production is used declines as the quantity of the factor of production used by a firm increases. The first group is not a source of diseconomies of scale as the term is used here. For the purpose of measuring the economies of scale, it is assumed that there is a perfectly elastic supply of factors of production available to firms: the quantity of factors they buy does not affect the price. In practice the costs of factors may rise with increasing scale.

(i) *Technical forces.* There are some technical forces which cause diseconomies of scale. As the capacity of individual units of plant is increased, stresses and strains and friction may result. A possible source of diseconomies connected with the use of larger units of capital equipment is that they may take longer to design, build and break in, particularly if the size is outside the manufacturer's existing experience. If large plants take longer to construct this will increase the cost of equipment because of the cost of capital tied up while the plant is built and broken in.

(ii) *Management.* It has been argued that the costs of management may increase more than proportionately with scale, or the effectiveness of management may diminish as scale is increased.[4] Either could set a limit to the optimum scale for plants and firms.

---

[4]If the effectiveness of management falls as scale is increased, the costs of production are increased, but not necessarily the cost of management itself.

The costs of coordinating and organizing production may rise more than proportionately with increases in scale. The effectiveness of management may decline as the chain of management is extended because of delays in taking decisions brought about by the length of the management chain and/or the tendency for those ultimately taking decisions to get out of touch with events affecting the decisions. Scale may also affect the motivation of managers. Whether or not the management and ownership of a large firm are separated, the determination to maximize profits at the expense of other objectives may decline as scale is increased. In some cases the managers of large firms may be able to shelter behind the technical economies of scale achieved by their firms, while their counterparts at small firms may be spurred to greater efficiency by the stark choice between economizing or being forced out of business.

Originally the effectiveness of management was seen as placing a limitation on the absolute size of firms. The growth of super giant companies with 'M' form management structures undermined this view. The emphasis changed to management limiting the rate of growth of a firm. It was claimed that the rate at which a company could train additional managers needed to expand its operations was limited. During the 1980s managers have focused their companies on 'core businesses' suggesting there are limits to how many different types of business a company can operate.

(iii) *Labor relations and supervision costs.* As scale is increased people may simply work less well. The possibility that the performance of employees declines with scale could apply to more than one dimension of scale. As the length of production runs increases this may result in specialized and/or repetitive work, as the size of factories is increased it may be difficult to retain a 'family spirit' and, similarly, in a large firm labor relations may be inherently worse. The larger the factory or firm, the longer the chain of command must be; employees tend to be further away from their employer, and they are less likely to be understood by their employer.

(iv) *Selling and distribution.* Selling and distribution costs are also possible sources of increased costs at higher scales of output. For example, if, as the scale of a plant is increased, the geographic spread of markets, and so the average length of haul, is increased, the average unit costs of transport will rise. If additional sales are obtained from a new, less concentrated market, the costs per unit of representation may also increase. On the other hand, if the additional sales are made to existing customers and the size of consignments increases, both selling and delivery costs per unit may be reduced. Whether there are increased costs at higher scales of output depends on the overall marketing dimensions.

Avoiding the Disadvantages of Small Scale

It is possible to avoid some of the disadvantages of operating on a small scale. One strategy for avoiding scale disadvantages is to specialize: to have a large share of the output of a product or products for which firms operating on a larger scale cannot gain significant technical economies of scale while making other products. Another avenue for avoiding the disadvantages of small-scale production, in the case of operations or components for which the economies of scale are large, is to obtain these from domestic suppliers or suppliers in other countries who manufacture on a large scale. The purchase and use of second-hand equipment, machinery, jigs and tools may also reduce the handicap of small-scale operations for capital costs.

Research and development costs are an important source of economies of scale; they can be spread over the output of products to which they relate. Small firms may specialize in products requiring little research and development. Also, firms may work together (and with the government) on research projects in order to spread development costs over a larger output. It may be possible to buy or license designs from a manufacturer in another country. Similarly, ownership of operations by international companies may result in some sharing of research and development costs. However, agreements to buy designs and overseas ownership may preclude exports by the licensee or subsidiary or limit the area to which they can export; domestic firms may have to develop their own designs to get access to all markets.[5] Another advantage of international companies is to be able to speed up the learning process for their operations in different countries.

Economies of Scale and Less Developed Countries

Economies of scale apply in less developed countries, but they vary from those for developed countries. First, the relative costs of factors of production are different. In LDCs the shadow price of unskilled labor is generally very low and that of imported capital goods much higher than in more industrialized countries, reflecting the relative scarcity of the latter. This provides an incentive for the adoption of more labor-intensive techniques or local adaptation of capital-intensive ones. In addition, capital-intensive techniques—especially those relying heavily on imported equipment—often prove relatively less efficient in LDCs

---

[5]The terms for acquiring designs usually include a lump sum payment which results in economies of scale based on the number of units produced, and a royalty which does not lead to scale economies for the producer in the LDC.

than when used in more industrialized countries (there are, of course, cases in which this is not so, and there are also cases where the capital goods required are produced locally and efficiently). There can be no general presumption that large capital-intensive plants will not be optimal in LDCs because of differences in relative factor costs and less efficient operation of capital-intensive plants as there are often large economies of scale for capital as well as labor inputs.

There are detailed as well as general differences in factor prices. Transport costs and costs of reerection for imported bulky capital equipment are examples of where differences in absolute and relative costs can arise. Similarly difficulty in getting spare parts for machinery quickly increases the relative costs of production for large-scale operations which depend upon the use of complex imported machinery. These are examples of differences which raise costs for operations in LDCs. In contrast, some LDCs have access to relatively low cost sources of raw materials and power.

The efficiency of factors and techniques of production vary between advanced industrial countries and LDCs (as well as within these groups) and some of these variations are related to scale. Small scale production and less sophisticated techniques of production may be operated relatively more efficiently in developing countries. Lack of experience in building and managing large plants and operating large-scale units increases the relative costs of setting up and running this type of operation.[6]

In developed countries, economies of scale are often created by spreading product development costs over large outputs. Keeping abreast of the latest fashions, look or technical developments is less important, at least for some products made in LDCs, and sturdiness and reliability are even more important in these markets. This can provide a source of advantage for LDC manufacturers when exporting to other LDC markets. The market for new advanced products in developed countries is generally much larger, and having a large home market for new products is very helpful for getting them established.

Implications

Economies of scale may create difficulties for LDCs competing with advanced countries simply because for many products their smaller output means higher costs. Very approximate comparisons of the total output of all manufactures in 1980 for Brazil, Colombia and advanced

---

[6]This lack of experience may be avoided by hiring foreign contractors (particularly for an initial period) or by having the investment managed by foreign firms, though the use of foreign contractors and firms would, of course, have balance of payments consequences.

Table II-1   Population and Manufacturing Output of Selected Countries in 1980
(Approximate terms)

		Brazil	Colombia	U.K.	E.E.C.	U.S.
Population	(millions)	120	25	55	250	225
Employment in manufacturing	(millions)	4	0.4	6	28	20
	index:					
Manufacturing	U.K. = 100	30	2.5	100	600	450
Value Added	U.S. = 100	7	0.6	22	133	100

countries are shown in Table II-1. The smaller total output of manufactures in Brazil and Colombia compared to the USA reflects those
countries' smaller populations, lower per capita incomes and lower manufacturing exports. The fact that Brazil's production of manufactures is
about ten times that of Colombia is also important. The output of manufactures varies among LDCs.

Table II-1 deals with output per year. The cumulative output of
many manufactures to which learning relates is also much lower in
developing countries because their industrialization started later.

So far, economies of scale have been treated as a handicap for
LDCs. If a producer in an LDC can once achieve rates of production
similar to, or greater than, in developed countries, economies of scale
become neutral or a source of advantage. Also producers in LDCs may
be able to achieve higher rates of growth of output and gain advantage
from this. Finally, the importance of LDC markets to developed countries is worth noting where large economies of scale apply. Manufacturers in developed countries seek markets to reap the benefits of economies of scale and this provides developing countries with some leverage
if they can get multinational companies to bid against each other for a
share in the developing country's market.

Entry

An important question for LDCs is the extent to which economies of
scale are barriers to entry to an industry. While engineering estimates
of economies of scale for new production units will show the effect of
scale on the competitiveness of a new production unit in an industry
composed of such units, firms already in an industry have equipment
which is partly written down. New entrants must first be able to finance
the full costs of new plant and equipment (though this may be reduced
if the firms can acquire equipment second-hand). Traditional accounting
treatment often loads the initial years of operation of machinery with
relatively high costs. Also there are substantial initial costs connected
with setting up new operations: developing products, training employees, solving teething problems with new equipment and initial selling

and marketing costs to break into markets are examples. Firms already in an industry will have written off these sunk costs. There may be some advantage of late entry, however. It is often less costly to install the latest techniques at a new production unit and it may be easier to set efficient manning levels at such a unit.

Market failure

To claim that economies of scale act as a barrier or impediment to the exports of LDCs suggests a kind of market failure. If production costs are potentially low at some LDC sites, why do international (or indigenous) companies not set up more optimum-size plants in such locales and export from them? In fact there are many examples of companies doing this. But the investment decisions of companies in, for example, Japan are not taken on the basis of costs of production alone. Where they are protected by technical development, economies of scale or product differentiation, these companies can select their sites for production and are not forced to use the least cost sites; they can allow national interest as well as costs to influence decisions. In addition, there are differences between private and social benefits and costs for investment decisions. Companies may choose not to invest in LDCs unless they can earn a risk premium because they perceive risks for such investment—political risks and/or economic risks associated with fluctuations in commodity prices, etc. In effect, the risk premium increases costs for developing new industries in LDCs. Other reasons why firms may not minimize costs by setting up operations in LDCs to an optimum extent may be simply inertia, lack of information or a reluctance of managers and experienced workers to work in an LDC.

Estimates of Economies of Scale

Many studies have been undertaken to assess the size of the economies of scale and the range of scale over which they extend. Often estimates of the economies of scale are related to estimates of the MES—the minimum efficient (or optimum) scale of production—or are summarized by estimates of the MES (or MOS). Although the meaning of the term MES speaks for itself, the definition is in practice arbitrary: for example, the minimum scale the doubling of which would reduce average unit costs by less than 5 percent.

Comparisons of Actual Costs

Estimates of costs for operating at different scales of production are required to estimate the economies of scale and the MES. An obvious source of information is the actual cost of production at varying scales of output. Apart from the difficulties of obtaining such confidential data, the main objections to this approach are that the data usually relate to equipment of varying vintages, the equipment may not be fully adapted to the level of production at which it operates, and best-practice techniques may not be used, especially in LDCs and other countries not subject to international competitive pressures. Inevitably the data relate to operations in existence and cannot provide estimates for scales of production outside that range. For some industries, cost data for actual plants have been analyzed to estimate the economies of scale; electric power is probably the industry most fully researched for this purpose.

Censuses of Production are a rich source of data on industrial structure and costs. Two examples of attempts to estimate the MES scale for industries from this source are: Bruce Lyons, "A New Measure of Minimum Efficient Plant Size in U.K. Manufacturing Industry," *Economica* 47 (Feb. 1980), pp. 19–34, and Peter F. Cory, "A Technique for Obtaining Improved Proxy Estimates of Minimum Optimal Scale," *Review of Economics and Statistics*, LXIII (February 1981), pp. 96–106.

The main limitations on using census data are that the definition of most census 'trades' includes a range of products for each of which economies of scale, market size and growth vary and affect the size of establishments. For example, one U.K. census trade includes the production of components for cars (seat belts and engines are included), and the assembly of cars, commercial vehicles, buses and battery-driven vehicles. Some components for vehicles can be manufactured very efficiently in a factory of very small absolute size, but for the assembly of standard cars substantial economies of scale entail an output of at least a quarter of a million cars a year on one site. Similarly, production of agricultural equipment is lumped together in one census 'trade' although there are wide differences in the complexity and hence economies of scale for different types of agricultural equipment such as plows and combine harvesters. Another limitation on census data is that they can be used to derive estimates of economies of scale related to only one, or possibly two, dimensions of scale: the sizes of establishments and possibly the size of firms. Generally they do not reveal the economies of scale related to large outputs of individual products. The advantage of census data is that they are costs for actual plants.

Engineering Estimates

Another approach to estimating the economies of scale is to assemble *estimates* made by managers, engineers, economists and accountants of the costs of operating at different scales of production, where full adaptation to the scale of production is allowed for. The best of the 'engineering' estimates are based on technical relationships and detailed costings and they relate to the production of specific ranges of products. The main objections to engineering estimates are that they are estimates for *hypothetical* operations and are not tested. In practice, costs for actual production vary from expected levels, and such variances could be related to scale. Where engineering estimates extend beyond scales of production for which actual experience of operation has been obtained, unforeseen technical problems could invalidate the estimates. Transport costs and market constraints are usually excluded from engineering estimates. Transport costs can be included but they have to be related to an actual or hypothetical distribution of markets. A particular weakness of engineering estimates is that they do not measure the effectiveness of management at different scales of output, including the effectiveness of management in getting a good performance from employees.

To summarize, the evidence concerning the economies of scale is open to question. It should be regarded like the evidence in a legal case rather than experimental evidence to prove a scientific hypothesis.

Engineering estimates of the economies of scale for a range of manufacturing industries are summarized in Appendix E. In this section we use estimates for a wider range of industries to draw some conclusions about the nature and extent of the economies of scale. The MOS estimates are summarized in Table II-2.[7]

Engineering estimates indicate the existence of widespread, persistent and significant economies of scale. The weakness of engineering estimates, that they do not estimate the effectiveness of management, was noted earlier. It is therefore important that other evidence should support the engineering estimates of large economies of scale. This evidence is found in international comparisons of labor productivity which include the effects of management performance. Prais has estimated that, in 1978, output per employee in manufacturing industries in the United States was more than three times the U.K. level and twice the German level.[8]

Comparisons of labor productivity are difficult and these estimates might exaggerate the differences in output per employee. Also there may be unique factors causing low productivity in Britain. Nonetheless there do seem to be significant differences in labor productivity between the United States and Germany which are not accounted for by differ-

---

[7]This summary is based on that given by F. M. Scherer in *Industrial Market Structure and Economic Performance, op. cit.*

[8]S. J. Prais, *Productivity and Industrial Structure. A Statistical Study of Manufacturing Industry in Britain, Germany and the United States.* (Cambridge: Cambridge University Press, 1981).

Table II-2 The Magnitude of Economies of Scale

	Minimum optimum scale (MOS) as percentage of U.S. market	Percentage increase in costs at ⅓ MOS
Textiles, clothing and footwear		
Cotton and synthetic broad woven fabrics	0.2	7.6
Non rubber shoes	0.2	1.5
Tufted rugs	0.7	15
Average	0.4	8
Synthetic fibers		
Cellulose fibers	11.1	8
Nylon, acrylic and polyester fibers	6.0	14
Average	9	11
Raw material processing industries		
Portland cement	1.7	26.0
Petroleum refining	1.9	4.8
Integrated steel mills	2.6	11.0
Soybean mills	2.4	3.0
Printing, paper mills	4.4	14.0
Linerboard mills		12.0
Average	3	12
Industrial material and component industries		
Sulfuric acid	3.7	2
Synthetic rubber	4.7	22
Iron foundries	0.3	15
Bearings	1.4	8
Average	2.5	12
Machinery building industries		
Consumer products		
Refrigerators	14.1	6.5
Passenger cars	11.0	9
Bicycles	2.1	n.a.
Average	9	8
Capital goods		
Turbo generators	23	n.a.
Diesel engines	21–30	6
Machine tools	0.3	8
Electronic computers	15	12
Electronic motors	15	22
Transformers	4.9	12
Aircraft	10	30
Average	13–14	15

Source: F. M. Scherer, *Industrial Market Structure and Economic Performance* (Chicago: Rand McNally, 1980). Some of the estimates of the increase in costs at lower than MOS given by Scherer are for ½ MOS. These have been adjusted to estimate the cost at ⅓ MOS.

ences in investment, and large economies of scale (including learning) are the most likely explanation for higher productivity in the U.S.A. Again the fact that nearly 40 percent of West Germany's exports of manufactures originate from 20 companies is suggestive of the potentially important role of *large enterprises* (Germany is Europe's leading exporter). Without the large enterprises many of their suppliers would be unable to export the components and other products they manufacture.

A point of interest about the estimates of the MOS in Table II-2 is that they refer to different dimensions of scale. Many of the estimates refer to the size of one factory or plant to make shoes, cement, etc. In the case of bicycles, turbo generators and aircraft they refer to the output of products. In these industries production can be separated among a number of locations, though final assembly has to be at a single site to capture the full economies of scale. Even in the case of shoes it is economically possible to have certain departments at a separate location.

There are wide differences in the proportion of the output of U.S. industry represented by a plant of MOS scale and the increase in costs below that scale. The MOS varies from 0.2 to 23 percent of the American market, and the rise in unit costs at one third the MOS scale from 1.5 to 30 percent. In part these differences represent differences in the definition of industries. For example, turbo generators are a narrowly defined industry which, for census purposes, is part of the industry which "manufactures machinery for generating, transmitting and distributing electric power and electrical machinery not reported elsewhere," while machine tools include a very wide range of products sold to all the engineering industries and form a separate census trade. However, this is only a part of the explanation. There are large differences in the magnitude of economies of scale, the size of markets for products and hence the MOS as a percentage of the output of products.

The increase in costs at less than MOS scale is interesting. For nearly half the industries, the increase in costs at one third the MOS scale is less than 10 percent. One reason for the low increase in average unit costs at less than the MOS is that economies of scale for material costs are generally reckoned or assumed to be minor and the latter are a major component of total costs in many industries.

The large MOS in relation to the U.S. market for capital goods is noteworthy. If these estimates of the MOS are related to the much smaller markets of Latin American countries, the MOS's are far larger percentages of the market. And there are key industries—automobiles are the outstanding example—for which very large scale is required for assembly to reap the full advantages of scale. These industries are supplied by a great many small establishments in other trades which would not be viable in the absence of the large assembly plants.

The Griliches and Ringsjad Study

One influential study based on census data by Z. Griliches and V. Ringsjad (G&R) estimates scale coefficients which imply generally small economies of scale.[9] This conclusion is reinforced by the fact that their study is based on Norwegian data, and establishments in Norway tend to be smaller than in the larger developed industrial countries. However, the principal finding of this elegantly developed and presented study "is the evidence *for* increasing returns to scale . . . ," so it does not cast doubt on the existence of economies of scale.

The objections to using census data as a source for estimating economies of scale previously outlined apply to the G&R study. The economic interpretation of a scale coefficient for data for establishments drawn from all of Norwegian manufacturing industry is not clear. In effect, small businesses making, for example, made-to-order products or breaking bulky consignments and repacking are compared with paper mills making newsprint and plants for the manufacture of bulk chemicals. One would expect approximate equality of value added per unit of (weighted) input across this spectrum. The scale coefficient perhaps measures the effects of the greater barriers to entry in trades with large plants compared to trades with small plants.

The authors also provide estimates for individual industries. But many of these industries are amalgamations of different trades (subject to varying market conditions in 1963). The problems of comparing different kinds of business apply within many industries as well as to all manufacturing establishments. For example, pulp and paper mills are grouped together, as are small paper mills making high quality special papers with large paper mills making newsprint and packaging paper. The authors recognize the problem. They also recognize other uncertainties which may bias the results to an unquantifiable extent. They admit that there is a great deal of variability in their microdata which is not explained by the variables at their command. They say that the estimates (of scale) resulting from the bias are as likely to be too low as too high. They do not examine the *economic* justification for this claim. Where large economies of scale exist, small establishments will have been forced out of business or the value of their capital stock will have been lowered. The use of insurance policy replacement values may not circumvent this problem of valuation, because these values may reflect expectations of profits. For example, a firm may not insure at full replacement value in the event of fire because a new plant would

---

[9]Z. Griliches and V. Ringstad, *Economies of Scale and the Form of the Production Function: An Econometric Study of Norwegian Manufacturing Establishment Data* (Amsterdam: North Holland Publishing Co., 1971).

not be profitable at full replacement cost. The authors note that if economies of scale exist, the output of large establishments may well be priced lower.

Further, Norwegian industry is concentrated in activities for which economies of scale are limited (for example, food and fish processing and sawmills), manufacturing processes relatively simple and transport costs (for concentrating production) high. As the Norwegian market is relatively small, the Norwegians have kept out of industries requiring large scale, such as motor vehicles.

We may conclude that it is not the practical implications of G&R's study that has aroused interest, but its methodological sophistication.

A possible use of estimates of MOS based on census data is to check engineering estimates. Certainly census data and the MOS estimates based on these data indicate that caution is needed when dealing with any evidence which purports to show that very large economies of scale are *universal* in manufacturing industry. Lyons has estimated the MOS for *establishments* based on data for the distribution of plant sizes for multiplant firms in the U.K. given in the Census of Production; the average MOS for establishments was only 160 employees for the 118 trades distinguished.[10] This suggests *establishments* of large absolute size are not the key to competitiveness in many trades.

Alternative Technologies

The estimates of the MOS in Table II-2 are based upon data for developed economies and the technologies appropriate to those economies. Information about technologies appropriate to LDCs where the shadow price of unskilled labor is very low and that of imported capital goods relatively high is only available for a limited range of industries. These industries include shoes and cotton spinning and weaving—industries where economies of scale are not a major problem for LDCs— and industries such as brickmaking, maize milling and beer, which are probably not potential export industries.[11]

The use of adapted technology (appropriate technology) and/or second-hand equipment improve the relative costs of production for LDCs compared to those for advanced countries, but they apply in most industries (the main exception are process-type chemical operations). Thus they are unlikely to significantly change conclusions, based on data for developed countries, about which industries are subject to substantial economies of scale when applied to LDCs. Also, one study of the choice

---

[10]Lyons, *op. cit.*
[11]Howard Pack, *Macroeconomic Implications of Factor Substitution in Industrial Processes.* World Bank Staff Working Paper no. 377 (Washington: The World Bank, 1980).

of technology has indicated that relative costs are a secondary factor in the choice of technology, at least in the important machine-building industries.[12] There are other reasons for doubting the effectiveness of the use of appropriate technology rather than the most technically efficient techniques for firms seeking to export. Extra people will be employed with appropriate technology and this could lead to more difficulty in supervising operations. International competitiveness requires efficiency and high-quality products, and there are advantages in a continuous unswerving drive for high labor productivity and quality. Capital-intensive technology may be required to achieve high quality standards.

Small firms

The evidence of widespread economies of scale does not imply that there is no place for small firms. The emphasis on encouraging small firms in all the developed industrial countries indicates that small scale is not a universal barrier to efficient operation. Circa 1982, the decision by many companies in Britain to devolve responsibility for their operations to subsidiary companies and profit centers, reducing the day-to-day control and management exercised from the head office, again emphasized the advantages of smaller units when companies have to contend with a recession.

In a wide range of industries, small firms with less than, say, 200 employees can operate efficiently. They can supply certain components and services to large firms in industries such as motor vehicles where there are economies of scale for assembly and for the production of many components. Small firms can compete by making specialist products for which the market is small, or products for which large markets in terms of number of units can be supplied by a factory of small absolute size, or products for which the economies of scale are limited. In developed countries small firms have advantages in developing new products for which the initial market is small. For many new products large teams of R&D staff are not required and would not greatly speed development. Small firms in LDCs have similar advantages in the area of product development.[13]

---

[12]Samuel A. Morley and Gordon W. Smith, "The Choice of Technology: Multinational Firms in Brazil," *Economic Development and Cultural Change* 25 (January 1977); 239–87.

[13]Editor's note. This may be best exemplified by the contributing role of small firms in the export successes of Taiwan. See, e.g. L. J. Lau ed., *Models of Development: A Comparative Study of Economic Growth in South Korea and Taiwan* (San Francisco, 1986; Institute for Contemporary Studies).

Conclusions

Two conclusions of Bela Gold's review article, "Changing Perspectives on Size, Scale and Returns," were that scale effects may differ widely between and even within industries, and that our knowledge of economies of scale is inadequate.[14]

These conclusions are apt. The difficulty of estimating economies of scale springs from the vast range of products and processes. Even for one industry the knowledge required to make investment decisions is very great. The estimates of economies of scale available can only be used to draw qualitative and general conclusions. They do not provide a menu of blueprints for detailed investment and policy decisions. The general conclusions which can be drawn are:

(i) The MOS scale of production forms a substantial share of the U.S. market for many industries, particularly for the manufacture of capital goods. For the production of complex and evolving products the MOS tends to be large.

(ii) There is a range of industries (textiles, clothing and footwear) where, for many products, the economies of scale are exhausted at modest levels of production.

Comparisons with the Countries of East Asia

Editor's Summary:

Appendix F presents the data assembled by Pratten on Latin American and East Asian trade, especially exports of manufactures. The data are for 1979–80, the latest available when the study was first prepared.

This seemingly outdated material was retained for two reasons. First, during the years immediately following—the initial years of the debt crisis—Latin American export performance was abnormally poor, both in absolute terms and in comparison with the Asian countries. Second, in 1984 and in several years since (especially 1987–88), several Latin American economies achieved extraordinary increases in manufacturing exports (see, e.g., the discussion of the Mexican and Brazilian cases in Appendix A and that of the Costa Rica in Chapter I) but, many of those increases seem to be attributable to the magnitude of some of the devaluations and the collapse of some local economies, and to have been more of a temporary phenomenon than that of recent exports from East Asia.

---

[14]Bela Gold, "Changing Perspectives on Size, Scale, and Returns: An Interpretive Essay," *Journal of Economic Literature* XIX (March 1981), pp. 5–33.

Data from the 1978–81 period provide a more representative base for general comparisons for the region. Such data may underestimate the international industrial competitiveness of some countries such as Mexico, Brazil and Costa Rica and overestimate it for Peru, Argentina, most of Central America, and a few others. The Introduction and the Appendix F cite more recent and comprehensive comparisons of Latin American and East Asian manufacturing exports, but the earlier data used by Pratten appear to provide a sufficient basis for drawing conclusions appropriate to this chapter. The relatively early stage of the learning curve at which some industries operated during the period to which the comparisons relate, doubtless, contributed to the strength of some of Pratten's criticism of import-substituting industrialization.

Pratten's comparisons of Latin American with East Asian exports of manufactures concludes that the composition of exports of the former has concentrated on products for which economies of scale are generally less important, whereas this has been less true for the countries of East Asia.

Economies of Scale and Latin American Export Performance Since 1970

We shall now analyze the likely role of the economies of scale in recent Latin American export performance. Here we attempt to answer the question whether economies of scale explain why Latin American countries were not more successful in exporting the type of manufactures they did in fact export. To answer this question we have to assess other factors besides economies of scale which influence Latin American exports. No attempt will be made to quantitatively analyze the impact of scale economies of the type "an x percent increase in plant size would lead to. . . . " We concentrate on a general assessment of whether the lack of large operations in Latin America seriously hampered her export performance, given the actual structure of Latin American exports and the other factors influencing Latin American exports. To do this we consider where Latin American countries lose out in competition with East Asian countries. For this comparison we concentrate on exports of textiles and clothing which are products for which the two groups of countries have been rivals. A serious qualification to this part of the paper is that it rests on a review of the literature and not a field study of firms in Latin America and East Asia. A further qualification is that the literature analyzing the competitiveness of Latin American exports is not comprehensive. The published studies give a view of the competitiveness of manufactured exports which is not necessarily applicable to all Latin American countries. A final comment to this part of the chapter concerns the reliability of the literature on which it is based. Many of the studies of differences in industrial performance lack rigor in the sense that the conclusions have not been tested statistically. They may omit factors which are important to explain differences in performance.

Factors Which Have Not Played a Major Role

Chart 1 outlines the maze of forces which affect competitiveness. It is perhaps best to start by getting rid of those factors which do not seem to have played a major role. *Transport costs* are an example: the proximity of the countries of the northern part of Latin America to the major developed markets enables some goods to be flown to the U.S. market for the same price as sea freight from other parts of the world, and in a fraction of the time. This latter is especially important in clothing— one of the Latin America's most important manufactured exports—due to the need to keep up with fashion trends. Potential transport costs from Latin America to the European market are roughly equal to those from East Asia. Communication costs are also similar (e.g. telephone, letters, telex, etc). Thus, if anything, Latin American countries have an advantage over other developing countries in this respect, thanks to the speed with which they can get goods to the U.S. market.

A cry often heard in Latin American countries has been that the successful East Asian countries compete purely on the basis of *cheap* (some say exploited) *labor* (see Morawetz, *op. cit.*). Yet, as Morawetz indicates in that study, Colombian wages even in the early 1980s were below those of the East Asian countries. It is certainly true that the latter's prices are far more competitive, 10–40 percent more so in the case of clothing.

Subsidies are also often pointed to as a source of East Asian advantage. Yet Morawetz maintains that far greater government subsidies were offered by Colombia than by East Asian governments, and while more recent studies have documented subsidies in East Asia, it is clear that this factor has been prominent in many Latin American countries as well.

Trade Policies

Latin American countries have tried a variety of international *trade strategies*. The experience of Colombia is fairly typical of many Latin American countries. Until 1967 the emphasis was on import substitution with a system of tariffs and taxes which was biased against exports.

Now in all developing countries a phase of import substitution is desirable; the home market is of major importance in the initial devel-

CHART 1
THE DETERMINANTS OF SUCCESS IN EXPORTS OF MANUFACTURES

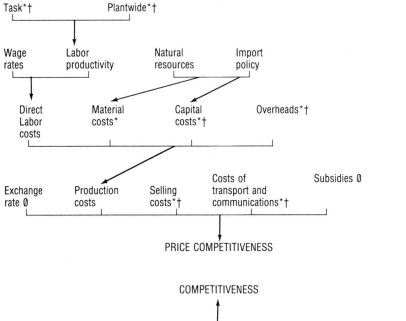

---

*Possible role for economies of scale
†Management factor important
ØRole of government important

opment of manufacturing industries. This has been as true for Japan, Korea and Taiwan (though admittedly not for Hong Kong) as for Colombia, Brazil and Chile. However, in the case of Japan, Korea and Taiwan, after an initial phase based on a build-up of industries making consumer goods and basic manufactures supplied to the home market, trade was reoriented to exports. In the Latin American countries, import substitution was carried further to the intermediate and capital goods industries. The MES applicable to the production of many of these goods is too large for the smaller Latin American countries to manufacture them efficiently for their domestic markets. Korea and Taiwan also have given attention to intermediate and capital goods industries, but not until the consumer goods industries was well enough developed to allow the profitable export of large proportions of output.

Between 1967 and 1973 the Colombian peso was devalued on a crawling peg system and many export incentives were introduced. There was a very noticeable improvement in the export position. The situation deteriorated again after 1973, chiefly because of a higher exchange rate following the increase in world coffee prices and the government's fear of the inflationary consequences of devaluation. While the inducements to export improved again by the mid-1980s, the situation from the mid-1970s until the mid-1980s was not unlike that of Britain in 1980, and the effect was similar: a heavy squeeze on exporters.

An *import substitution policy* has been followed to varying degrees in the Latin American countries (more so, for instance, in Chile prior to the change of government in the 1970s, as can be seen by the decline in the share of exports in total output during the early-to-mid seventies). The policy has had more far-reaching consequences than just the initial price effects. To the extent that the intermediate and capital goods industries are heavily protected, the export industries which they supply are trapped. The domestic industries charge higher prices for home sales than for export sales (see Morawetz *op. cit.*). The obvious reaction is to import—yet high tariffs make these goods massively expensive. What is worse, it is claimed that inefficient port and customs officials often delay imports (and exports). As a result Latin American export industries have higher raw materials costs than East Asian ones, and are less certain of the quality and delivery of raw materials.

Labor Productivity

It was noted that Latin American wages are, on average, not markedly higher than those in East Asia. What of *labor productivity, the other determinant of unit labor costs*? Labor productivity can be divided into "task productivity" and "plantwide productivity." The former is concerned with the efficiency with which individual tasks are performed given the relevant machines, operating schedules, plant organization, etc. Plantwide productivity measures the effect of varying the factors which are assumed to be given for measuring task productivity.

Task productivity can be further subdivided into output per minute, say, on a set task and output per operative day. The former measures the efficiency of the worker himself, how good he is at a given task. Results for LDCs show quite good performance in this respect. The second part, however, shows LDCs operating with a considerable amount of "X-inefficiency," i.e. below the technical potential of worker and machine. This is due to such things as lack of technical know-how and skill, which lead to an underestimation of the potential of machines and failure to plan and organize production efficiently.[15]

According to the Morawetz study cited above, plantwide productivity was the source of the most dismal performance by Latin America in comparison to East Asia.[16] Common inefficiencies were poor layout of machines, lack of shift work, excessive inventories, cluttered floors, crowded floor space and poor linking of production processes. The result is that labor productivity is said to be up to 50 percent lower in Latin America than in East Asia. This then is a major source of price uncompetitiveness for Latin America relative to the East Asian countries. Such differences are not limited to Latin America. For example, productivity in the Japanese motor industry is reckoned to be about twice that of the European industry.

Markets

It is important to be able to offer a competitive price, but that is half the battle at most, particularly for exports to developed markets. We shall look now at the many constituents of this aspect of successful exporting. Latin American firms face many problems in first getting themselves recognized as potential exporters. There is a credibility problem: the Latin American countries have not yet as a group, or individually with the possible exception of Brazil, Argentina, and recently Mexico, built up strong enough reputations as exporters. Keesing, *op. cit.*, suggests foreign buyers will look for their imports from countries which have commercial and industrial experience, high levels of skill and education, political stability, a sound institutional infrastructure and good transport and communication facilities. The existence of these factors in the East Asian countries, for example, has led to a convergence

---

[15]Editor's Note: See also Pack, 1987, cited in Chapter I.
[16]See also Howard Pack, *Fostering the Capital-Goods Sector in LDCs: A Survey of Evidence and Requirements.* World Bank Staff Working Paper no. 376 (Washington: The World Bank, 1980).

of views among businessmen that the best LDCs to buy from are Hong Kong, Taiwan, Korea, etc. In this way, their hand is strengthened further.

Another aspect of the process is the interconnections amongst firms in the same industry in a given country. Large chain stores deciding where to buy from may initially lean towards one specific item of clothing made in Colombia. However, if the whole range of garments they wish to buy is not available from Colombia but is available in Hong Kong, they may choose to optimize across all purchases, rather than buy one from a different place. Thus they may take all their business to Hong Kong. Countries such as Colombia then have to be especially good at manufacturing the few items they do produce in order to lure the large importers away from Hong Kong.

The other side of the buyer-location problem is sales specification, i.e., *fashion* or *design* performance. Finding an importer who is interested in buying clothes or machinery from Latin American firms is one thing; making sure the firms can produce exactly the right sorts of clothes or machines is another. As noted in Chart 1, this requires prior sales information on "fashion trends" (where these are relevant), technical advances, etc., and the concomitant production flexibility to adapt to changes in trends. Evidence suggests that Latin American firms have been less adept at achieving fashion consciousness than their East Asian rivals, and that this is known amongst major developed country importers.

Fashion and punctuality are linked. A firm can be completely up-to-date in its observation of and response to fashion trends, but if it cannot get its product to market in time, the sale is lost. We have already discussed the speed of Latin American deliveries to the United States market compared to that of deliveries from East Asian countries. One cause of poor delivery performance pinpointed in several studies is slowness in moving the goods out of the exporting country. Poor management, leading to low productivity (with the emphasis here on the relevant time implications rather than the cost), production muddles and inefficient export bureaucracies are the other major causes of bad performance in this area.

Quality

Quality control is the last item we deal with from Chart 1. Problems here can be split into two parts: those on the production side, and those on the sales side. The former arise through a phenomenon already discussed, the difficulties of exporters in obtaining raw materials. In the clothing industry, for example, certain textile producers are inefficient and small, and thus unable to achieve economies of scale. Their own quality control is weak, but because of high import barriers they can sell poor quality goods to clothing manufacturers. There is also a major problem in the capital goods sector, where import substitution policies in the machinery sector have led to low quality machinery.

Sales problems are also linked to product specification difficulties outlined earlier. Some Latin American firms have used exports as a means of getting rid of excess production, rather than seeing them as an end worth pursuing in their own right. Accordingly, they try to sell goods of the same specifications and quality which they sell at home, the result being a bad name for themselves and further damage to the reputation of Latin American exports in general.

Economies of Scale

The estimates of economies of scale quoted in earlier sections of the paper show that Latin American countries need *not* be at a substantial disadvantage in the textile, clothing and footwear industries because of the small scale of their firms and plants. Given their total output of textiles, clothing and footwear, Latin American countries are not precluded from organizing production to achieve the minimum optimum scale for production runs, factories and firms. In practice, economies of scale could have been a source of handicaps in these industries. For example, there are considerable economies to be obtained by organizing long production runs. However, we do not have the requisite information to examine the extent to which these economies have been achieved in Latin American countries. In general, Latin American textile mills produce an extensive range of products in short production runs.[17] In addition, the competitiveness of the textile and clothing industries depends on a competitive supply of fibers, dyes, thread, etc. Large economies of scale apply to the production of these commodities, and failure to achieve them could be a serious handicap. The economies of scale with respect to synthetic fibers are summarized in Table II-2. Importing, of course, provides a possible escape from this handicap.

It is obvious that for some factors influencing exports, such as the setting of exchange rates and export promotion policies, no economies of scale apply. Furthermore, poor management has been identified as a major source of low labor productivity, but since economies of scale depend on effective management rather than the reverse, their absence could not be blamed for problems in this department.

---

[17]Editor's note. Visits to textile mills in a number of Latin American countries tend to support this. An early 1980s consultant report prepared at the request of one of the larger mills in Colombia recommended production of a smaller number of items in longer runs as a means of reducing costs and increasing the proportion of output exported. No major changes were made in that regard, however.

New Trade Theories

The "new" trade theories[18] suggest that the size of the home market will be one important determinant of successful exporting. As trade barriers are reduced the importance of the size of domestic markets diminishes also. The emphasis in the new theory is on marketing strategies and innovation, i.e., market knowledge, entrepreneurial know-how, production process planning, design, etc. which are hypothesized to be sensitive to scale. These economies, moreover, are dynamic, i.e., they grow out of cumulative production through time, from learning and experience in producing for a market which must be penetrated more deeply once the initial breakthrough has been made. These economies do provide cumulatively increasing barriers to competitors; they are a result of sunk costs. They are the source of advantage to many manufacturers based in advanced countries.

There are advantages of scale which can aid market penetration. The existence of large firms in a developing country means that finance is available for setting up marketing organizations and sales information offices in the developed countries. There is no doubt that the relatively small size of some Latin American firms, in contrast to say, Japanese organizations, badly hampers their ability to break into developed markets because of the high product development and marketing costs associated with such an effort. In the U.K., for example, some Japanese firms offer six months' free credit to buyers of steel products. It is difficult for relatively small firms in Latin America or elsewhere to compete on those terms.

These handicaps must be put in perspective if we are to measure the importance of economies of scale accurately in determining the success of exports. Brazil, for instance, has a large home market, yet until the early 1970s its pattern of exports was similar to smaller Latin American countries. Also, firms can grow to a size where the setting up of marketing facilities in the developed countries becomes feasible, but, if quality, punctuality and design are not up to standard, no one in the advanced countries will buy their products. Firms domiciled in the advanced countries may also market imports for exporters from LDCs.

Conclusion

Our conclusions on the historic role of economies of scale are that larger scale operations would have reduced production costs and made it easier

---

[18]The new trade theories emphasize the nonprice and dynamic nature of modern international comparative advantage. They stress the advantages gained by technological developments, the concept of human capital, and product life cycles.

to finance marketing, which would have helped to establish footholds in foreign markets. But the relatively weak cost position and the poor quality, design and punctuality records make it doubtful whether the net advantage from larger scale per se would have appreciably affected Latin American export performance. In brief, the principal reasons for past differences in export performance between Latin American and East Asian countries are not economies of scale. They originate with the other factors. The East Asian countries have been used for comparison because they have been the most successful countries in increasing imports.

Economies of Scale and Latin American Exports in the 1990s

To assess the impact of economies of scale on Latin American exports during the 1990s, it is necessary to consider whether there will be changes in the incidence and extent of economies of scale in the near future. New technical developments are reducing the optimum scale of production. Examples of these are numerically controlled machine tools which reduce the costs of producing parts in short runs, and computer type setting and new printing machinery which reduce the costs of printing books and newspapers and thus the handicaps inherent in short print runs of books and newspapers with limited circulations. A recent study of the automobile industry suggests that more general changes may be afoot. Altshuler claims that for motor vehicle production "new hardware on the plant floor, in combination with computer aided design, engineering and tooling" is resulting in "receding scale economies."[19]

In advanced countries there is some evidence of a leveling off or even some decline in industrial concentration. A factor suggested to explain this change of trend is the increasing importance of science-based technical progress. Large companies, it is claimed, have greater difficulty organizing research and motivating and rewarding managers and research staff than do smaller firms. However, it is far from clear that the overall advantage of the large corporations will be broken. Many of the new small firms act as sub-contractors and suppliers to giant companies. This policy provides opportunities for firms in LDCs; they may act as suppliers of components and services to the giant companies.

In practice, economies of scale may be of *increasing* importance in international trade in spite of the changes which are reducing them. Industrial restructuring is taking place in both the developed industrial

---

[19]Alan Altshuler et al., *The Future of the Automobile Industry*. The Report of MIT's International Automobile Program (London: The MIT Press, 1984), p. 182.

countries and the LDCs to take advantage of the enlarged markets made possible by the enlargement of the EEC, the general reduction in tariffs, and the rapid industrialization in LDCs. The recession following the second oil price shock in 1979/80 speeded the process of restructuring. Restructuring increases the importance of economies of scale by increasing the scale of some production units and organizations, eliminating less efficient producers and applying pressure for increased efficiency—including taking advantage of the economies of scale.

Industries with Limited Economies of Scale

Although our conclusion was that economies of scale had not been decisive in shaping Latin American competitiveness in such industries as textile, clothing and footwear during the 1970s, we pinpointed the length of production runs as an area where there is scope for taking advantage of economies of scale. Further, the lack of large-scale domestic operations supplying the textile, clothing and footwear industries may handicap these industries. A third way in which these Latin American industries may be competing with a scale disadvantage is that they may not have firms of sufficient size to develop overseas markets. The relevance and importance of these sources of economies of scale require further study. If detailed study were to reveal that changes in industrial structure would improve competitiveness, further research to establish the most effective methods of bringing about the changes would be necessary.[20]

Resource-Linked Manufacturing Industries

The summary of the economies of scale in Table II-2 suggests that economies of scale are more important in the resource-linked industries such as steel and paper than in the textile, clothing and footwear group. Resource-based industries have not been a focus of this paper but they are important sources of Latin American exports, and a number of them supply other manufacturing industries and therefore influence the latter's competitiveness. Economies of scale certainly are of importance for processing plants and bulk transport of some resource-linked products, and those activities require further study.

---

[20]Editor's note: In countries with small domestic markets, a relatively concentrated industrial structure may be necessary to take advantage of economies of scale and enable enterprises to compete internationally. See C. D. Jebuni, J. Love and D. J. C. Forsyth, "Market Structure and LDCs Manufactured Export Performance," *World Development*, vol. 16, no. 12, (December 1988) pp. 1511–1520.

Industries with Large Economies of Scale

The industries in which the developed countries have an advantage are speciality chemicals, advanced machinery, electronics and vehicles. Their advantage is not based on economies of scale related to the size of production units or markets alone. In our view, knowledge and acquired skills are more important than scale differences in many of these industries. If, as Altshuler claims, a new entrant to international markets has to make a "breakthrough in production systems or products," the importance of this aspect of competitiveness is reinforced.[21] Can Latin American countries compete in some of these industries, and how are they to gain entry to them?

Plainly the larger Latin American countries have better prospects of entering and competing in such industries. Nevertheless, it is worth noting that in Europe some of the smaller countries, most notably Switzerland and Sweden, have been remarkably successful in achieving strong positions in these industries by specialization and overseas investment to achieve large scale and to secure markets.

One possibility for Latin American countries would be to have more industries subject to large scale economies set up by international companies. Multinationals can reduce the initial cost disadvantages for their operations in LDCs by supplying them with product designs, blueprints for factories and components for which the economies of scale are large. They can also source components in different countries to take advantage of the economies of scale. In the short term it serves the interests of the LDC to have a number of multinational companies providing competition in each industry. But there are advantages in limiting competition to take maximum advantage of the economies of scale. This applies to regions as well as separate countries. That having been said, it must be acknowledged that the role of multinational corporations has been greater in Latin America than in most of the developing countries of East Asia. Moreover, for the long term, control by foreign companies may have disadvantages: they may limit exports to other markets in which they have production facilities or to markets they supply from third countries. There may be advantages in associating with established multinationals based in the smaller industrial countries, or in associating with new or small multinational companies in the advanced countries as the latter may more readily share world markets.

International agreements among LDCs to give reciprocal advantages for entry to their markets would be helpful for the development of the new industries. For advanced products, transport costs represent

---

[21]*op. cit.*, p. 39.

a lower proportion of total costs, so trading blocs need not be limited to geographically adjacent countries. Some advanced countries have used the setting of standards as an effective temporary barrier to imports while home producers consolidate their position. LDCs might join together to develop a system of standards appropriate to conditions in their countries and provide their industries with temporary support in this way.

In the chemical industry, firms of engineering consultants have played an important role in transmitting technological expertise and knowledge to LDCs. It may make sense for international organizations to subsidize the setting up of more firms of this type to supply LDCs with information about mechanical and electrical engineering products, and manufacturing facilities. The formation of such firms may have high real returns, in part by reducing the prices of products in which the advanced countries specialize. It could be profitable for a group of LDCs to invest in these firms, if not for an individual LDC. It is the role of entrepreneurs to find such niches in markets, but many industrialists and businessmen in LDCs lack the close knowledge of markets to identify the right products.

The most productive approach for governments in Latin America to encouraging the development of new industries may be to improve the supply of qualified and skilled employees, thus providing the means for firms to enter new industries. New information technology makes it possible for LDCs to speed the process of industrialization by supplementing traditional training methods.

Final Conclusions

We conclude that economies of scale will become a progressively more important factor influencing the competitiveness of Latin American exports. Firstly, as other countries take advantage of economies of scale, that will intensify the pressure on Latin American countries to do so. Secondly, as Latin American countries move into more advanced manufacturing areas, including capital goods, they will be entering industries subject to greater economies of scale.

CHAPTER III

THE ROLE OF TECHNOLOGICAL LEARNING IN FACILITATING THE EXPORT OF BRAZILIAN CAPITAL GOODS

Morris Teubal
Hebrew University[1]

Introduction

The object of the study is to explain the evolution of Brazilian capital goods exports in terms of at least two sets of variables: technological learning within the sector, and government policy.[2] For several reasons, the learning variable is emphasized at the expense of more traditional economic variables, such as size of sector (or level of activity) and government policy, on which most studies of exports put emphasis.[3] The

[1] I am grateful to Hugh Schwartz for having made this study possible and for his comments throughout its execution. I appreciate the help of Carl Dahlman in providing both important material and useful comments on a wide variety of issues addressed by the study. The collaboration of Sylvio de Aguiar Pupo, Helio Nogueira de la Cruz, Nuno de Figueiredo, and Jorge Katz is much appreciated. Nadav Halevi, Ruth Klinov-Malul, Francisco Sercovitch, Simon Teitel and William J. Tyler made useful suggestions on various points. I am also grateful to a considerable group of Brazilian entrepreneurs and to Susanne Freund, who provided very useful editorial assistance. The field work for this study was conducted in July-August 1981. A different version of this chapter appeared as an article in *World Development*, vol. 12, no. 8 (August 1984), published by Pergamon Press, Oxford, UK, under the title, "The Role of Technological Learning in the Exports of Manufactured Goods: The Case of Selected Capital Goods of Brazil."

[2] A third important variable is the environment facing the sector, principally the domestic and export markets. Some of these will be referred to indirectly; e.g., a principal component in the domestic market for capital goods was the demand for equipment by state-owned enterprises (a government policy variable).
[3] An example is Tyler's study of Brazilian exports: William T. Tyler, *Advanced Developing Countries as Export Competitors in Third World Markets: The Brazilian Experience* (Washington, D.C.; Center for Strategic and Advanced Studies, Georgetown University, 1980). An important exception is Jorge Katz and Eduardo Ablin, *Tecnología y Exportaciones Industriales: Un análisis microeconómico de la experiencia argentina reciente* (IDB/ECLA/UNDP/IDRC Regional Program of Research on Scientific and Technological Development in Latin America, Working Paper no. 2 (Buenos Aires, 1976).

technological learning variable has received very little attention from economists, although intuitively it is of significance for exports of non-homogeneous products. It is also a critical variable for understanding the development of infant industries and the emergence of dynamic comparative advantage, and its conceptualization will therefore have policy implications. However, the study does not concentrate on technological learning to the exclusion of government policy variables. While the direct effects of the latter on exports are pretty well known, the indirect effects, via the effect on learning, have not been investigated.[4] This paper attempts to illustrate and illuminate the nature of these relationships.

The approach followed is to identify relevant learning processes for eventual introduction into export behavior equations or as a basis for theoretical models. Its starting point was a series of microeconomic case studies of technologically sophisticated firms (eight firms were interviewed in Brazil and five in Argentina). Such studies concentrate on a small number of variables focusing on the learning processes of firms, and in particular on the indirect contribution (spin-offs) of early activities or products to later activities or products. Among the specific issues addressed in the case studies are the following: (1) What is the nature of technological learning? Are there recognizable sequences? Does it generally lead to products of increased technological complexity or sophistication? (2) How, if at all, has technological learning benefited exports? (3) To what extent have other endogenous firm spin-offs, principally from reputation effects, been important for increased efficiency and for the emergence of exports? (4) What can be said of the economic value of the firm's accumulated experience, and the factors determining it?

The learning process within the firm relates to a whole series of activities: manufacture and plant operation; investment or project execution; product design and R&D. The case studies document all aspects of learning but some of those more commonly found should be emphasized here. A basic distinction, which is particularly relevant for metalworking industries, is between learning to manufacture, or *the acquisition of manufacturing capability*, and *the acquisition of design capability*. The former refers to the gradual mastery of an increasing range of manufacturing processes, such as machining and other metalforming processes, welding and assembly. It also involves increasing knowledge of and experience with the many materials used. The acquisition of

---

4Some policy instruments, such as exchange rates and subsidies, directly affect the share of output which is exported. Others, such as output subsidies and protection of the domestic market, may have only an indirect effect on exports, e.g., via learning, economies of scale, etc. Econometric work on exports has emphasized exchange rates and subsidies.

design capability enables the firm to specify the equipment required for a particular manufacturing process, and the product needed for a particular user. This requires a much deeper knowledge of materials in order to be able to select the best for each purpose. It also requires knowledge about the use to which the product will be put. For example, the manufacturer of chemical industry equipment must be familiar with the entire process carried out by the customer, not merely that part of it in which his equipment is involved. It is customary to distinguish detail-design capability from basic capability. The former tailors a product to a particular application without modifying the general type or class. Basic design capability, on the other hand, may enable a firm to adapt existing product types or to launch completely new products (innovation). R&D is the set of activities (such as the construction and testing of prototypes or pilot plants) which, in firms that have basic design capability, leads to product or process innovations.

Learning may or may not lead to product or process adaptation, depending on a number of factors. Developing an ability to handle manufacturing processes is probably insufficient to sustain product or process adaptation, although minor adaptations may be possible. On the other hand, the acquisition of design capability does not by itself ensure that more than minor adaptations (and tailoring) will take place. This depends on other factors as well, some of them related to the market. However, the presence of design capability increases the probability of major adaptations. Here, the main reason for focusing on capital goods industries in Brazil was their impressive development, especially during the 'Brazilian miracle' period (1968–74), not only quantitatively but qualitatively as well. The array of goods being produced and exported and their increasing sophistication are prima facie evidence of intensive technological learning and identifiable adaptation. In addition, capital goods, broadly defined to include all transport equipment, have in the last decade become the most important component of exports of relatively sophisticated products.[5] Other *a priori* considerations (some of them not specific to capital goods) were that: (i) machinery or metal products are non-homogeneous products and the large number of different features increases the probability of product

---

[5]See Carl J. Dahlman, untitled draft on Brazilian capital goods (Washington, 1981) p. 40; "relatively sophisticated" products were defined as manufactured products (ISIC definition) excluding: semiprocessed basic products such as brown sugar, frozen meat, and processed mineral ores; semimanufactured products such as crystallized sugar, natural wax, vegetable oils, cut woods, cacao paste, processed hides, paper pulp, and iron and steel in crude form and in simple products; and other products using relatively simple technology such as food products, beverages, textiles, clothing, leather goods, footwear, and wood products. The share of capital goods in total exports of relatively sophisticated products rose from 30 percent in 1970 to around 50 percent in 1979.

adaptations; (ii) process adaptations in other industries (such as raw-materials processing) may involve machinery adapted by the capital-goods sector; (iii) machinery production may be divided into a set of elementary tasks common to a wide range of machinery types.[6] Thus the probability of learning and adaptation would seem to be high. Needless to say, I do not claim that all the relevant learning processes are concentrated in the capital-goods sector (although this may in part depend on what is classified as capital goods).[7]

The second section gives an overview of the development of the capital-goods sector and its exports. It is shown that the increased share of capital-goods exports is part of a general increase in the sophistication of total Brazilian exports. The work of others on the effects of government policy in explaining the evolution of exports is summarized in the third section. It is argued that while direct, often short-term foreign-trade instruments such as tariffs, exchange rates and export subsidies offset the tendency towards currency overvaluation, thus permitting sales to export markets to take place, they cannot explain the rise in the share of capital goods output exported, since they do not seem to have affected the relative profitability of the export and local markets for capital goods.[8] This points to other measures and factors, such as increased efficiency in the sector (for which there is independent evidence). One cause of this increased efficiency—the learning processes within the firm—is investigated in the fourth section. The last section summarizes the original study and spells out some implications of the analysis for productivity (and export) growth and for the theory of the infant firm. It should be said at the outset that the present work does not lead to a clear-cut theoretical model of learning and export growth, nor to a quantitative empirical relationship between them. The epilogue provides a broader context to take account of the developments of the 1980s.

Capital Goods Exports: An Overview of the Brazilian Case

The growth of Brazilian capital-goods exports should be related to the growth of manufactured goods exports in general and to the growth of

---

[6]See Nathan Rosenberg, *Perspectives on Technology* (Cambridge, England, 1976: Cambridge University Press).

[7]Points (i) and (iii) are common to metal products in general. Also some of the factors favoring product adaptations in non-homogeneous products may favor process adaptations in the chemical and petrochemical industries.

[8]Editor's note: While this appears to have been true for many industries, including those analyzed in this study, the measures did amount to major subsidies for some industries (notably transportation goods), and the subsidies do appear to have fostered more exports in the latter favored industries than otherwise would have taken place. See Appendix A.

relatively sophisticated manufactured exports, of which capital goods are an important group. Table III-1 summarizes Table 1 of the Dahlman Report (1981). The first two columns show the development of total Brazilian exports between 1970 and 1980. Nominal exports in 1980 were 7.4 times the 1970 level, while real exports trebled between 1970 and 1979, an impressive record by any standard. The shares of various definitions of manufactured or industrialized products in total exports are shown in columns (3), (4) and (5). The ISIC definition of manufactures (column 3) includes anything which is manufactured and thus includes processed foods, most of which relies on relatively simple technology. The Brazilian definition of industrialized products (column 5) excludes a number of semiprocessed products, while the Brazilian definition of manufactured products (column 4) subtracts semimanufactures from industrialized products (see note 5 above). The figures in these three columns show that while the share of manufactures (ISIC) in total exports has risen by about 10 percentage points, the share of the industrialized and manufactured products (Brazilian definition) doubled and trebled, respectively. The increasing sophistication of Brazil's exports stands out when we look at the share of the last two categories of Table III-1. Capital goods (column 7) are an important component of relatively sophisticated exports, and their share in total exports quadrupled between 1970 and 1979. Thus the increasing importance of capital goods exports can be viewed as part of a wider trend of increasing technological sophistication. This is also true of the output of capital goods.

The central feature of Brazilian capital-goods[9] exports during the last 15 years is their impressive growth, both in absolute terms and relative to the output of the sector. From $87 million in 1970, representing 2.2 percent of output, exports grew to $800 million (1970 dollars) in 1978, or 9 percent of the output of that year.[10] Real exports grew at an annual rate of 28 percent during the period. The growth in the share of output exported took place in a sector whose real annual growth rate (11 percent) exceeded that of manufacturing industry in general: the share of capital goods in total manufacturing output increased from 11.5 percent in 1965 to 15.1 percent in 1977 (World Bank, 1980, p. 65).

The composition of capital-goods exports, including automobiles, between 1962 and 1979 is seen in Table III-2. The largest categories are

---

[9]Unless otherwise stated, the definition of capital goods used is that appearing in World Bank, *Brazil: Protection and Competitiveness of the Capital Goods Producing Industries*, Report no. 2488–BR. (Washington, 1980). It includes metal products, mechanical and electrical equipment, and transport equipment other than automobiles.

[10]See World Bank (1980), p. 67. Exports of a broader category that includes transport equipment, boilers and machinery, electrical equipment, and steel manufactures grew from $213 million in 1972 to $1,920 million in 1978 and $2,595 million in 1979. See World Bank, *Country Economic Memorandum: Brazil* Report no. 3275a-BR (Washington, 1981). A summary of some of the information can be found in Table III-2 below.

Table III-1. Development of Brazilian Exports: 1970–1980

	Total exports		Percentage of total exports				
	Millions of current US$ (1)	Millions of 1970 US$ (2)	Manufactured products		Industrialized products (Brazilian definition) (5)	Relatively sophisticated products[a] (based on ISIC) (6)	Capital Goods[b] (7)
			ISIC definition (3)	Brazilian definition (4)			
1970	2,739	2,739	70.4	15.2	24.3	10.9	3.4
1971	2,904	2,792	69.9	20.0	28.3	11.4	4.3
1972	3,991	3,695	76.6	22.9	30.6	12.7	4.9
1973	6,199	5,437	72.8	23.6	31.3	9.3	3.6
1974	7,951	6,260	70.4	28.5	40.0	12.9	6.8
1975	8,670	6,282	66.2	29.8	39.6	19.1	9.0
1976	10,128	6,889	69.3	27.4	35.7	16.1	8.2
1977	12,120	7,769	74.4	31.7	40.3	18.6	10.1
1978	12,659	7,535	79.4	40.2	51.4	25.0	13.4
1979	15,244	8,195	80.0	43.6	56.0	31.1	14.7
1980	20,132			44.9	56.5		
1979/1970 (Ratio)	5.6	3.0	1.1	2.9	2.3	2.9	4.3

[a]The category of relatively sophisticated products includes—in addition to capital goods—paper products, printing and publishing, industrial and other chemicals, petroleum refining, rubber and plastic products, basic ferrous and non-ferrous metal products, etc.

[b]Inclues motor vehicles.

Source: Carl J. Dahlman, untitled study on Brazilian capital goods (Washington, 1981) Table 1.

Table III-2 Production and Exports of Capital Goods, 1970–79

| | Total[a] (millions of 1970 US$) | | Exports[b] (current prices) | | | | | |
	Output	Exports	Total	Metal products	Non-electrical machinery	Electrical machinery	Transport equipment	Scientific and other equipment
Millions of $								
1970	3,203	87	105.7	9.8	63.6	16.5	14.9	0.9
1971	3,610	114	148.8	11.5	76.2	27.9	30.8	2.4
1972	4,366	182	239.7	18.8	98.4	38.7	80.9	2.9
1973	5,920	241	336.1	25.0	128.9	83.4	94.1	4.7
1974	6,849	466	702.7	43.1	251.3	182.2	215.2	10.9
1975	7,195	602	984.7	61.8	366.6	162.9	373.6	19.8
1976	8,441	553	1,032.3	50.3	326.7	196.1	443.2	16.0
1977	8,173	757	1,498.2	78.7	473.0	286.0	636.8	23.7
1978	8,800	800	2,087.2	109.3	636.1	315.7	984.3	41.8
1979			2,652.2	134.8	864.3	340.8	1,247.6	64.7
Percent								
1970	100.0	2.2	100.0	9.3	60.2	15.6	14.1	0.3
1971	100.0	3.1	100.0	7.7	51.2	18.8	20.7	1.6
1972	100.0	4.1	100.0	7.9	41.1	16.2	33.8	1.0
1973	100.0	4.0	100.0	7.4	38.4	24.8	28.0	1.4
1974	100.0	6.8	100.0	6.1	35.8	25.9	30.6	1.6
1975	100.0	8.3	100.0	6.3	37.2	16.5	37.9	2.1
1976	100.0	6.5	100.0	4.9	31.6	19.0	42.9	1.6
1977	100.0	9.2	100.0	5.2	31.6	19.1	42.5	1.6
1978	100.0	9.0	100.0	5.2	30.5	15.1	47.2	2.0
1979			100.0	5.1	32.6	12.9	47.0	2.4

a Excluding automobiles.
b Including automobiles.
Source: Dahlman (1981).

transport and non-electrical machinery, followed by electrical machinery, metal products and scientific instruments (within transport, the largest item is motor vehicles). The subsectors which exported more than $10 million in 1970 and whose exports increased rapidly thereafter are special industrial machinery, office machinery, machinery not otherwise classified and motor vehicles. As can be seen, there was a significant change in the composition of capital-goods exports (broad definition) in the period.

Exports and Government Policy: A Summary of Research

The export performance of the Brazilian capital goods sector in the 1970s can be summarized as follows: a high annual rate of real export growth (28 percent—well above the country average of 11 percent) and a more than fourfold increase in the share of sector output exported. In analyzing the role of technological learning it is important to assess to what extent this can be explained by direct export incentives and other measures having a direct effect on the volume and direction of trade.

One would expect a significant rise in the ratio of capital goods exports to output to be associated with an increase in the profitability of exports relative to local market sales (given the overall profitability of the industry). Government policy would affect this ratio if export subsidies rose more than the level of protection. Furthermore, the policy variable which will have a direct effect on the growth of exports (and, via export demand, on the growth of output) is the effective real exchange rate (that is, the real exchange rate plus export subsidies). Two important studies, one focusing on capital goods and the other on exports in general, reached the conclusion that these incentives have not been sufficiently strong to explain the growth of capital-goods exports. Referring to the period 1969–78, the first of these studies states that "while export incentives were important in these sales, their magnitude offset the overvalued cruzeiro. Moreover, there were no changes in the benefits provided during this period which can explain this growth."[11]

Tyler (1980) arrives at essentially the same conclusion for the 1970s. He also points out that exports have to contend with discrimination which "can also be seen through a comparison of the protection afforded

---

[11]World Bank (1980), pp. vi and vii. Nominal subsidies on most capital exports for 1975 ranged between 20 and 36 percent (see Table III-4 below); in 1978 the cruzeiro was regarded as overvalued by 25–35 percent, and the extent of overvaluation had not changed substantially between the end of 1973 and mid-1978 (see World Bank, 1980, pp. 10, 11 and 13). Editor's note: See, however, footnote 8.

to production for the domestic market and the subsidization provided to export production" (Tyler, 1980, pp. 56–57). Both studies conclude that the development of Brazilian capital-goods exports was made possible by increased productivity or competitiveness, and provide some direct evidence in support of this view (Tyler, 1980, Chapter 5; World Bank, 1980, pp. 39–43). An alternative hypothesis would be that in the 1970s export growth was fueled by an increase in the sector's excess capacity and that the price received probably covered marginal rather than total average costs. This hypothesis cannot be tested, but I suggest that its significance would be limited in so far as exports depend relatively less on price and more on quality, product specifications and firm reputation, particularly, as will be seen later, with respect to many capital goods.[12] Finally, another factor which may have influenced exports is changes in demand. If anything, the local demand for capital goods increased during most of the period (a fact due to the investment demand of state-owned enterprises, see next subsection), in which case its direct effect on exports would be negative.

What caused this increase in productivity and hence in exports? An answer to this question requires a close look at the supply and demand factors impinging on the Brazilian capital goods industry. The importance of skill acquisition and technological learning is suggested both by the changing array of commodities produced and exported by the sector and by the case studies of individual firms. Some of these studies show, first, that exports may be associated with an increased capability to supply more sophisticated products, and second, that this capability is in part a spin-off from earlier activities involving less sophisticated products supplied to the local market (see the section on technological learning). It seems to me that these phenomena are important for explaining both the absolute and the relative growth of exports.[13]

---

[12]Editor's note: Teubal's thesis also appears to be supported by the findings of Teitel and Thoumi which shows that this export growth reflects statistically significant growth trends over the decade of the 1970s, and thus, presumably long run profitability independent of the shifting export promotion arrangements. See Simón Teitel and Francisco E. Thoumi, "From Import Substitution to Exports: The Manufacturing Exports Experience of Argentina and Brazil," *Economic Development and Cultural Change*, vol. 34, no. 3 (April 1986).

[13]Another factor that could explain the sector's export performance is a rise in the world price of capital goods supplied by Brazil; a basic issue here is the price index that should be used. The effects of a change in world prices cannot always be separated from the effects of technological learning. For example, a fall in the relative price of a simple good currently being exported may have a positive or a negative effect on exports according to whether the sector is or is not able to shift to a more complex good whose world price has increased.

Other Measures Favoring the Capital-Goods Sector

The export performance of the capital goods sector has also been greatly influenced by government measures affecting the overall (private) profitability of capital goods firms rather than causing changes in the relative profitability of exports and local sales. These measures may be divided into those increasing the domestic demand directed to local producers and those that favor the supply of capital goods (output and investment). The most important was the increase in government demand for locally produced capital goods. This followed from the expansion programs in the basic industries and infrastructure, in conjunction with clear directives to the state-controlled firms to purchase domestically produced equipment. I have found no figures on the extent of this demand or on the proportion of total domestic capital-goods demand originating in government or government-owned enterprises. In some peak years as much as two-thirds of the total demand for capital goods was filled locally. Other measures that increased demand include tariffs and nontariff barriers to imports, tax exemptions, and cheap loans for the purchase of locally produced capital goods and other such incentives that are part of government approved investment packages. Concerning tariffs, there are figures on the average rate collected on capital goods for selected years between 1964 and 1977: it ranges from 6.9 to 16.2 percent (World Bank, 1980, p. 16), the higher figure reflecting the increased protection of 1976 and 1977 that followed Brazil's balance-of-payments difficulties.

Additional 1976 figures on tariffs can be found in Table III-4 below. Nontariff barriers to imports were much more important in increasing the demand for locally produced capital goods (the prior deposit required for importation was equivalent to a 50 percent tariff). Table III-

Table III-3   Composition of Investment Approvals and Share of Local Equipment Required for Approval: Brazil 1974 and 1978

	Percentage of total fixed investment		Required percentage of local equipment	
	1974	1978	1974	1978
Capital goods	8.5	7.8	37.5	50.9
Basic and intermediate metal industries	23.1	61.0	48.4	75.9
Chemicals and petrochemicals (including pharmaceuticals)	20.9	11.4	48.7	97.6
Nonmetallic, intermediate products, paper and cement	23.0	11.0	54.3	80.5
Automotive industry (including components)	7.9	6.0	36.5	74.7
Consumer goods	16.5	2.8	30.5	56.5
Total	100.0	100.0	44.3	75.9

Source: World Bank (1980).

3 shows the percentage of locally purchased capital goods required for government approval of special investment programs; as can be seen, this proportion has increased. Measures favoring locally produced capital goods include the investment incentives mentioned above (which favor several other sectors as well) and direct fiscal subsidies (see Table III-4). I have found no figures for the rate of subsidy implied by the investment incentives, although some estimates may be available from Brazilian sources.

Some Implications

The description presented above suggests that government has had a significant effect on the development of Brazilian capital-goods exports. Most of this effect, however, was indirect: it came about through a set of protection and subsidy measures whose immediate object was import substitution (or the avoidance of an unduly high rate of import growth) and the development of what economists would regard as an infant industry. These measures enabled the sector to accumulate physical

Table III-4   Tariff and Subsidy Rates for Capital Goods[a]

	Average[b] tariff rate, 1976	Export subsidies[c]		
		Fiscal subsidies	Tax rebates on capital goods	Total
Pumps and motors	13.0	22.4	0.1	22.5
Machine parts	28.3	20.8	-	20.8
Industrial equipment and machinery	9.2	21.0	13.5	34.5
Agricultural equipment and machinery	11.7	16.8	10.9	27.8
Office and domestic equipment and machinery	17.1	24.9	2.0	26.9
Tractors	4.9	23.0	13.5	36.5
Equipment for electric energy	17.1	19.4	2.1	21.5
Electric conductors	20.5	20.0	1.4	21.4
Electrical equipment	34.4	20.2	4.5	24.7
Electrical machinery	28.1	25.7	4.6	30.3
Electronic equipment	18.8	20.0	-	20.0
Communications equipment	42.0	26.5	5.0	31.5
Trucks and buses	8.7	26.0	9.7	35.7
Motors and vehicles parts	26.5	25.8	4.3	30.1
Shipbuilding	0.1	23.5	5.9	29.4
Railway and aircraft equipment	2.1	15.5	7.3	22.8

[a]IBGE classification.
[b]Calculated as actual tariff collections divided by imports c.i.f.
[c]The fiscal subsidies via the IPI and ICM tax credits are estimates made with 1975 data.
Source: World Bank (1980), p. 74.

capital, technology and experience while for the most part supplying the local market.

Exports, whose growth accelerated significantly after 1973, should be regarded as a spin-off from what was essentially a domestically oriented activity (see next section). They should also be regarded as a consequence of underutilization of capacity, especially in the later years when, because of the energy crisis, the government cut back its expansion plans for basic industries.[14] In other words, two factors should explain the acceleration of exports; the capabilities accumulated during the import-substitution and infant-industry states—physical capital, technological knowledge, experience and skills—and the subsequent reduction in domestic demand. This emphasizes the dual relationship between the local and export markets: in the short run they are substitutes, i.e., a reduction in domestic demand will, for a given level of capacity or output, tend to increase exports; on the other hand, stimulation of local demand (and/or protection of the local market) will, by making it possible to increase efficiency, eventually increase exports. In other words, the local market and exports may be regarded as complementary in the long run.

The microeconomic studies summarized in the next section suggest that an important technological learning effect underlies the productivity increase in the Brazilian capital-goods sector. Together with enhanced firm reputation, this explains why a preliminary stage of supplying the local market has contributed to exports in the long run. It would be interesting to know the conditions under which an efficient export-promotion strategy should conform to this pattern. Static trade theory suggests that if exports are to be encouraged at all, it should be via direct subsidization of exports (or devaluation). The Brazilian experience suggests that under certain conditions, export promotion need not be specifically geared to exports in the short run.

There would seem to be two such conditions. The first holds when exporting is more difficult (or expensive) than supplying the local mar-

---

[14]Figures published in *Conjuntura Econômica* (July 1981) show that the rate of capacity utilization in the mechanical industry declined after 1976, ranging from 76 to 80 percent during 1977–81 (these are simple averages of quarterly figures). The figures for 1971–76 are closer to 90 percent and in 1973 the average stood above 92 percent. A broadly similar pattern is observed for the metallurgical and electrical, electronic, and telecommunication materials industries (the classification used here does not correspond to the standard industrial classification). Excess capacity in capital goods should be regarded as the 'natural' outcome of a policy of promoting basic industries and infrastructure with an increasing reliance on local supplies. This assumes that, once these programs are terminated, the shift to exports is not automatic and takes time. The excess-capacity situation will be more serious if government cuts in investment are unexpected (as they seem to have been in Brazil), and if initial firm strategy was not explicitly geared to the eventual supply of exports.

ket. This may be due to the difficulty of achieving reasonable product quality, to the need to produce more complex or sophisticated products, to the greater firm reputation required, to the greater difficulty in understanding user needs, or to other factors, such as longer delivery times, supply of spare parts, or arranging for servicing. The second holds when the experience, capabilities, and reputation acquired by supplying goods to the local market have the spin-off effect of benefiting exports.

These conditions will probably hold for some products and countries and not for others. For example, nonhomogeneous products such as machinery, instruments and systems may satisfy the first condition since it may be inherently difficult for users to evaluate their functional utility or reliability. It will be even more difficult to export if the prospective purchaser runs the risk of substantial losses by making the strong choice of products or supplier. In this case the local market will enable local firms to enhance their world reputation as reliable suppliers of equipment, thereby eventually permitting them to penetrate export markets. A large domestic market is necessary but not sufficient for the second condition. The indirect strategy is probably less efficient for small or even medium-sized developing countries than for large ones such as Brazil, Mexico and India.[15,16]

Technological Learning: a Summary of Some Enterprise Interviews

The microeconomic interviews focused on learning processes and their relationship to export potential. This relatively narrow focus made it possible to interview a fairly large number of firms (given the time available) and to collect a large amount of information on the topic analyzed. Although a great deal of the information is qualitative (e.g., descriptions of endogenous firm spin-offs), some quantitative information was obtained on their economic value. More important, a good deal of the groundwork for theorizing about the nature of the spin-offs and their economic value to the firm has been laid, and it has become much more clear what additional quantitative information will be needed.

---

[15]If both conditions hold, the efficiency of direct export subsidization of an infant industry or firm will be relative low, i.e., both the absolute effect on exports and the ratio of exports generated to subsidies will be lower, at least relative to what it would be after having supplied the local market for a while. Note that indirect export strategy is not inconsistent with export or outward orientation even in the early phase. In addition, it does not imply that tariff or nontariff protection is preferable to output subsidization in that phase, nor does it exclude export requirements as part of the investment incentive package.

[16]In the above discussion we reviewed the strategy for export promotion under the assumption that the country in question possesses a dynamic comparative advantage in the sector analyzed. It may, however, be impossible to separate the two issues.

The Firms Interviewed

A total of thirteen firms were interviewed, eight in Brazil and five in Argentina.[17] In addition, background information on five other firms was obtained, and these firms can be interviewed in any follow-up of this project. Most of the firms belong to the capital-goods industry.[18]

A brief description of the product lines and areas of the firms interviewed follows:

Carvallo: a successful Argentine producer of bottling equipment for the domestic and foreign markets.

Confab Industrial: originally a boiler shop which has evolved into Brazil's most important welded steel pipe producer. It also produces general industrial equipment (boilers, tanks, furnaces, etc.) and equipment for the steel* and cement industries.

Dedini: a group of Brazilian companies having a dominant share of the market in equipment for the alcohol* and sugar* industries. It also produces equipment for cement* and steel* plants; boilers and turbines; steel rolls/bars for reinforced concrete, etc.

Equipetrol: a Brazilian producer of pipes and accessories for petroleum exploration and production.

Meitar Aparatos: an Argentine firm supplying components, equipment, and complete plants* in the food processing area. It specializes in machinery for the processing of citrus fruit, milk and milk products, tomatoes, apples, etc.

Metal Leve: a major Brazilian supplier of pistons* and bearings for the automobile market. It also produces pistons* for diesel and aircraft engines.

Pescarmona: an Argentine firm producing heavy capital goods to order, such as overhead cranes,* components for hydroelectric projects,* components for nuclear power stations, tanks, and other equipment for the process industries, equipment for the steel industry, etc.

Phoenicia: an Argentine trading (and subsequently engineering consultancy) firm specializing in the export of various types of equipment (bottling equipment, bakeries, equipment for the plastics industry, etc.).

---

[17]Editor's note: The author, who is more familiar with Argentine than Brazilian industry, interviewed firms in both countries in order to have a firmer basis for assessing the spin-off phenomenon. Spin-offs appear to have contributed to some export capacity among enterprises in Argentina as well as in Brazil, but the general policy environment was so much more propitious for industrial growth in Brazil than in Argentina—and that is such an important component of the overall, indirect-stimulus-to-exports thesis put forth by Teubal—that the role of technological learning in helping to foster exports is developed here only for Brazil.

[18]The exceptions are Promon Engenheria, a Brazilian engineering consultancy firm, and Phoenicia, an Argentine capital-goods trader and engineering consultant.

*Asterisk indicates design capability or ability to offer complete installations.

Promon Engenharia: a very large Brazilian engineering consultant offering comprehensive engineering and management services for a variety of sectors (civil engineering,* construction,* petrochemical industry,* telecommunications,* transport, etc.).

Sei Ingenieria: an Argentine firm supplying food-processing equipment (e.g., for bakeries).

Treu—Máquinas e Equipamentos: a relatively small Brazilian company producing mixers* for the pharmaceutical, petrochemical and nuclear-power industries and a wide variety of other special equipment for these and other industries (food, paint, etc.).

Villares: one of the most important locally owned industrial groups in Brazil. It produces automobile elevators,* motors, parts, special steels, steel-industry equipment, mining equipment, heavy capital goods,* transport equipment, overhead cranes,* and other goods. The group's original area was elevators.

Zanini: a group of Brazilian companies originally centering on sugar and equipment for sugar production. It later diversified into industrial equipment (cement plants, overhead cranes, etc.) and equipment for the production of alcohol.*

The firms interviewed vary greatly in size[19] and cover a wide variety of capital goods and associated areas. For a number of reasons, however, the sample is not representative. First, there are some important capital-goods areas where no firm was interviewed in either Argentina or Brazil. These include electrical equipment, automobiles or trucks, ships, machine tools, agricultural equipment, equipment for the pulp and paper industries, road-building and heavy earthmoving equipment and textile machinery.

Second, most of the firms were either leaders in one or more or the areas in which they were active (Confab in pipes, Dedini in sugar and alcohol production equipment, Villares and Pescarmona in overhead cranes and in a variety of other heavy capital goods, Promon in engineering services), or were important in these areas (Zanini in alcohol equipment). This reflects the view that relatively successful firms are those which have realized potential spin-offs from past activities and should therefore be interviewed when a qualitative understanding of the nature of such processes is sought. A follow-up sample would have to cover less successful firms as well.

---

[19]Size measured by annual sales range from approximately $500 million (Villares) to $2 million (some Argentine firms, but this represented a size smaller than in the 1970s, reflecting the economic crisis in that country). The smallest Brazilian firm was Treu with sales of the order of $10 million. All firms interviewed stated that they currently have underutilized capacity (relative to 'normal levels'). All the manufacturing firms which eventually exported had supplied the local market for some time before entering the export market.

Third, all the firms interviewed were locally owned. This is particularly problematic in view of the predominance of multinational enterprise (MNE) in some of the most important and fast-growing areas in the Brazilian capital-goods industry (automobiles, trucks, and other equipment).[20] This is the main weakness of the sample. The firms were chosen because they were successful or interesting (and available).

The main reason why no attempt was made to interview MNEs was my *a priori* belief that the main dynamic effect of MNEs is not technological learning but the externalities they generate in the process of supplier development (this would require a different focus). I have since revised my view about the learning process in MNEs: although they have easier access to foreign technology (often from the parent company) than the locally owned firm, there need be no perceptible difference in the efficiency of learning and absorbing it.[21] Thus a study focusing on learning processes should also try to cover MNEs and consider external effects.

Endogenous Firm Spin-offs

The field work focused on identifying and conceptualizing endogenous firm spin-offs, principally technological learning. Of all the indirect or dynamic effects of economic activity, it was felt that those materializing within the firm were the most direct and easily ascertainable.[22,23] These effects are also very significant and, given the imperfections of LDC capital markets, may have important policy implications.

Spin-offs from early products of the firm which significantly benefited subsequent products were detected in every one of the cases studied. In all but one case (where the only spin-off was enhanced firm reputation) significant technological learning was involved.[24] They also led to the emergence of export potential and to actual exports. Appendix G summarizes some examples that were reported (taken from case studies completed for seven firms of the sample).

---

[20]See Dahlman (1981), p. 12, Table 4. Metal Leve, included in our sample, is, however, an important producer of parts for the automobile industry.

[21]I owe the distinction between access and efficiency to S. Teitel. He also pointed out that the pool of experience in their home countries enables the MNEs to develop suppliers in LDCs more efficiently than locally owned firms.

[22]A study illustrating this is Morris Teubal, "The R&D Performance Through Time of Young, High Technology Firms: Methodology and an Illustration," *Research Policy*, vol. XI (1982), pp. 333–346.

[23]This is not to deny that external effects are important. On the contrary, I am fully aware of their significance as well as of the difficulty of identifying them and of measuring their economic impact. A follow-up of case studies on MNEs would have to focus on some of the relevant externalities (see note 21 above).

[24]The exception was Equipetrol, where the founders had gained experience working in similar firms. I shall try to identify the nature of this externality in a follow-up of the present study.

The summary of each case starts by identifying the particular instance or instances where learning or other endogenous spin-offs were identified. The mechanisms involved are then described: e.g., the manufacturing abilities learned in producing X at t make possible higher profits (than in the absence of X) from producing Y at t + 1. An asterisk indicates that the spin-off has had an effect on exports. The 'remarks' section provides background and other relevant information (which may be supplemented by referring to the firm descriptions given above). It should be emphasized that the possibility of comparing different cases may be limited, owing to the heterogeneity of cases and to differences in terminology.

Summary of Results

Eleven endogenous spin-off mechanisms—most of them related to learning in one way or another—were detected in the firms interviewed. It may be useful to group them into those related to manufacturing, those related to design, and others.

Learning related to manufacturing: (i) the accumulation of manufacturing capabilities (in most firms); (ii) operating experience (in Confab's pipe plants); (iii) experience derived from similarity of equipment (Treu's mixers of increasing size); and (iv) improvement of quality control procedures (in Metal Leve for aircraft pistons, Pescarmona).

Learning related to design: (i) development of a mechanical design capability (Confab's equipment division); (ii) development of a process design capability;[25] (iii) development of a total project management capability[26] (Promon's hydroelectric power projects and Dedini's alcohol plants).

Other mechanisms: (i) enhanced firm reputation (Metal Leve due to its success in supplying aircraft pistons to the local market); (ii) improved capability to plan and execute investments (Confab, pipe division); (iii) increased knowledge of markets; and (iv) development of a network of suppliers (Meitar Aparatos).[27]

---

[25]It may sometimes be difficult to separate the two types of design capability; in other cases, the distinction is less relevant.

[26]Including capability to supply turnkey plants. This includes but goes beyond the capabilities associated with mechanical or process design.

[27]The spin-off processes indicated here differ from those reported in Teubal (1981) for a successful electronics firm. These were recorded at two levels: within generations of a given product class; and between one product class and another. The phenomenon of equipment generations does not occur in many of the mechanical goods produced in the Brazilian capital goods sector (the rapid substitution of one product class for another also occurs rarely). Moreover, in electronics, the most significant spin-offs were related to market feedback and R&D, rather than to manufacturing capabilities. These differences reflect other more basic differences between the highly dynamic electronics systems/equipment areas and the metalworking industries.

The most common spin-off mechanisms are related to manufacturing capabilities: they were present in all firms except consultants such as Promon; they seem to have been extremely significant in some cases; and they generally emerge before design capabilities. Operating experience, which was relevant to Confab's pipe plants, refers to the operation of whole plants (e.g., aspects of layout) and should therefore be distinguished from the accumulation of manufacturing capabilities on the part of individual operators. This factor is presumably more important in continuous or semi-continuous production processes than in assembly type industries (though more knowledge about the differences in technology between the two types of industry is required before we can be sure about this). An important implication is that operating experience directly improves the capability to plan and execute investments; that is, investment is not only a function of past investments. This feature has been observed in microstudies of steel plants.[28] The phenomenon of capacity stretching is also to a large extent a result of operating experience.[29] A final point is that in manufacturing, the capability to produce products with more exacting specifications (or heavier items of equipment) followed from the production of simpler and smaller items.

A natural sequence of events in successful capital goods firms seems to be, first, the acquisition of manufacturing capabilities, and second, the acquisition of design capabilities in a narrower set of products. Sometimes, although this should be further documented, the link between the two is the producers, equipment, and personnel involved in quality control (this is what seems to have happened in Metal Leve, where quality control personnel staffed the R&D laboratory set up by the firm; it seems to have happened in the Usiminas steel plant, too). The interviews also suggested that the full development of a design capability may be jeopardized by a reduction in local demand for the product, apparently because of the fixed costs incurred.[30]

---

[28]See Philip Maxwell, *Learning and Technical Change in the Steel Plant of Acindar S.A. in Rosario, Argentina*. IDB/ECLA/UNDP/IDRC Regional Program of Research on Scientific and Technological Development in Latin America. Working Paper no. 4 (Buenos Aires, 1976) and Carl J. Dahlman and Fernando Valderes Fonseca, *From Technological Dependence to Technological Development: The Case of the USIMINAS Steel Plant in Brazil*. IDB/ECLA/UNDP/IDRC Regional Program of Research on Scientific and Technological Development in Latin America. Working Paper no. 21 (Buenos Aires, 1978).

[29]See Samuel Hollander, *The Sources of Efficiency Growth: A Case Study of Dupont Rayon Plants* (Cambridge, Mass., 1965: MIT Press); Jorge Katz, M. Gutkowski, M. Rodríguez and C. Goity, *Productividad, Tecnología y Esfuerzos Locales de Investigación y Desarrollo*. IDB-ECLA-UNDP-IDRC Regional Program of Research on Scientific and Technological Development in Latin America. Working Paper no. 13 (Buenos Aires, 1977) and the items of footnote 28 on capacity stretching.

[30]A consequence of this may be reduced export capability at a subsequent stage.

A very important distinction suggested by some of the examples is that between simple learning or process learning and what might be called *product learning*.[31] The former enables the firm to produce existing equipment at lower cost or to introduce relatively minor technological improvements. The latter, on the other hand, enables it to shift to new but, in some respects, technologically related types of equipment which are more difficult to produce or which require a design capability as well. Examples of simple learning are those accumulated by Dedini on its original lines of sugar processing and alcohol production equipment. Simple learning enables the firm to exploit fully the (temporary) expansion in its existing market. Most of the other instances of spin-offs are due to product learning. They involve either more exacting specifications (e.g., Confab's X-70 grade pipes, Metal Leve's diesel-engine pistons) or the manufacture of larger items (Treu's mixers, some of Pescarmona's products), or a design capability, or a capability for offering complete packages (Dedini's and Zanini's turnkey alcohol plants, Metal Leve's diesel-engine pistons, or Promon's and Meitar's project management and turnkey projects).[32]

The essential difference between the two types of learning is that while simple learning makes possible fuller exploitation of the market(s) and user segment(s) currently served by the firm, product learning enables the firm to better exploit the existing set of submarkets or user segments related to its area of expertise. Thus, it does not have to be dependent on expansion of the specific submarket/user segment served in order to increase sales. Moreover, it will be better able to exploit new opportunities in the world and domestic markets and to avoid some of the pitfalls. The policy implications of this distinction for exports and for industrial development may be far-reaching.

It is interesting to note that in all cases except one (Treu) spin-offs involving product learning have led to exports. In some cases, the world market requires more sophisticated products than those currently supplied to the domestic market (some of Confab's pipes made of high grade steel and piping for transporting fluorine, for which the firm has obtained prequalification —see next paragraph— and possibly some of

---

[31]Thanks to Larry Westphal for having suggested the terms used.

[32]While our simple learning category is part of the elementary learning category outlined by S. Lall in "Developing Countries as Exporters of Industrial Technology," *Research Policy*, vol. IX (1980), pp. 24–52, there is no similar correspondence between our product learning and his intermediate and/or advanced learning categories. This product learning includes transitions to the manufacture of more complex or sophisticated products. This may occur *without* process or product adaptations (from a world point of view) and therefore would be considered by Lall as elementary learning.

Dedini's turnkey alcohol plants or some of Promon's turnkey projects).[33] In other instances, the firm is exporting less sophisticated products than those it currently supplies domestically (Pescarmona's hydromechanical components and Promon's exports of hydroelectric projects), but even the more sophisticated products were the result of the accumulation of this type of manufacturing and other capabilities while serving the domestic market. In some cases, it seems that the reputation acquired by supplying sophisticated products to the local market (e.g., nuclear-power components, whose production was made possible by product learning) opened up some export markets for less sophisticated products.[34]

No instance was detected of exports which were not preceded by sales of the same or similar equipment to the local market. The acquisition of firm reputation was a major reason why supply to the domestic market was important for exports. Enhanced reputation enables the firm to *prequalify* for the supply of goods in international tenders (Confab, Pescarmona, Promon) or to gain access to a foreign license which would enhance its export acceptance (Metal Leve). Another important spin-off from supplying the local market was learning how to assemble and offer turnkey projects or sophisticated products, a critical factor in some (especially less sophisticated) export markets (Promon).[35]

Table III-5 presents some qualitative information pertaining to the economic value of the spin-offs reported earlier. Very little quantitative information is available at this stage, so the table focuses on the factors mainly responsible for a 'high' or 'low' economic value (as reported in the interviews). The preponderance of cases with a high economic value reflects the fact that the sample includes relatively successful firms. Needless to say, there are some serious conceptual problems in determining the value of the spin-off flowing from a particular activity.[36]

Except in cases of simple learning and in firms providing services, the materialization of potential spin-offs from a particular activity requires complementary effort and investment (the exceptions were Dedini, Promon, and Meitar Aparatos). Some of that should be planned and executed in advance and this may require successful market fore-

---

[33]This includes situations where the trend in (rather than the state of) international markets favors more sophisticated products.

[34]It is not clear whether the examples given here contradict the Linder hypothesis. In both cases, the domestic market is a proving ground for export production, primarily because of skill acquisition (and firm-reputation effects), and not necessarily similarity in demand.

[35]Although there are instances in other countries of capital-goods exports without a prior phase of supply to the local market (e.g., ships from Korea), my hypothesis is that it is much more difficult with capital goods than with manufacturing in general.

[36]The value of the spin-off from product i to product j is the difference between profits actually obtained from j and those that would have been obtained in the absence of product i. The latter is problematic because in the absence of i the firm might not undertake j. The formula for calculating the value of spin-offs will differ in each case.

Table III-5 The Economic Value of Spin-Offs

Spin-off and main contributory factors	Value of spin-off
CONFAB, equipment division	Not high
Reduced local market for equipment before full mastery of a design capability.	
CONFAB, pipe division	High
Market trends favored a more sophisticated pipe. There was a very significant reduction in risk and in time for planning and executing investments (a newcomer needs 8 years for a new pipe plant, CONFAB maybe half that). A newcomer incurs high costs of purchasing know-how.	
DEDINI	
Diversification from original activities (A1)[a]:	Low
Narrow market, at least up to now. Possibility of losing part of design capability (no economic justification for maintaining a large team of engineers).	
Diversification within traditional lines (A3):	High
Shorter delivery times (1–1/2 years less than new entrants) in a market predicted to reach satiation in a few years. Although the technology is not very complex, purchase of know-how is expensive for new extrants. With Dedini's volume, savings could reach $22 million.	
MEITAR APARATOS	
Spin-offs from first turnkey plants (A3):	Low
Overvaluation of the Argentine peso did not permit the firm to sell more than a small number of turnkey plants after the first order.	
METAL LEVE	
Spin-offs from aircraft pistons (A1, A2):	High
Market trends favored high quality piston with more exacting specifications (e.g., heavy-duty diesel-engine pistons).	
PESCARMONA	
Production of heavier and more sophisticated items (A1):	High
Bigger items cannot be produced without previous experience with smaller items (manufacturing risks, reputation needed for orders, etc.). The firm avoided excess capacity and was able to supply markets for sophisticated products which expanded while those for simpler items declined. There is less competition in new markets.	
PROMON ENGENHARIA	
Increasing complexity of projects undertaken (A1):	High
It is too risky to undertake such projects without prior experience with simpler projects.	
TREU	
Spin-off from mixers (A1):	High
It is too risky to produce big mixers without previous experience with smaller ones. The market for big mixers expanded and that for smaller ones contracted; the firm would have had much more excess capacity if it had not entered the new market. The market for bigger mixers is less competitive than the market for smaller ones.	

[a]The numbering refers to the case histories in Appendix G.

casting on the part of the firm. For example, in the 1960s, Metal Leve complied with Caterpillar's H-D piston requirements. The firm was particularly successful in the 1970s, when market trends favored the H-D over the gasoline engine pistons, which had accounted for a majority of sales a decade earlier.

Others require heavy investment in physical capital and involve considerable risks (Confab pipes; Pescarmona; Metal Leve). Finally, know-how agreements with foreign firms may be a necessary condition for shifting to a more complex, but technologically related, product (Pescarmona, Treu). This situation also required the introduction of more stringent quality control procedures and investments in instrumentation for quality control (and/or testing facilities).[37]

Conclusions

The Brazilian capital-goods industry experienced a very high rate of export growth during the 1970s, together with a significant rise in the share of output exported. The sector's output and exports both grew faster than the output and exports of the manufacturing sector as a whole. A brief survey of existing work on government policy towards the sector shows that export subsidies did not unambiguously increase during the period; that they only compensated for an overvalued cruzeiro, and that they did not discriminate in favor of the export market. Therefore changes in these instruments of government policy do not provide an adequate explanation of the sector's export performance, and others must be sought. Previous work has assembled quantitative information on the costs of production of various capital goods product classes. This paper has provided information on endogenous firm spin-offs in a sample of capital goods firms. The most commonly found and significant spin-offs involve the accumulation of manufacturing capabilities (learning to manufacture), with the development of design capabilities following in certain cases. A nontechnological spin-off was enhanced firm reputation; all the firms interviewed believed that this played an important role in their growth. The interviews also suggested that exports benefited from the increased capability to supply either more sophisticated products, products with more exacting specifications, or turnkey plants. There were, in addition, important reasons why, in the firms analyzed, exports of capital goods benefited from prior activities associated with supplying the local market. It should be noted that capital goods exports of other countries, such as Korea, also developed after learning and enhanced reputation were acquired while supplying local markets, according to the references cited in Chapter 1, although we are not aware of a precisely comparable analysis of spin-offs and exports for other developing countries.

The pattern indicated here may not be applicable to the capital-goods sector as a whole, nor does it prove that capital-goods exports must, on efficiency grounds, follow a stage of supplying the domestic

---

[37]A more detailed description of complementary efforts can be found in the complete write-ups of the firm interviews. These are available from the author on request, subject to permission from the firms.

market.[38] It only suggests the need to link exports (and the emergence of export potential) with the theory of the infant firm.[39] The resulting framework would deal with the following issues.

Strategy for promoting exports: The characteristics of most capital goods suggest that the export-promotion strategy for those goods whose production is justified in the long run should give considerable attention to, indeed probably emphasize, indirect measures, at any rate in large LDCs.[40] In Phase 1, prior to the acquisition of manufacturing and design capabilities and firm reputation, infant-industry measures (protection, subsidization, or whatever meets the case) should be implemented.[41] Direct export subsidization will fail to promote exports or at best will do so only at very high cost, especially when exports require greater technological sophistication than is required to supply a less demanding local market and when export firms have to be prequalified (as is often the case with capital goods, especially heavy capital goods). The effectiveness of export promotion will increase in Phase 2 once the firm has acquired sufficient experience and reputation. This strategy would seem to be applicable to other experience goods, where the economic consequences of inappropriate choice are likely to be high, and in situations where (a) exporting is significantly more difficult than supplying the domestic market, and (b) where the latter generates a spin-off benefiting the former.

Infant industries: price versus other incentives: The preference for output subsidization over other incentives, derived from static trade theory, is far less unambiguous when firm-reputation effects are also critical in Phase 1. Under these conditions, even very high output subsidies may do very little to stimulate output (and indirectly learning). Therefore, given that competition basically rests on the user's confidence in the supplier which the local firm does not enjoy in Phase 1, there is a case for nontariff protection (such as the Brazilian domestic input schedules imposed on firms receiving government support). Considerable effort is still required to determine the conditions under which it would be optimal. Factors such as market size and the efficiency and learning motivation of entrepreneurs may be critical. Any optimum solution should take these aspects into account as well.

---

[38]Editor's note: Indeed, there are examples of capital goods enterprises representing foreign investment which have exported from the initiation of production activities—though this has been less common in Latin America than in Asia, particularly since the onset of the Debt Crisis in 1982.

[39]Thus confirming the overall approach followed by J. Katz and E. Ablin (1976).

[40]Since preparing this study, Teubal's research along the lines dealt with here has developed two additional themes, which are summarized in the Editor's Comment at the end of this Chapter.

[41]Editor's note: This needs to be qualified. See Ch. I, Section 4a.

Finally, the learning and spin-off processes observed do not seem to be those which are traditionally used in productivity studies. For example, use of the weighted average of a firm's past R&D efforts as an indicator of its stock of knowledge[42] does not seem to be adequate for capital goods firms in developing countries, since formal R&D activities, if undertaken at all, are rarely initiated by a newly-established firm.[43] Significant learning has nevertheless taken place, learning which should not always be represented by cumulated output. Skill acquisition, in both manufacturing and design, seems, at least in some cases, to be related to the firm's current degree of sophistication (rather than to cumulated output) and to current investment in upgrading skill and purchasing or absorbing new technology.[44]

Epilogue

The study focuses on the learning process in capital-goods enterprises, and has implications for infant-industry and export promotion. I believe that the spirit of the conclusions remains appropriate for Newly Industrializing Countries (NICs) or countries of potential NIC status, especially those of the size and sophistication of Brazil and Argentina. However, a number of additional factors should be taken into consideration in order to provide a broader context and to take account of the developments of the 1980s.

This epilogue considers, first, certain findings on the effects of the domestic market on export performance. Those findings, from Denmark, tend to reinforce the conclusions from the analysis of Brazil, although the implications of the current, worldwide communications

---

[42]See Zvi Griliches, "Research Expenditures and Growth Accounting," in B.R. Williams ed., *Science, Technology and Economic Growth* (New York, 1973: Wiley), for the use of this variable at the aggregate level. Subsequent studies by him and others have used it at the sector and firm levels.

[43]We have already noted that the acquisition of design capability does not imply R&D. In any case, there are usually no consistent data on R&D expenditures. This study further reinforces an important implication of microeconomic case studies of firms, namely, that technological effort should not be identified with R&D (see Hollander, *op. cit.*; and the studies conducted under the IDB/ECLA Research Program in Science and Technology for Latin America; especially Katz, *Domestic Technology Generation in LDCs: A Review of Research Findings*. Working Paper no. 35 (Buenos Aires, 1980), and Katz, "Domestic Technological Innovation and Dynamic Comparative Advantage: Further reflections on a comparative case study program," *Journal of Development Economics*, vol. 16 (1984), pp. 13–38.

[44]The cases of Treu and Pescarmona suggests this in connection with the size of capital goods. The larger the product currently supplied the easier it is to acquire the technology and additional skills needed to supply other large or larger items. This pattern can be found in other firms of the sample with respect to other product dimensions (e.g., precision requirements in pipes and pistons; complexity of engineering projects).

and transportation revolution are less clear. Second, note is taken of policies followed by countries such as Japan, which have protected the local market in the first phase but whose strengthened production capabilities have led to exports in a second phase. Finally, I discuss other aspects of export and infant-industry promotion, in particular those related to the infrastructure, skills and capabilities which seem to be essential for the implementation of such export-oriented policies. These may be termed the Structuralist Perspective to Economic Growth and Development, and are consistent with the experience of Japan.

Domestic Markets and Revealed Comparative Advantage

Possibly the best study documenting the relationship between local markets and export performance is that reported from Denmark by Anderson and Dalum and interpreted by Anderson and Lundvall (1988).[45] These authors report a connection between the specialization patterns and technical competence of the engineering (i.e. capital goods) sector and the country's primary sectors. As many as seven or eight of the ten engineering product categories with the highest export specialization indexes[46] are connected either directly with agriculture or with the associated food processing industry. The five groups with the highest specialization indexes for 1975 were: milking machinery and dairy equipment (with an index of 15.2), mineral-crushing and glassworking machinery (an index of 5.2), agricultural machinery for planting and harvesting (4.7), food processing machinery, excluding household equipment (4.3), and agricultural machinery not otherwise specified (4.0). Data for 1961, 1973 and 1985 show that the highest export specialization indexes for the Danish economy as a whole can be found in the primary sectors, best exemplified by bacon, pork, beef, diary products and animal feeds. The capital goods sector is linked with these primary products not only through market size but also by virtue of the close relationship between producer and user required from innovation and productivity growth (Anderson and Lundvall, *op. cit.*). These data are thus consistent with a two-phase process of development in Danish capital goods similar to

---

[45]E.S. Anderson and B.A. Lundvall, "Small National Systems of Innovation Facing Technological Revolutions: An Analytical Framework," in Christopher Freeman and Bengt-Ake Lundvall eds., *Small Countries Facing the Technological Revolution* (London, 1988: F. Pinter), which draws on E.S. Anderson et al., "The Importance of the Home Market for Technological Development and the Export Specialization of Manufacturing Industry," and B. Dalum et al., "Long Term Economic Development: A Discussion of the Structural Implications of Technology," both papers presented to an IKE Seminar on Technical Innovation and National Economic Performance in Aälborg in 1981.

[46]The export specialization index refers to the share of the product in Danish exports in relation to its share in total exports of all OECD countries. Index values higher than 1.0 thus reflect relatively great specialization in a product.

that shown in the analysis of Brazil. The development of of capital goods occurred first in response to the growth of a domestic market (the emerging needs of Denmark's primary exports in the last quarter of the 19th Century), and this was followed by export specialization in those same capital goods which helped facilitate the primary sector exports.

Japanese Industrial Policies

In the postwar period, and as late as the second half of the 1960s, Japanese industrial policies included (i) the designation of infant industries for preferential support ("targeting"), and (ii), a policy package containing protection of the local market among its various instruments (see Okuno and Suzamura 1987).[47] Since many of these industries subsequently became successful exporters, the overall pattern conforms to the "indirect" approach to export promotion outlined in the analysis of Brazilian capital goods. Alternatively, what we have is complementarity between supplying the domestic market first and exporting at a later phase of the sector's life cycle. This applied to numerous sectors in Japan, including machinery, automobiles and capital goods generally.

The importance of market size in justifying the two-phase export promotion, infant-industry policy is treated rigorously by the same authors in a related paper (see Okuno and Suzamura 1988).[48] The framework of the analysis is a two-good economy (X and Y) using only one factor of production: labor. Good X is characterized by Marshallian external economies, i.e., the unit costs of each firm depends upon the output of the industry as a whole (this is precisely the configuration of the metalworking, automobile and capital-goods industries, where the size of the industry influences the extent of the parts and components suppliers network—which is a factor in determining firm costs). Under the conditions given, the maximization of GNP requires an "industrial policy" which assures that the domestic output of X exceeds a certain critical level XB*. When the requisite equilibrium output is large enough, then the maximization of GNP may be met by a temporary prohibition on imports of X. Success depends upon the existence of a large domestic demand for X, since otherwise domestic producers would be unable to survive after trade liberalization. It is clear that Japan is an example of a country whose domestic market is large enough to justify protection to promote infant industry. The argument also may hold for the larger

---

[47]M. Okuno and K. Suzamura, "Industrial Policy in Japan: Overview and Evaluation," unpublished paper, 1987.
[48]Okuno and Suzamura, "The Economic Analysis of Industrial Policy: A Conceptual Framework Through the Japanese Experience," unpublished paper, 1988.

NICs such as Mexico and Brazil, in particular with respect to capital goods, but the market-size requirement would limit its applicability within the developing-country group.

The Structuralist Perspective on Economic Growth and Development

The structuralist perspective on economic growth and development maintains that structural change is a cause at least as much as it is a consequence of economic growth (see Justman and Teubal, 1989).[49] It argues for government involvement in promoting growth, particularly at "nodes" of structural change since "market failure" may be a pervasive phenomenon at these nodes. This perspective implies that the aggregate production function may be "scalloped" rather than smooth and that the process of growth is punctured by indivisibilities of various kinds. Government involvement must first and foremost assure the creation of a multiple component infrastructure for structural change embracing physical infrastructure, knowledge and technological capabilities, human capital (e.g., the availability of a critical mass of mechanical and electrical engineers for a successful shift to capital goods), export marketing capabilities and a variety of critical institutions (engineering firms, venture capital firms, consultation mechanisms between the public and private sector, etc.).

Given this perspective, the establishment of a successful capital-goods sector is not only a matter of infant-industry promotion and protection and of designing the right set of "direct" policies such as low-interest loans and accelerated depreciation for capital investment, import restrictions and (eventually) export subsidies. It also involves establishing the appropriate "infrastructure" which need not be specific to any one product group or sector but may serve as class or category of sectors. To assure an appropriate supply of electrical engineers and technicians may require new professional training institutes at the secondary-school level and the establishment of a Department of Electrical Engineering at the university level, or, alternatively, a massive program for sending people abroad to acquire the requisite training.

Concerning technological capabilities, authors like Westphal, Dahlman, Bell, etc.,[50] and the experience of Japan and Korea, suggest turning to alternative inducement mechanisms—establishing export targets for individual enterprises, using direct incentives to create technological

---

[49]Moshe Justman and Morris Teubal, "The Structuralist Perspective to Economic Growth and Development: Conceptual Framework, Final Aspects and Policy Implications," paper presented at AID Conference on Science and Technology for Development, Washington, 1989.

[50]Editor's note: See references in Chapter I.

capability at the firm level, and rationalizing industrial structures. One interesting example of a program to stimulate an infrastructure for the adoption and diffusion of information technology is Denmark's Technology Development Program, enacted and implemented in the period since 1984–85. The objective of this program is to facilitate the shift of Danish industry from conventional technology to Computer Integrated Manufacturing (CIM), a set of technologies involving CAD, CAM, the introduction of robots, etc. The program involves both the strengthening of the existing set of Technological Service Institutes, whose objectives are to support small and medium-sized enterprises, to set up demonstration projects, and to direct support for cooperative projects to the adopting and implementing of new technologies related to products or production processes.

These examples suggest that the approach to developing the capital-goods sector in the 1990s should extend far beyond our traditional infant-industry perspective. We should address the issue of structural change with explicit consideration given to the critical new infrastructure needs emerging from both the technological revolution and the need to generate an export capability at a certain stage of production. Export-oriented output should become a salient feature of the capital-goods sectors of most countries.

Editor's Remarks

Since preparing this study in 1981–82, Teubal has developed two additional themes relevant to this chapter. One expands directly on the role of learning in facilitating manufacturing exports, and the other, as noted in Teubal's 1989 Epilogue, relates to the kinds of indirect government measures which encourage technological learning.

In "Learning and the Rise of Israel's Exports of Sophisticated Products," prepared with N. Halevi and D. Tisiddon (*World Development*, vol. 14, no. 12, (Dec. 1986) pp. 1397–1410), one of several articles Teubal has authored or co-authored on high-technology firms in Israel, it was argued that the nature of the learning process is different and potentially more significant in what are referred to as sophisticated industries (S) than in conventional industries (C). S industries develop and diffuse key technologies, while C industries generally only use them. Moreover, the underlying 'key' technologies tend to improve more continuously in S than in C industries (it is acknowledged, though, that 'simple' learning also can be important in S industries such as those related to metal goods). For S industries, which are characterized by more product heterogeneity and product innovation than C industries, Teubal *et al.* maintain that traditional static comparative advantage considerations are not as important in explaining exports as "sufficient past accumulation of intangibles (including those from R&D);" the latter are held to be more important for S industries than the availability of cheap production factors. Moreover, in S industries, a preexisting market may not be present or sufficiently well defined; export success depends upon whether technology can be geared to current needs, which involves multifaceted learning and the accumulation of intangible factors. Intangible accumulation is deemed necessary to begin exporting and is the main factor behind the acceleration of S exports. Finally, Teubal *et al.* maintain that, while rises in export prices and changes in government policies such as devaluations and export promotion measures are likely to have major direct effects on C industry exports in the short run, the overall effects in the case of S industries may be even greater, but the most important are likely to be indirect and to occur only in the long run.

The second and now major theme of Teubal's work concerns the nature of indirect government measures for fostering technological learning, and is perhaps best represented by Moshe Justman and Morris Teubal, "A Framework for an Explicit Industry and Technology Policy for Israel and Some Specific Proposals," which appeared in Christopher Freeman and Bengt-Ake Lundvall eds., *Small Countries Facing the Technological Revolution* (London, 1988, F. Pinter). This provides a background for the subsequent paper by the two authors just referred to in the Epilogue to this Chapter.

Justman and Teubal set out to define what they characterize as an appropriate industrial and technological policy for a basically export-oriented country. They propose that the role of government be limited to correcting for market failure—"dynamic market failure," in their terms —and to promoting structural change, stressing the development of scientific and technological infrastructure. The authors propose that government take action with respect to: (a) industrial policy (defined as comprising industrial R&D, capital investments and technological diffusion); (b) capital markets; (c) universities and the science and technology infrastructure; and (d) strategic coordination for very large investment programs with clear "coordination failures." They stress the need to integrate the requirements of industrial and technological development into macroeconomic policy, to create new frameworks for strategic coordination at the intersectoral level, and to establish "administrative market-enhancement mechanisms" at the microeconomic level. Thus, they propose moving from an implicit industrial technology policy (such as that supported in the text of this chapter) to an explicit policy—with targets for parameters such as technological effort and structural change, and with the capacity to relate policy measures to these parameters, and through them, to trace their growth implications. This implies identifying the analytical justification for policy and ascertaining the effects of implementation—in a quantitative simulation model if possible. The long-term perspective would make it feasible to anticipate future structural problems and take appropriate action before the problems become crises and partisan pressures for immediate remedies reduced the chances of finding a "constructive growth-promoting solution."

Integration with macroeconomic policy would entail a formulation of the latter, much broader than the usual short-term framework of monetary and fiscal measures to achieve price stabilization, balance-of-payments equilibrium and full employment. It would be necessary to incorporate industrial and technological goals, and could entail setting long-term quantitative targets for the accumulation of human capital and other measures of technological capacity. With respect to microeconomic correction for market failure, Justman and Teubal maintain that the efforts should be broadly based, and universally if not neutrally applied, with attention—at least in the Israeli example—to policies regarding R&D, venture-capital promotion, technology adoption and diffusion, the projection of skilled-manpower needs along with education policies geared to those needs, mobility and retraining requirements, support aspects of a national export-marketing policy and integrated assistance measures for small firms. The authors conclude that the appropriate industrial and technological policy is one in which government attempts market stimulation and strategic coordination (perhaps even occasionally "picking winners"), but does not engage in central planning.

CHAPTER IV

GETTING STARTED AS AN INDUSTRIAL EXPORTER: THE CASE OF PERU

Shane Hunt
*Boston University**

Introduction

Since World War II, economic policy in Latin America has been marked by contentious debate over a number of basic issues. No issue has been more debated than the role of foreign trade in development. Should the process of development be inward-looking or outward-looking? Should nations seek the security which would come from minimizing dependence on imports, or should they seek the gains from specialization according to comparative advantage?

Although the policy prescriptions have varied greatly, points of common agreement have emerged. One such point concerns the indispensable role of foreign exchange in Latin American economies. Foreign exchange availability has been seen, in most circumstances, as the binding constraint on policies for full employment and high economic growth.

As early as 1960, the agreed-upon need for foreign exchange has led to an agreed-upon need for export promotion. This was so because the alternative strategy of import substitution was in fact seen to be a net user of foreign exchange. How, then, could exports best be promoted? On this point the consensus evaporated and the old dichotomies reasserted themselves: elasticity optimism versus elasticity pessimism, neoliberalism versus neostructuralism.[1]

*The author wishes to thank Hugh Schwartz for guidance and criticism, and also Concepción Colpe, Vivian Brady, Pilar Rivero, Sonia Carey and Joel de Graff for research assistance.

[1]Export pessimism is analyzed in Jagdish Bhagwati, "Export-Promoting Trade Strategy: Issues and Evidence," *World Bank Research Observer*, January 1988. For an earlier discussion of elasticity optimism and pessimism, see Carlos Díaz-Alejandro, "Trade Policies and Economic Development," in Peter Kenen, ed., *International Trade and Finance: Frontiers for Research* (Cambridge: Cambridge University Press; 1975), esp. pp. 108–122. Neoliberalism and neostructuralism are discussed in Albert Fishlow, "The State of Latin American Economics," in Inter-American Development Bank, *Economic and Social Progress in Latin America*, 1985 Report, Chapter 5.

The neoliberal view of foreign trade policy has been based on elasticity optimism combined with the conviction that real devaluation is both feasible and desirable. It has been buttressed by a massive effort of research and policy advocacy emanating from the principal centers of North Atlantic academia plus the more affluent of international institutions. That effort has focused on the policy deficiencies in Third World countries themselves, and has documented the high levels of protection for industry, the bias against exports, and the pernicious effects of trade control regimes.[2]

Studies of the efficacy of different policy regimes have been supplemented by more narrowly focused econometric studies of export supply, oriented particularly to the question of price elasticity. Most of these studies have tended to support the elasticity optimists, indicating that relative price adjustments through real devaluation is an effective measure of export promotion.[3]

The counterpoised neostructuralist view was founded in part on elasticity pessimism.[4] This view reflected an assessment not just of the shape of foreign demand curves, but of other factors as well. It saw feasible export prospects concentrated in those sectors of labor-intensive production for which protectionist sentiment was already very strong in the developed countries. Therefore the initial export successes brought about through real devaluation would be stopped cold by new measures

[2]Some of the major efforts in this voluminous bibliography are: From the World Bank, Bela Balassa and Associates, *The Structure of Protection in Developing Countries* (Baltimore: Johns Hopkins University Press, 1971); and Bela Balassa and Associates, *Development Strategies in Semi-Industrial Economies* (Baltimore: Johns Hopkins University Press, 1982). From the OECD, I.M.D. Little, Tibor Scitovsky, and Maurice Scott, *Industry and Trade in Some Developing Countries* (London: Oxford University Press, 1970). From the National Bureau for Economic Research, Jagdish Bhagwati, *Anatomy and Consequences of Exchange Control Regimes* (Cambridge, Mass.: Ballinger, 1978), and Ann Krueger, *Liberalization Attempts and Consequences* (Cambridge, Mass.: Ballinger, 1978). The state of current thinking has been effectively summarized a number of times, e.g., Carlos Díaz-Alejandro, "Trade Policies and Economic Development," in Peter Kenan ed., *International Trade and Finance* (Cambridge University Press, 1975; Donald Keesing, *Trade Policy in Developing Countries (Washington: World Bank, 1979); I.M.D. Little, Economic Development: Theory, Policy, and International Relations* (New York: Basic Books, 1982); Anne O. Krueger, "Trade Policies in Developing Countries," in Ronald Jones and Peter Kenen, eds., *Handbook of International Economics*, volume 1 (Amsterdam: North Holland, 1984), pp. 519–569; Howard Pack, "Industrialization and Trade," in Hollis Chenery and T. N. Srinivasan, eds., *Handbook of Development Economics*, volume 1 (Amsterdam: North Holland, 1988), pp. 334–380.

[3]This literature is reviewed in Morris Goldstein and Mohsin S. Khan, "Income and Price Effects in Foreign Trade," in Ronald Jones and Peter Kenan, eds., *Handbook of International Economics*, volume 2 (Amsterdam: North Holland, 1984). The best estimates for Peru are in Carlos Paredes, "Política económica, industrialización y exportaciones de manufacturas en el Perú," GRADE (Lima), processed, 1988.

[4]Neostructuralist approaches are well summarized in a number of contributions in Paul Streeten and Richard Jolly, eds., *Recent Issues in World Development: A Collection of Survey Articles* (Oxford: Pergamon Press, 1981).

of protectionism. By this view, the problem of export promotion was not one of getting the prices right but rather of establishing sufficient political power in international negotiations to secure guaranteed access to the markets of developed countries. Beginning with the structuralism of CEPAL, this viewpoint provided the intellectual foundation for UNCTAD in the 1960s, and the call for the New International Economic Order in the 1970s.

Neostructuralist thinking has also given greater emphasis to the social implications of different foreign trade regimes. This is one reason why the East Asian example, often advanced as a paragon by neoliberals, has encountered strong resistance in Latin America, even while it has helped effect significant change in Latin American attitudes on the viability of export-oriented policies.[5] Observing that the East Asian exporting countries are in general politically conservative and authoritarian, Latin American critics have been inclined to see an intimate relation between the economic strategy and the political system. This might be the case particularly when the early stages of a successful export strategy involve labor-intensive production which can thrive only if wages are kept low.

Recent years have seen the neoliberal view in the ascendancy.[6] Policies relying on market mechanisms have acquired new respectability and new converts. Time and again government economic intervention has produced disappointing results, giving rise to phenomena as disparate as Perestroika and Thatcherism.

Buoyed by neoliberal conviction, perhaps supplemented by the precision of econometrically estimated export supply functions, governments of developing countries have therefore become more inclined to promote exports through real devaluation. Yet neither policy makers nor policy critics would like to entrust export earnings to the workings of one policy variable alone. Export earnings are surely affected by variables other than price. Product quality, market knowledge, and punctuality of delivery are three which come quickly to mind. They might be thought of as additional variables in a properly specified export supply function. They are, however, variables which resist quantification. Studies of their effect on export earnings tend to be both qualitative and highly specific to the institutional peculiarities of a given export sector.

Some studies have examined these variables at the most detailed level possible, focusing on the various determinants of export perform-

---

[5]See, for example, William Cline, "Can the East Asian Model of Development be Generalized?" *World Development*, February 1982.
[6]For a recent review of this trend, see "Desperate, Latin Nations Discover the Free Market," *New York Times*, July 30, 1989, p. E2.

ance for just one product in one country. The study by Morawetz of Colombian clothing exporters, and how they failed where East Asian exporters succeeded, is perhaps best known.[7] At a different level of generality, Keesing's work summarized the experience of all developing countries with regard to the influence of marketing and product quality variables on industrial export performance.[8]

These institutional approaches have proven attractive for two principal reasons. First, the price variable of real devaluation is associated with liabilities which governments desire to avoid. It exacerbates inflation problems and often sharpens distributional conflict. If exports can be promoted through other, less costly instruments, governments would like to know about them. Second, many who are skeptical of neoliberal prescriptions find the coefficients of export supply functions far too abstract and problematical to be convincing. Case studies rich in historical and institutional detail have often proven more convincing to noneconomists, and to economists as well.

Precisely because detailed studies of this sort emphasize the institutional specifics of each case, thus making generalization more difficult, a variety of studies is needed to establish the universality of observed phenomena. The present study examines the export experience of only one country, Peru, giving particular attention to two variables: product quality and marketing capability.

Since their significance may be expected to vary from product to product, they can best be examined by reviewing the export experience of a sample of products. The sample chosen for this study, set forth in Table IV-1, is limited to six products: canned fish, cotton textiles, electric motors, pumps, batteries, and industrial chemicals. The concluding section of the study will however make reference to the export experience of additional products.

All exports considered are classified in Peru as nontraditional. Their export experience will be examined particularly during Peru's first major surge of nontraditional exporting, from 1975/76 to 1980/81. Subsequent

---

[7]David Morawetz, *Why the Emperor's New Clothes Are Not Made in Colombia* (London: Oxford University Press, 1981). See also Ernst Feder, *Strawberry Imperialism* (Frankfurt: Suhrkamp, 1980), and Harvard Business School works on agribusiness, e.g., James Austin, *Agribusiness in Latin America* (New York: Praeger, 1979), J. David Morrissey, *Agricultural Modernization through Production Contracting, The Role of the Fruit and Vegetable Processor in Mexico and Central America* (New York: Praeger, 1974); Ray Goldberg, ed., *Agribusiness Management for Developing Countries - Latin America* (Cambridge: Ballinger, 1974).

[8]Donald Keesing, "Exporting Manufactured Consumer Goods from Developing to Developed Economies: Marketing by Local Firms and Effects of Developing Country Policies," Washington, World Bank, mimeo, 1982. Also "Linking Up Distant Markets: South to North Exports of Manufactured Consumer Goods," *American Economic Review*, May 1982, pp. 338–342.

Table IV-1. Exports Included in Sample
(Thousands of dollars)

Nabandina Code	1965	1970	1975	1977	1980	1981	1986
Product:							
Canned fish 16.04	0	2,737	4,048	15,849	63,546	74,032	15,263
Cotton textiles 55.05; 55.09[a]	1	615	1,768	23,063	94,574	86,844	
(55.09 only)[a]	(0)	(565)	(1,524)	(13,380)	(42,079)	(52,125)	(42,106)
Electric motors 85.01	0	136	1,141	1,481	4,547	3,130	1,168
Pumps 84.10	285	63	850	922	3,023	3,543	2,000
Batteries 85.03	0	122	117	580	6,417	2,085	55
Industrial chemicals 28.27, 28.38	81	537	776	2,467	4,960	3,961	3,082

[a]55.05 is cotton yarn; 55.09 is cotton fabric.
Sources: 1965–1977: *Estadística del Comercio Exterior*, various issues.
1980–1986: Computer tabulations of OFINE (data processing office of Ministerio de Economía).

experience, better described as attempted export maintenance rather than export expansion, will also be reviewed.

Within the fishing sector, canned fish was both the most important and the fastest growing nontraditional export during the 1970s boom. Within textiles, cotton textiles are historically the most important, but certain clothing lines have shown faster export growth in recent years.

The metalworking and machinery sector is overrepresented in the sample only because so many hopes have been placed on its development, both in Peru and in Latin American countries generally. The three products chosen for examination within this sector—pumps, electric motors, and flashlight batteries—are simply three products which have had some success in export development, and about which a story can therefore be told.

The remaining product chosen for examination comes from the chemical sector. This means that, because of time and space limitations, no products from sectors such as agricultural products, non-metallic minerals and metallurgical products have been considered for study.

The export experience of this sample of products is examined in detail through analysis of both export statistics and interview data. No formal hypothesis testing is attempted; rather the analysis proceeds at a more primitive stage which can be viewed as hypothesis generation regarding constraints on export expansion. In the case of each product in the sample, the analysis seeks answers to the following questions:

(i) What is the logic of the observed distribution of exports by country of destination?

Table IV-2. Exports of Selected Latin American Countries
(Annual averages)

	Peru	Chile	Colombia	Argentina	Brazil
Exports as percentage of GNP					
1950–54	20.5	9.4[a]	13.9	6.6[a]	8.6[a]
1955–59	20.7	11.3	15.4	9.3	7.7
1960–64	23.6	11.5	13.0	10.1	7.5
1965–69	19.1	16.0	12.6	8.1	7.6 (6.3)[e]
1970–74	16.5	13.2	14.2	9.0	7.2 (7.1)
1975–78	16.5	20.2	16.8	10.3	7.5 (7.0)
1979–80	29.6	23.8	15.8	8.1	8.3 (7.9)
1981–82	20.7	19.1	11.5	12.3	(8.7)[b]
1983–85	24.5	28.1	12.4	16.2[c]	(12.9)
*Value of Exports**					
1950–54	224	373	517	1,031	1,529
1955–59	308	439	574	970	1,354
1960–64	550	499	500	1,207	1,345
1965–69	789	903	587	1,506	1,837
1970–74	1,097	1,286	1,056	2,530	4,696
1975–78	1,580	2,088	2,425	4,733	10,712
1979–80	3,704	4,270	3,714	7,916	17,688
1981–82	3,271	3,771	3,136	8,383	21,725
1983–85	3,047	3,762	3,631	8,110	24,845
1986–87	2,568	4,712	5,516	6,604	22,392[d]
Income Terms of Trade					
(Peru, 1981–82 = 100)					
1950–54	19[a]	33[a]	44[a]	81[a]	213[b]
1955–59	24	34	45	76	187
1960–64	45	41	41	99	187
1965–69	70	80	52	134	246
1970–74	79	92	76	181	468
1975–78	71	93	109	212[a]	592
1979–80	127	147	127	272	663
1981–82	100	115	96	256	664
1983–85	94	116	112	250	860
1981–82/1950–54	5.3	3.5	2.2	3.2	3.1

[a]1951–54
[b]1952–54
[c]1983
[d]1986
[e]Alternative series in parentheses.
*Value of exports in millions of current U.S. dollars. Income terms of trade, or purchasing power of exports, is dollar value of exports divided by a dollar index of import prices. A dollar unit value index of imports for Colombia, published in *International Financial Statistics* (e.g., 1988 Yearbook, pp. 136–137) was used for Brazil, 1952–60, and all other countries for all years. For Brazil, 1961–82, a Brazilian unit value index was used from the same source.
Source: *International Financial Statistics*, 1988 Yearbook and earlier issues. 1986–87 figures for Peru from Banco Central de Reserva, *Memoria 1987*, p. 159.

(ii) What is the quality of the Peruvian product compared to that of the principal competition?
(iii) What capacity for product improvement can be identified among Peruvian exporters?
(iv) What marketing patterns typify particular product lines and countries of destination?

(v) Does the Peruvian exporter (or the associated importer) have a market development strategy for a given country of destination?
(vi) Does the Peruvian exporter have a mechanism for seeking out new markets?
(vii) Finally, to what extent do factors of product quality and marketing know-how constrain export expansion, independent of more quantifiable factors such as the real effective exchange rate and price-cost margins?

In the second section of this study, Peru's experience in industrial exporting is summarized, both in statistical terms and through a review of the policy strategies pursued by different governments. The third section summarizes the export experience of the products examined. Aside from the statistical sources referred to, it is based on interviews conducted in 1982 and 1989. The fourth section readdresses the questions just posed and the fifth section presents some conclusions regarding the Peruvian experience in export promotion.

Peruvian Industrial Exports: a Statistical Review

The importance of foreign exchange for determining the level of domestic economic activity may be seen in the emphasis often given in economic studies to the "import coefficient," i.e., the ratio of imports to GNP. Lowering the import coefficient, so as to get more GNP for a given level of imports, has been the objective of import substitution policy.

With balance in the merchandise trade account, an import coefficient implies an export coefficient of equal magnitude. Table IV-2 shows export coefficients for a number of South American countries. While the ratios differ greatly among countries, the table shows that, for any given country, the export coefficient has remained remarkably stable over the past three decades. This is surprising, because in all these countries the period has been marked by substantial effort at import substitution.

Economic structure is hard to change, however, and most of the variation observed over time is clear and merely cyclical. Indeed, the time periods were chosen so as to isolate cyclical effects, particularly for Peru.[9] As a result, in the Peruvian case there is no evidence of long-

---

[9]The break points are the following: Troughs of U.S. business cycles, with the correspondingly low commodity prices, in 1954 and 1959; topping out of Peru's export boom in 1964–65; two more troughs in the U.S. business cycle in 1969 and 1974, with the first phase in between; Peruvian depression during 1975–78; copper price boom in 1979–80; and another massive depression during 1983–85.

run change in this ratio. The high figures of 1960–64 and 1979–80 correspond to export booms, with a less drastic expansion of GNP, while 1970–74 was marked by an import substitution process which could not be sustained and ended in foreign exchange crisis. The high figure for 1983–85 corresponds to the high trade surpluses which characterize the debt crisis.

Among Peru's neighbors, the ratio of exports to GNP has been remarkably stable in the case of Brazil, and also in Argentina since the fall of Peron in 1955. The only variation in the Colombian ratio can be related directly to booms in coffee prices in 1954–57 and 1976–80. Aside from the post-1982 debt crisis, the only evidence of substantial structural change in the table is the case of Chile since 1973, where the liberalization policies of the Pinochet regime are reflected in a near doubling of the ratio of exports to GNP.

The immobility of these export/GNP ratios may give the impression of general stagnation in these economies. The middle and bottom panels of Table IV-2 are intended to disabuse the reader of such ideas. The annual value of exports, expressed in dollars, expanded more than tenfold in Peru, Chile, and Brazil, eight-fold in Argentina and by a factor of six in Colombia. The dollar has also suffered its inflation, however, and the bottom panel adjusts for this by presenting data on the income terms of trade, i.e., the dollar value of exports deflated by a dollar index of import prices. The income terms of trade thus measure trends in the purchasing power of exports.

The results are somewhat surprising: The Brazilian miracle is rather hard to find, and until the debt crisis, the Peruvian expansion was the strongest of the countries listed. Most of the Peruvian export growth occurred in the early period, however, from 1950–54 to 1960–64. The recent lamentable export performance of Peru is seen in the post-1985 figures of export values, which show Peru's export earnings in decline while those of Chile and Colombia expanding greatly.

Peru's export growth since 1975 has been accomplished mostly through product diversification. Table IV-3 shows the growing significance of nontraditional exports in Peru's total export earnings. The table shows that nontraditional exports acquired significance only after 1976, when increased Certex rates, a strongly devalued real exchange rate and a depressed domestic market combined to foster export growth in a wide range of products.[10]

---

[10]For further analysis of the determinants of export growth during this period, see Daniel Schydlowsky, Shane Hunt and Jaime Mezzera, *La promoción de exportaciones no tradicionales en el Perú* (Lima: Adex, 1983), Chapters 2 and 3. See also Carlos Paredes, "Política económica, industrialización y exportaciones de manufacturas en el Perú."

Table IV-3. Nontraditional* Share of Total Exports
(Percentages)

	Peru	Colombia	Brazil
1950	5.6	—	—
1960	—	23	13
1961	—	21	17
1962	—	23	15
1963	—	16	16
1964	—	16	18
1965	4.3	20	28
1966	3.4	23	25
1967	2.5	27	28
1968	2.4	33	29
1969	3.4	36	32
1970	3.5	33	37
1971	3.6	41	46
1972	5.2	49	49
1973	12.8	51	57
1974	9.5	58	58
1975	7.2	61	60
1976	10.2	52	61
1977	13.0	41	64
1978	17.9	40	67
1979	22.0	36	71
1980	21.6	42	70
1981	21.6	51	78
1982	23.1	45	77
1983	18.4	37	—
1984	23.1	49	81
1985	24.0	42	81
1986	25.5	32	81
1987	27.5	49	—

*Traditional exports are defined differently in each country. For Colombia: coffee beans and crude petroleum only. For Brazil: coffee beans, cotton, sugar, cacao, lumber, ores of iron, manganese, and other minerals. For Peru: concentrates, ores, and refined metals, petroleum products, fishmeal and fish oil, coffee, sugar, wool, cotton, and hides.

Sources: Colombia: IMF, *Balance of Payments Statistics Yearbook*, various issues. Brazil, 1960–71: William Tyler, *Manufactured Export Expansion and Industrialization in Brazil* (Tubingen: J.C.B. Mohr, 1976), pp. 123,126. Brazil, 1972–82: Banco Central do Brasil, *Boletim Mensual*, various issues. Perú, 1950–74: Superintendencia General de Aduanas, *Estadística de Comercio Exterior*, various issues. Peru 1975–82: Banco Central de Reserva, *Memoria 1984*, p. 145; *Memoria 1987*, p. 159.

Perspective is given to the Peruvian numbers by comparison with similar figures for Brazil and Colombia. Each country defines new or nontraditional exports somewhat differently. Nevertheless, Table IV-3 shows that both Brazil and Colombia began export diversification programs substantially before Peru, with results already perceptible during the 1960s. In fact, Brazil and Colombia were perhaps the first Latin American countries to reverse the pendulum away from import substitution and back toward more balanced growth, including export growth. The principal policy mechanism chosen in both cases involved the use of minidevaluations to maintain a real exchange rate more favorable to exporting. At the same time, the real exchange rate would be made less liable to wide fluctuations as compared to earlier regimes, when periodic

Table IV-4. Bilateral and Aggregate Real Exchange Rates
(1975 = 100)

	Germany	Ecuador	Colombia	Venezuela	Bolivia	U.S.A.	Aggregate Index
1950	117[a]	170[a]	321	205	226	156	186[a]
1955	113	180	273	223	893	155	282
1960	112	169	177	223	114	165	153
1965	80	110	127	117	94	107	103
1970	85	109	101	110	113	110	105
1971	87	93	97	105	110	107	99
1972	92	93	97	102	98	103	97
1973	106	96	105	102	78	101	98
1974	107	102	111	103	109	105	106
1975	100	100	100	100	100	100	100
1976	107	117	116	114	110	112	112
1977	126	140	146	135	126	127	132
1978	174	184	191	172	164	161	173
1979	172	175	193	163	166	157	169
1980	151	160	174	162	164	147	157
1981	109	156	157	156	177	136	145
1982	108	151	168	170	158	140	144
1983	115	168	184	202	178	156	160
1984	108	158	172	147	184	162	153
1985	128	218	183	190	186	195	184
1986	121	107	117	147	115	134	122
1987	93	66	76	73	80	90	81
Price Index	(1)	CPI	WPI	(2)	CPI	(1)	
Value Weights in Aggregate Index	0.203	0.216	0.092	0.073	0.155	0.261	

[a]1951.
Key to price indexes: (1) Industrial goods; (2) Home goods.
Source: IMF, *International Financial Statistics.* Value weights from computer tabulations for 1979, for total nontraditional exports to countries indicated. Germany's weight refers to imports of Inner Six countries of EEC.

major devaluations offset the effects of internal inflation.[11] The Colombian government introduced a minidevaluation system in March 1967; the Brazilians followed in August 1968. Almost coincidentally, fiscal incentives for exports were either introduced or strengthened.[12]

---

[11]In the interest of terminological standardization, the terms "real exchange rate" and "real effective exchange rate" will be used as they were in Morawetz, *The Emperor's New Clothes.* That is, the real exchange rate is the financial exchange rate adjusted for price level change both overseas and in the domestic economy, while the real effective exchange rate is the real exchange rate further adjusted for taxes and subsidies on exports.

[12]*Coyuntura Económica* (Fedesarrollo), March 1984, p. 110; Carlos Díaz-Alejandro, *Foreign Trade Regimes and Economic Development: Colombia* (New York: Columbia University Press, 1976); J. D. Teigeiro and R. A. Elson, "The Export Promotion System and the Growth of Minor Exports in Colombia," *IMF Staff Papers,* July, 1973, pp. 419–470. Also Eliana Cardoso, "Incentivos as exportações de manufaturas: serie historica," *Revista Brasileira de Economia,* abr/jun 1980, pp. 241–250; Jose Augusto Arantes Savasini, *Export Promotion: The Case of Brazil* (New York: Praeger, 1978), Ch. 2; William Tyler, *Manufactured Export Expansion and Industrialization in Brazil* (Tübigen: J.C.B. Mohr, 1976), Ch. 7.

In the meantime, Peruvian policy-making seemed rather behind the times, as it had been for some years. Earlier, in the 1950s, while other countries pushed hard for import substitution, Peruvian policy-makers had expanded mining ventures and kept tariffs low. A CEPAL study calculated Peru's average tariff in 1959 at 28 percent as compared to figures of 41 percent for Colombia, 40 percent for Brazil, 92 percent for Argentina, and 49 percent for Chile.[13] Ten years later, while other countries were moving in the opposite direction, Peru embarked on its most aggressive period of import substitution under the military government of Velasco. Exports were discouraged by an unfavorable real exchange rate and also by an uncooperative bureaucracy.[14] After 1975, however, economic conditions were substantially different. Peru was afflicted with a foreign exchange crisis which had plunged the country into a severe depression. Under such circumstances, the policy shift toward export promotion was almost foreordained.

The real devaluation which gave such sharp impetus to exports after 1976 is shown in Table IV-4, which presents bilateral real exchange rates with the major importing countries for Peru's nontraditional exports.[15] The increase of the real exchange rate during 1975–79 is remarkable: from 57 percent to 93 percent for the countries shown, with an aggregate increase of 69 percent.[16] Clearly so considerable a shift of relative prices had to increase greatly the attractiveness of exporting.

Subsequently, the real exchange rate was not kept very stable, but at least it was kept devalued, relative to the levels of the early 1970s. The rate was allowed to appreciate during the copper price boom of 1979–81, and, not coincidentally, nontraditional exports leveled off and

[13]Santiago Macario, "Protectionism and Industrialization in Latin America," *Economic Bulletin for Latin America*, vol. IX, no. 1, March 1964. The figures are unweighted averages of the various import categories. If weighted by the value of imports, the figures are lower (22 percent for Peru) but the ordering is the same.

[14]For an elaboration of the failure to give sufficient consideration to export promotion during the Velasco era, see Daniel Schydlowsky and Juan Wicht, *Anatomía de un fracaso económico* (Lima: Universidad del Pacifico, 1979). See also E.V.K. Fitzgerald, *The State and Economic Development: Peru since 1968* (Cambridge: Cambridge University Press, 1976); and *The Political Economy of Peru, 1956–78; Economic Development and the Restructuring of Capital* (Cambridge: Cambridge University Press, 1979).

[15]The bilateral real exchange rate is given by $(Pf)(E)/(Ps)$, where Pf is a foreign price index, E is the appropriate bilateral financial exchange rate, and Ps is a Peruvian price index, in this case the CPI. Pf is taken as an indicator of prices that Peruvian producers could receive from exporting to the country in question, while Ps is taken as an indicator of trends in Peruvian production costs. Thus the real exchange rate is an approximation of trends in price-cost margins for actual and potential exporters. It is only an approximation because of unresolved problems of aggregation and also because of failure to allow for changes in trade taxes and subsidies.

[16]These cases of sharp real devaluation also tend to be cases of economic misfortune, with unemployment so widespread that workers do not press for money wage increases as compensation for real income losses, and with capital flight causing the financial exchange rate to become devalued more than warranted by trade flows.

started to decline during this same period (see Table IV-5). Some stability was restored to the rate in the last years of the Belaunde government, but since 1985 the real exchange rate has followed an erratic course.[17]

The devalued real exchange rates of recent years are sometimes thought to be an abnormality, reflecting the abnormally depressed economic conditions. This impression is given superficial support by the use of 1975 as the base year of Table IV-4, since there is a natural tendency to think of the base year as a normal year. Indeed, 1975 was quite representative of the decade 1965–75, a period in which bilateral real rates were in general very stable. The earlier years of Table IV-4 —1950, 1955, and 1960— give a rather different picture, however, and suggest that for Peru 1965–75 was the abnormal period characterized by a sharply overvalued exchange rate.

1976 saw major changes in Certex rates as well as in the real exchange rate. The average Certex rate for nontraditional exports rose from 13.8 percent in 1975 to a high of 27.2 percent in 1978, all rates being related to the FOB value of exports. Average Certex rates were lowered to 13.4 percent by 1982, but were subsequently increased in 1984.[18]

Because of Certex, the change in the total policy package after 1976 had substantially greater effect in promoting nontraditional as opposed to traditional exports. This is seen in the sharply rising share of nontraditional in total exports, from 7.2 percent in 1975 to 22.0 percent in 1979 and even higher figures in the 1980s (see Table IV-3). In current dollars, this represented an increase from $107 million to $809 million, i.e., by a factor of seven in only four years.

Of what do these nontraditional exports consist? Although conventional wisdom tends to think of traditional exports as primary goods and nontraditional exports as industrial goods, this association is not entirely correct. On the one hand, most traditional exports, even when thought of as primary products, are subjected to some degree of industrial processing before export. Ores are smelted, cotton is ginned, sugar is refined. On the other hand, Peru's nontraditional exports have included a scattering of primary products such as corn, timber, and marble. Nevertheless, aside from these rather unusual cases of nontraditional primary products, most of which are agricultural, the division between traditional and nontraditional exports is most often an arbitrary division between lesser and greater degrees of industrial value added.

---

[17]The real exchange rate estimates for 1985–87, based on the *International Financial Statistics*, must be viewed with some skepticism, since that source makes reference to just a single rate for each country. For Peru, however, the post-1985 period witnessed a lavish use of multiple exchange rates.

[18]Schydlowsky, Hunt, and Mezzera, *La promoción de exportaciones no tradicionales*, pp. 29, 192.

Table IV-5. Peru: Nontraditional Exports
(Millions of U.S. dollars)

	1971	1975	1978	1979	1980	1981
Agriculture	7	13	39	75	72	61
Fisheries	8	19	62	104	117	107
Textiles	1	13	103	247	224	234
Other	14	62	139	384	432	299
Total	31	107	343	810	845	701

	1982	1983	1984	1985	1986	1987
Agriculture	70	56	74	93	72	87
Fisheries	98	80	167	124	111	103
Textiles	281	186	258	244	232	257
Other	313	233	227	253	230	269
Total	762	555	726	714	645	716

Sources: 1971–78: Perú Exporta (Asociación de Exportadores), July 1980, p. 57. 1979–87: Banco Central de Reserva, Memoria 1987, p. 159.

Thus fish meal, unrefined fish oil, and electrolytically refined copper are traditional, but canned fish, refined fish oil, and copper alloys are nontraditional. In the end, it must be said that a principal motivating factor in establishing the division was to keep major export categories in the traditional area, so as to avoid excessive fiscal drain in the subsidy payments. This is the most likely explanation why, for example, coffee is counted as a traditional export but tea is nontraditional.[19]

Table IV-5 shows the evolution of nontraditional exports in dollar values by major product categories. The data show that the sharp growth of such exports during 1975–79 and the subsequent stagnation of the 1980s affected major product lines in about equal proportion. Nontraditional exports depicted in more specific detail in Table IV-6, which groups products by major export sector. Within each group, the products are listed according to the value of exports in 1979, the first of the peak years and therefore the year marking the end of the 1970s boom.[20]

The table brings out a number of points with respect to the variety of products exported. First, it will be seen that the line between processed and unprocessed agricultural products is quite arbitrarily drawn, and that a number of the so-called unprocessed products, e.g., tara, Brazil nuts, barbasco and flour, require grinding or shelling. The so-

---

[19]Another possible explanation is that Peruvian coffee is perceived as having a lower demand elasticity in foreign markets than Peruvian tea.

[20]These detailed data come from computer tapes giving a separate record for each shipment from January 1, 1976 to September 15, 1980. The data refer to export authorizations, however, which generally exceeded actual exports by about 10 percent. Unfortunately, there is no guarantee that key punching error has not been incorporated into the tapes, but neither can it be guaranteed that published documents are error-free.

Table IV-6. Peru: Nontraditional Exports: Detail for 1979

Product Group and Sub-Group Product	Nabandina* Code	1979 Value of Exports ($000)
Agriculture		
Unprocessed Agricultural Products		
Cocoa beans	18.01	4,891
Onions	07.01	4,449
Cochinilla	05.15	4,182
Tara	13.01	3,740
Brazil nuts	08.01	3,175
Tea	09.02	2,137
Barbasco	12.07	2,055
Maize	10.05	1,930
Beans	07.05	1,519
Fertile eggs	04.05	1,514
Horses for breeding	01.01	1,259
Baby chicks	01.05	1,224
Flour	11.01	1,135
Olives	07.03	1,129
Processed Agricultural Products		
Cocoa paste	18.03	6,055
Cocoa butter	18.04	3,341
Canned fruit	20.06	3,105
Milk products	04.02	2,759
Soluble coffee	21.02	2,551
Canned vegetables, esp. asparagus	20.02	2,514
Margarine	15.13	1,815
Jams and jellies	20.05	1,730
Confectionery	17.04	1,034
Fishing Products		
Canned fish	16.04	45,383
Frozen fish	03.01	30,016
Enriched animal feeds	23.07	23,719
Hydrogenated fish oil	15.12	8,062
Salted fish	03.02	4,733
Animal feeds	23.01	2,838
Shellfish	03.03	2,753
Whale meal	02.04	1,377
Processed fish oil	15.08	1,327
Textiles		
Cotton fabrics	55.09	46,734
Cotton yarn	55.05	33,344
Wool of sheep and alpaca, carded and combed	53.05	31,344
Woolen fabrics	53.11	24,005
Men's outer garments	61.01	14,379
Shawls (mantas)	62.01	10,371
Women's outer garments	61.02	10,001
Sheets, blankets, coverlets	62.02	9,260
Cables for discontinous synthetic fibers	56.02	7,675
Discontinuous synthetic fibers, not combed	56.01	5,707
Yarn of sheep's wool	53.07	5,252
Knitted clothing	60.05	4,554
Yarn of sheep and alpaca wool, for retail sale	53.10	3,915
Fabrics of synthetic fibers	56.07	3,717
Velvet	58.04	2,966
Bags and sacks	62.03	2,501
Fishing nets	59.05	2,489
Yarn of synthetic fibers (blends)	56.05	2,284

Table IV-6. Peru: Nontraditional Exports: Detail for 1979 (continued)

Product Group and Sub-Group Product	Nabandina* Code	1979 Value of Exports ($000)
Discontinuous synthetic fibers, carded and combed	56.04	2,027
Knitted fabrics	60.01	1,897
Rugs and tapestries	58.01	1,733
Yarn of alpaca wool	53.08	1,586
Yarn of continuous synthetic fibers	51.01	1,252
Cotton yarn for retail sale	55.06	1,213
Men's undergarments	61.03	1,014
Manufactured Metal Products		
Fishing boats	89.01	20,133
Batteries	85.03	6,099
Autos, buses, trucks	87.02	4,666
Pumps	84.10	4,452
Refrigerators	84.15	4,328
Electric motors and transformers	85.01	3,333
Plumbing fixtures	84.61	2,763
Kitchen stoves	73.36	2,653
Auto parts	87.06	1,519
Pulleys	84.22	1,512
Bicycles	87.10	1,281
Motorcycles	87.09	1,125
Other machinery	84.59	1,034
Chemicals		
Detergents	34.02	7,514
Cosmetics	33.06	6,696
Explosives	36.02	5,785
Soap	34.01	4,648
Stearin and other esters	15.10	4,136
Medicines	30.03	3,316
Monosodium glutamate	29.23	3,196
Sulfates, esp. of copper	28.38	3,130
Lead oxides	28.27	2,915
Dyes derivate from chochinilla	32.04	2,468
Plastic products	39.07	2,343
Tires	40.11	2,202
Polymerized plastics, esp. acetates	39.02	1,501
Fuses for explosives	36.03	1,478
Lemon extract	33.01	1,402
Percussion caps	36.04	1,290
Other oxides, esp. of copper	28.28	1,011
Foundry and Metallurgical Products		
Copper wire and bars	74.03	28,056
Zinc alloys	79.01	12,474
Lead alloys	78.01	6,614
Steel bars	73.10	4,058
Zinc calots and anodes	79.06	3,491
Steel plates and sheets	73.13	3,090
Insulated cables	85.23	2,465
Copper alloys[a]	74.01	1,949
Processed bismuth and cadmium[a]	81.04	1,613
Copper sheets	74.04	1,397
Copper cables, without insulation	74.10	1,383
Lead sheets	78.03	1,366
Containers made from steel sheets	73.23	1,215
Alloyed steel products	73.15	1,103
Steel beams	73.11	1,029

Table IV-6. Peru: Nontraditional Exports: Detail for 1979 (continued)

Product Group and Sub-Group Product	Nabandina* Code	1979 Value of Exports ($000)
Nonmetallic Minerals		
Cement	25.23	31,327
Barite	25.11	12,247
Glass products for home use	70.13	2,909
Safety glass	70.08	1,368
Tiles and paving stones	69.08	1,190
Wood and Paper Products		
Books	49.01	4,698
Sawed lumber	44.05	4,388
Wood sheets less than 5 mm. thick	44.14	4,156
Paper, especially kraft paper	48.01	3,335
Plywood	44.15	1,980
Toilet paper	48.05	1,503
Wood pulp sheets	48.09	1,116
Hides and Leather Products		
Footwear[b]	64.02	7,214
Goatskins	41.04	2,107
Prepared hides	43.02	1,965
Leather clothing accessories	42.03	1,390
Other prepared hides and skins	41.05	1,374
Handicrafts		
Handicrafts	99.01	33,296
Other Products		
Objects of gold	71.12	30,027
Objects of silver	71.13	4,143
Non-leather footwear	64.01	2,223
Metallic objects for home decoration	83.06	1,712

*Nabandina Code is the Brussels Tariff Nomenclature as modified by the Andean Group Secretariat, Junta del Acuerdo de Cartagena (JUNAC).

[a]Approximately half the value of these items, consisting of "matas cobrizas" and bismuth crystals, are classified as nonmetallic minerals.

[b]Approximately one third of this category is assigned to "Other Products," i.e., leather is not the principal raw material.

Source: Computer tabulation of export authorizations, described in text.

called unprocessed products are largely specialty items, many of them from the jungle regions east of the Andes. Nontraditional fisheries exports are dominated by canned fish and frozen fish, while the textiles consisted largely of alpaca and cotton products, both derived from raw materials of particularly fine quality. Many other nontraditional exports, in other product groups, are seen to derive from Peru's abundance of nonferrous metals. These include structural shapes and alloys of copper and zinc, lead oxides, copper sulfates, gold and silver jewelry, and, incorporating still higher levels of industrial value added, copper cables and zinc-based flashlight batteries. A few products, such as fishing boats and pumps, had become Peruvian specialties not because they incorporated natural resources but because they were capital goods required in the extraction of natural resources. Still other products had no particular relation to particular natural resources but simply represented import substitution industries which, faced with a depressed domestic market, sought additional sales through exporting, particularly to nearby countries. This category included items such as refrigerators, soap and detergents, and kitchen stoves.

Table IV-7 takes these same export products at a more aggregated level and reorders them by decreasing share of exports directed beyond Latin America. This is a crude approximation to an ordering by comparative advantage, since it should be expected that only those products with strong comparative advantage would be able to compete successfully in world markets. Other, higher-cost products with limited comparative advantage would be confined to nearby countries, protected from the winds of world competition either by the Andean Group external tariff or by transportation costs.

The table shows a clear pattern relating the nature of the product to the principal region of destination. In general, exports which are natural-resource-intensive have a larger share of their exports directed to markets outside Latin America. This is, in a sense, hardly surprising. Traditionally, Latin American economies have held comparative advantage only in the production of primary products. These are products

Table IV-7. Peru: Nontraditional Exports by Product Group and Country of Destination, 1979

Product Group	Nabandina Chapter	Share Exported to: (percent)		
		Nearby Countries	Rest of Latin America	Rest of World
1. Wool of sheep and alpaca	53	2.9	0.8	96.3
2. Animal feed	23	0.8	5.9	93.3
3. Cacao and derivatives	18	2.7	4.4	92.9
4. Cotton yarn and fabric	55	8.1	3.9	88.0
5. Frozen fish	03	12.7	3.6	83.7
6. Zinc products	79	22.0	15.9	62.1
7. Fish products, esp. canned fish	16	28.0	22.6	49.4
8. Copper products	74	28.3	29.5	42.2
9. Lumber and wool products	44	47.5	10.3	42.2
10. Fish oil	15	47.2	13.2	39.6
11. Nonmetallic mineral products	25	63.0	10.5	26.5
12. Iron and steel products	73	80.9	0.7	18.4
13. Electrical machinery	85	86.2	1.5	12.3
14. Wearing apparel	61	70.1	18.3	11.6
15. Inorganic chemicals	28	61.4	28.7	9.9
16. Nonelectrical machinery	84	86.2	6.2	7.6
17. Ships	89	62.6	32.8	4.6
18. Shanks, spreads	62	87.8	8.3	3.9
19. Synthetic textiles	56	87.9	9.2	2.9
20. Soap, detergents	34	99.9	0	0.1

Note: "Nearby Countries" refers to Chile plus the Andean Group.
Source: Computer tabulations of export authorizations. See also Schydlowsky, Hunt and Mezzera, *La promoción de exportaciones no tradicionales*, p. 16.

which are either entirely natural resources, or which incorporate a limited industrial value added share to reduce shipping weight and lower transport costs, as in the case of refined metals. With the development of nontraditional, largely industrial exports, the greatest export successes have been achieved by incorporating industrial value added to additional primary products, such as the agricultural specialties listed in Table IV-6, or by incorporating additional value added to primary product exports of longer standing. Thus, for example, copper ore is not only refined; it is also processed further into alloys, structural shapes, industrial chemicals such as copper sulfate, wires and cables.

By contrast, the products exported largely to nearby countries appear not to be natural-resource-intensive. Instead, they come from industries created during the more extravagant periods of import substitution. Based on modern industrial technologies involving substantial economies of scale, such industries have often been high cost producers because of inability to capture such economies within the confines of Peru's limited domestic market. Under such circumstances, rational investors will tend to build plants which are relatively large given the size of that domestic market, and then to operate them at low levels of capacity utilization. In this way some scale economies can be realized. But at the same time such industries suffer chronically from the problem of unused capacity, and this problem becomes magnified when the domestic market shrinks, as it did during the recession of the late 1970s. Thus pressures to export in order to make use of available capacity become very strong.[21]

The competitiveness of such industries in export markets is affected by three separate factors. On the one hand, the technical efficiency of such industries tends to be low, in part because of the failure to exploit economies of scale and in part because of other inefficiencies spawned in a highly protected environment. This is counterbalanced, however, but a second factor, which is that such industries find it profitable to export at prices covering only marginal costs, since the capacity is already installed and unused. Third, competitiveness is further limited by the high cost of inputs. Whereas the natural-resource-intensive industries such as canned fish or industrial chemicals have access to inputs which are low-cost and high-quality by world standards, the import substitution industries are in quite the opposite position.[22]

---

[21]For further elaboration of the economics of capacity utilization, see Daniel Schydlowsky, "Capital Utilization, Growth, Employment, Balance of Payments, and Price Stabilization," in Jere Behrman and James A. Hanson, eds., *Short-Term Macroeconomic Policy in Latin America* (Cambridge: Ballinger Press, 1979), pp. 311–355. Also Roger Betancourt and Christopher Clague, *Capital Utilization: A Theoretical and Empirical Analysis* (New York: Cambridge University Press, 1981).

[22]The special position of the canned fish industry in this respect should be noted. With regard to its inputs, it has access to low-cost fish, but must also buy high-cost tin plate.

Table IV-8. Peru: Production and Exports of Fish Products and Preparations
(Thousands of metric tons, thousands of dollars)

	Production				Exports	
	Pilchards	Bonito, tuna	Mackerel	Total	Volume	Value
1948					5.0	2,648
1958	1.2	14.7	0	15.9	13.3	5,299
1960	2.3	21.0	0.1	23.4	15.4	5,686
1965	2.3	12.7	0.5	15.5	11.1	4,874
1970	8.9	8.4	0.3	17.7	4.3	2,746
1971	9.1	13.5	0.4	23.3	7.2	4,253
1972	12.47	13.4	0.9	27.0	10.2	6,342
1973	14.6	10.2	2.7	27.8	7.7	6,935
1974	16.8	2.1	9.3	29.9	5.2	4,967
1975	17.8	4.8	5.4	28.2	4.5	4,083
1976	22.0	2.4	1.3	32.4	9.5	8,079
1977	36.1	3.0	3.5	49.6	21.8	16,287
1978	44.5	2.8	5.8	64.3	35.8	23,678
1979	69.6	2.6	3.7	84.3	43.4	33,625
1980	129.9	1.7	3.5	140.0	85.7	64,091
1981	133.6	1.9	2.0	139.8	85.8	74,647
1982	61.1	1.2	1.3	64.3	58.0	44,636
1983	23.4	1.5	0.4	25.9	19.4	15,634
1984	42.9	0.4	0.6	44.9	26.0	21,103
1985	37.1	0.1	0.1	37.7	16.0	14,026
1986	60.9	0.1	0.6	62.5	16.5	13,746
1987	76.3	1.3	0.4	78.5	18.6	15,500

Note: For 1965 and earlier years, the mackerel figure includes small quantities of other fish products. For 1976 and subsequent years, the mackerel figure pertains to horse mackerel (jurel) only.
Source: FAO, *Yearbook of Fishery Statistics*, 1984, pp. 150–157, 169, and other issues.

Thus it is apparent that natural-resource-intensive exports may be more competitive in world markets for two reasons: they may possess a true comparative advantage, but they are also favored by access to low-cost inputs.

Export History of Selected Products

Canned Fish

Growth and Change in the Fishing Industry
This study examines one particular fish product—canned fish—because it embodies a higher share of industrial value added than do the other major fish products and because of its strong growth during the 1970s export boom.

Fish products are among the oldest of Peru's industrial exports. Judging from the industry's size, its capacity for innovation, the dispersion of its markets throughout the world, and its longevity, it might

Table IV-9. Peru: Production and Exports of Fishmeal

	Production (1,000 tons)	Exports (1,000 tons)	Value of Exports ($000)
1948	—	0.7	42
1957	—	62.9	7,225
1958	129.5	107.5	11,761
1959	336.2	281.4	31,681
1960	563.4	509.8	38,997
1961	844.5	713.5	49,819
1962	1121.5	1059.7	100,138
1963	1135.2	1041.8	104,755
1964	1556.0	1428.6	143,632
1965	1284.1	1414.9	155,700
1966	1472.8	1304.1	181,914
1967	1816.0	1594.8	173,286
1968	1925.3	2081.3	204,670
1969	1614.0	1711.2	200,464
1970	2255.8	1903.4	295,141
1971	1934.6	1762.1	277,863
1972	897.0	1625.9	234,402
1973	423.0	356.7	137,375
1974	880.1	618.0	198,754
1975	689.0	783.5	161,068
1976	886.4	594.1	185,938
1977	497.0	442.3	183,516
1978	669.7	484.8	192,280
1979	688.0	530.9	199,311
1980	458.1	463.7	207,314
1981	478.3	387.2	174,484
1982	665.5	615.9	202,606
1983	251.7	209.6	81,418
1984	568.4	389.2	134,226
1985	717.1	507.6	118,054
1986	973.1	698.5	200,088
1987	821.4	730.4	248,000

Source: FAO, Yearbook of Fishery Statistics, 1984, pp. 228, 243, and other issues.

be considered a particularly well-established industry. Nevertheless, it has been so beset by instability, for both ecological and economic reasons, that its future remains in doubt.

The ecological instability has been provided by El Niño, the warm coastal current which went astray in 1973 and again in 1983, each time with devastating effects on the fish supply. The effect of El Niño is seen clearly in the long-term series of Tables IV-8 and IV-9. Fishmeal production plummeted in 1973, as did production of canned bonito. As the anchovy (anchoveta) and bonito were driven away by warmer waters, their place was taken by the Pacific sardine (pilchard). Thus the canning boom based on the pilchard in the late 1970s was accompanied by depression among fishmeal producers.

The 1983 Niño then proceeded to decimate pilchard supplies as well. A more recent return of cooler waters has brought a recovery of anchovy stocks, while pilchard fishing remains concentrated in the warmer waters near the Ecuadorean frontier.

The world market for canned fish is highly fragmented, partly because the various types of canned fish are imperfect substitutes for one another, partly because of transportation costs, which give incentive for home markets to be served before exporting begins, and for exports to be made first to nearby destinations in the same part of the world. Table IV-10 gives figures on production and exports for South America alone (plus Mexico) as a means of indicating Peru's competitive position on a regional basis. The table shows that for many years, Peru's production of canned fish was little more than 10 percent of the South American total, except for the boom years around 1980 when its share rose to nearly half. Argentina, Brazil, Mexico, and Venezuela all have sizeable canned fish industries, but with production directed almost entirely to the respective domestic markets. Only in Peru, Ecuador and, more recently Chile has production substantially exceeded domestic consumption so that there has been surplus available for export.

The table also shows that Chile escaped the effects of El Niño in 1983, while canning industries in Peru and Ecuador suffered sharp reductions in both production and exports. The relative importance of ecological and economic policy factors in explaining the differential experience of the three countries is, unfortunately, not clarified by the table.

More detailed export figures for Peru alone, in Table IV-11, show that the boom and subsequent collapse of the canning industry was particularly a matter of canned pilchards packed in either oil or tomato sauce. Separate data for three important and interesting countries of destination—Brazil, USA, and South Africa—are shown as well. Particularly in the case of pilchards, the extraordinary variety of countries of destination could not be fully reflected in the table. Twelve countries were listed as export destinations in 1976, but by 1979 this figure had increased to 47 and included fifteen countries in Latin America, seven in North America and the Antilles, nine in Europe, one in the Middle East, three in Africa and twelve in Asia and the Pacific Islands. Peruvian pilchards were shipped to places as scattered as Antigua, Finland, Zaire, and New Caledonia. In fact, a substantial market was established across the South Pacific, from Tahiti to New Guinea.[23]

The marketing and product quality dimensions of export development are best seen in the growth of canned pilchards during the 1970s. Unfortunately, the classification available in export statistics, reproduced in Table IV-11, does not effectively separate new products from

---

[23]Various issues of *Estadística del Comercio Exterior* reveal that in the 1960s bonito exports were equally widespread.

Table IV-10. Production and Exports of Canned Fish

	1960	1965	1970	1975	1980	1981	1982	1983	1984	1985	1986	1987
Production (thousands of metric tons)												
Peru	23.4	15.5	16.8	28.2	140.0	139.8	64.3	25.9	44.9	37.3	62.5	78.5
Chile	2.9	7.8	9.9	7.3	34.7	26.6	21.9	38.2	45.4	40.5	56.9	60.4
Ecuador	1.6	4.1	5.5	13.0	44.0	63.0	44.8	22.4	36.8	39.6	35.8	34.0
Venezuela	14.4	25.0	21.4	21.0*	28.0	22.5	32.9	28.6	42.0	47.0	39.4	45.6
Argentina	20.4	18.0	13.0	20.6	13.5	14.6	12.7	13.1	12.4	16.6	16.6	15.2
Brazil	13.4	31.6	39.3		61.2	43.7	40.7	46.4	52.0	56.0	51.2	51.5
Mexico	8.0	18.0	46.6	41.8	65.0	80.6	52.7	36.7	57.7	75.3	49.4	54.9
South America	85.7	122.5	158.1	232.3	382.9	347.2	276.1	225.9	286.0	—	263.0	285.8
Peru as a percentage of South American total	27	13	11	12	37	40	23	11	16	—	24	27
Exports (thousands of metric tons)												
Peru	15.4	11.1	4.3	4.5	85.7	85.8	58.0	19.4	26.0	16.0	16.5	18.6
Chile	0	0	0	0	14.7	16.2	10.1	21.4	24.2	13.9	35.5	37.3
Ecuador	1.2	2.0	2.2	5.8	35.6	36.2	31.5	9.9	10.3	14.7	13.6	21.9
Venezuela	0	0.3	0.5	0.6	0	0.1	0.1	0.3	0.2	0.8	6.3	2.5
Argentina	0	0.1	0.1	0.3	0.6	0.3	0.3	0.2	0.3	0.7	0.5	0.6
Brazil	0	0	0	1.0	2.3	2.8	0.7	1.0	1.4	1.2	1.0	1.2
Mexico	0.3	0.5	0	0.9	1.0	0.2	0.2	1.3	0	0.2	0.2	1.7
South America	17.3	18.6	9.0	15.0	138.9	141.5	100.8	52.2	62.4	47.3	73.5	82.2
Peru as a percentage of South American total	89	60	48	30	62	61	58	37	42	34	22	23
Exports (millions of U.S. dollars)												
Peru	5.7	4.9	2.7	4.1	64.1	74.6	44.6	15.6	21.1	14.0	13.7	15.5
Chile	0	0	0	0	11.2	12.7	8.2	17.2	19.8	10.4	26.2	28.6
Ecuador	0.5	1.2	1.3	6.6	73.6	54.7	44.3	15.1	16.1	21.0	19.3	29.0
Venezuela	0	0.1	0.2	0.6	0	0.6	0.6	0.4	1.1	2.8	21.4	2.8
Argentina	0	0	0.1	0.4	2.4	1.1	1.1	0.6	1.1	1.2	1.2	2.5
Brazil	0	0	0	0.9	4.4	5.0	1.6	1.4	2.5	2.0	2.0	2.9
Mexico	0.1	0.1	0	1.1	7.7	0.5	0.7	1.8	0.2	0.5	0.4	2.7
South America	6.4	8.7	6.1	16.5	155.8	148.6	110.4	51.2	61.0	51.5	83.8	81.3
Peru as a percentage of South American total	89	56	44	25	41	50	44	30	35	27	16	19

*1974

Source: FAO, *Yearbook of Fishery Statistics*, 1984, pp. 150, 169–171, and other issues.

Table IV-11. Peru: Exports of Canned Fish by Country of Destination
(Thousands of dollars)

	1976	1979	1980	1981	1982	1983	1984	1985	1986	1987
Tuna										
Brazil	758	391	24	13	69	0	6	0	0	0
USA*	0	1,182	0	0	0	0	0	0	0	0
South Africa	0	0	0	0	0	0	0	0	0	0
Other	1,120	3,749	982	405	375	232	108	0	260	96
Total	1,878	5,322	1,006	418	444	232	114	0	260	96
Bonito										
Brazil	117	652	375	720	1,124	286	44	225	47	19
USA*	13	39	43	56	45	48	0	19	0	0
South Africa	0	0	0	0	0	0	0	0	0	0
Other	572	1,044	1,308	989	1,007	110	168	47	0	25
Total	702	1,735	1,726	1,765	2,176	444	212	291	47	44
Pilchards (sardines)										
Packed in Oil										
Brazil	248	1,317	—	—	—	—	2,186	1,245	2,255	1,597
USA	0	1,151	—	—	—	—	279	152	201	546
South Africa	0	217	—	—	—	—	0	0	0	0
Other	90	8,928	—	—	—	—	3,414	1,606	1,532	2,627
Packed in Tomato Sauce										
Brazil	0	10	—	—	—	—	23	9	0	12
USA	0	2,764	—	—	—	—	1,845	1,521	1,751	2,009
South Africa	0	2,770	—	—	—	—	1,889	1,239	0	1,468
Other	403	10,650	—	—	—	—	7,461	2,504	3,386	4,420
Packed in Brine										
Brazil	0	137	—	—	—	—	0	0	130	1,443
USA	74	695	—	—	—	—	1,097	698	735	1,085
South Africa	0	0	—	—	—	—	184	81	0	0
Other	318	252	—	—	—	—	636	598	817	2,718
Total, Three Sauces	1,133	28,891	—	—	—	—	19,014	9,652	10,807	17,925
All Canned Pilchards										
Brazil	—	—	3,633	3,801	4,208	1,197	2,364	1,747	3,410	4,881
USA	—	—	8,747	14,291	10,515	1,459	3,669	3,408	2,885	4,121
South Africa	—	—	13,228	22,475	1,948	1,255	2,409	1,320	0	1,468
Other	—	—	29,760	29,059	24,147	9,951	12,823	6,979	6,999	11,705
Total	2,308	29,057	55,368	69,626	40,818	13,862	21,265	13,294	13,294	22,175

*USA figures for 1976 and 1979 include Puerto Rico.

Sources: 1976, 1979: Computer tabulations of export authorizations, Ministerio de Economía y Finanzas. 1980–1987: Computer tabulations of OFINE.

old. The major innovations of recent years have been based not on the sauce but rather on the shape of the can and the way the fish is prepared. The traditional product was the 15–ounce oval can with the fish packed in tomato sauce. The two new styles are "tipo atun" (tuna) and "tipo tall." In the case of "tipo atun," the fish is skinned and filleted and only the meat is packed in a tuna-type can. In the case of "tipo tall," the can is of a shape associated with soup or vegetables, the fish is cut in pieces and packed with bone and skin still attached, and a tomato sauce is added. Thus the figures related to tomato sauce in Table IV-11 include nearly all the "tipo tall," but also some of the traditional 15–ounce oval cans, while the figures related to packing in oil contain most but not all of the tuna-type production. The production methods, economic consequences, markets, and marketing problems of these two new products have been completely different from one another. They will be discussed in turn.

Exporting to the United States and South Africa

By the mid-1970s, Peruvian producers had acquired years of experience in processing bonito in a manner similar to tuna, that is, as a boneless fillet packed in a small can. Bonito had always kept a small but secure market in countries such as Brazil and among special groups such as the Hispanic population in the United States. Around 1975 this same approach was begun with the vastly larger supplies of the Pacific sardine (or pilchard). Much smaller than the bonito, its 6 to 8–inch length places it at the margin of filleting possibilities. Thus production is highly labor intensive and requires a dexterous labor force. The resulting output is differentiated according to the size of the pieces in a manner similar to tuna and bonito, viz., solid pack (lomito), chunk, flakes, and grated, although in different proportions, with much more of the grated, because of fish size.

Many of the early marketing contacts for this new product were those developed through earlier export business, either in fishmeal or in bonito and tuna canning. Through experimental marketing efforts by a few Peruvian exporters using established channels, the new Peruvian product became sufficiently well-known in the United States to attract attention among fish processors and distributors. Many such processors and distributors chose to add a line of Peruvian pilchards to their offerings, and started visiting Peru. Thus most Peruvian producers never had to go abroad to look for buyers. The buyers came knocking on the factory door.

As with other consumer products described by Morawetz and Keesing, the importer-wholesaler became the principal marketing strategist for the export of canned sardines to the U.S. market.[24] The typical importer-wholesaler firm purchased on its own account, carried inventory in its North American warehouse, and accepted the responsibility for all marketing and sales activity within the United States.

The marketing strategies of different importer-wholesalers differed in detail, but all followed the same general thrust. In possession of a tuna-type product in a tuna-sized can, all emphasized that the product was "just like tuna," not just in shelf appearance but also in taste, and that it cost much less. This basic tuna-substitute strategy meant that importer-wholesalers sought to sell Peruvian pilchards not just to a specialized group such as the Hispanic population, but to the great North American mainstream, as defined by the consumption of tuna-fish sandwiches.

This marketing strategy could be carried out at the national level or within a regional or local market. A promotional effort at the national level would appear unattractive to importer-wholesalers, because in the absence of central coordination only a small percent of the benefit would be recaptured by the company making the effort. Nevertheless, some importer-wholesalers did try a national strategy, targeting U.S. supermarkets through advertising in national food trade journals and consumers through the sponsoring of taste tests on television, in which blindfolded participants proved unable to tell the difference between tuna and pilchard.[25]

Marketing technique at the local level may be illustrated with the case of Miami, Florida. One importer-wholesaler company, using just one salesperson, attempted a low-budget push in the Miami area. The technique was to persuade food editors of local newspapers to run stories on the pilchard, and then to persuade supermarkets to carry pilchards as specially advertised items for a trial period. The national advertising was perhaps a necessary preliminary to this local marketing effort, since the national discussion gave newspaper food editors a reason for giving attention to the product in their columns. All this was accomplished; at least some supermarket chains in the Miami area ran advertising specials on pilchards and were reasonably pleased with the results. However, they were less pleased six months later when pilchard sales had slumped

---

[24]David Morawetz, *The Emperor's New Clothes*; Donald Keesing, "Exporting Manufactured Consumer Goods."

[25]This prompted an analysis by *Consumer Reports*, in whose judgement "pilchard neither tastes nor looks like tuna," but "is tuna's peer when it comes to nutrition." The article concluded, "You probably won't 'think you're eating tuna,' but you may want to give pilchard a try nonetheless. It is nutritious and relatively cheap, and you just might like the taste. Mixed with mayonnaise, onion, and celery, pilchard makes a nice sandwich filling." *Consumer Reports*, January 1982, pp. 5–6.

badly. One supermarket buyer concluded that consumers had tried the product once but did not come back a second time. As early as mid-1982, some supermarkets had decided to drop the product, while others were leaning toward that same decision.

A year earlier, in 1981, Peruvian pilchards could be found in the canned tuna section of nearly every supermarket in the United States. A year later, in 1983, they were gone. Not just in Miami but throughout the country, the marketing strategies for making pilchards "just like tuna" had foundered.

Two factors explain this reversal. First, tuna prices had plummeted, partly as a result of vastly increased supplies from countries such as Thailand and the Philippines. By historical standards, tuna prices had been anomalously high in the late 70s and early 80s, but importer-wholesalers had not incorporated reasonable tuna-price projections into their pilchard-marketing plans.

Consumers were willing to purchase pilchards but only at a substantial discount from tuna. That discount evaporated as the price of tuna fell. Opinions differ, but it seems that a discount of 20 to 30 cents per can was needed in order for pilchards to retain a small but acceptable share of the market for tuna and its substitutes. At a time when pilchard sales were particularly buoyant, the price was scarcely more than half that of tuna. The *Consumer Reports* article, for example, gave a range of pilchard prices between 50 and 69 cents at a time when the average price for chunk light tuna was $1.05. In mid-1982, however, that same tuna could be purchased for as low as 69 cents as a loss leader in Miami supermarkets. At that price, the gap was too diminished and pilchards were squeezed out of the market. This is so particularly because the rent deriving from fish as a natural resource is a very small percent of final sale price. In other words, the supply curve for pilchards at the retail level was fairly elastic.

The second factor explaining the collapse of the tuna-substitute strategy was the reappearance of El Niño, which decimated the fishing industry once again in 1983. The blow of El Niño, combined with the credit crunch in the depression of that year, tempted some producers into accepting orders for which they had little chance of making delivery on time, presumably as a means of obtaining desperately needed credit. As a result, some deliveries were as much as a year late. Most importer-wholesalers in the U.S., faced with declining tuna prices, serious supply problems, and, in some cases, unreliable producers, simply dropped the Peruvian pilchard from their product lines.

The development of "tipo-tall" came at the initiative of buyers from South Africa, who had turned to Peru and Chile as alternative supply sources after the pilchard fisheries off the coast of Namibia had suffered a catastrophic decline in fish supplies. Thus South African canners had found themselves with a distribution network and a developed market, but with no fish.[26] Within a short time, however, the expansion of the Peruvian pilchard canneries attracted the attention of the South Africans, who were determined to make up for what they had lost in Namibia through massive purchases in Peru and Chile. The traditional Peruvian product was however quite unlike what the South African consumer was accustomed to. The preparation of the fish, the sauce, the shape of the can, all had to be adapted to established tastes in South Africa.

In South Africa, canned pilchards are a staple of the poor black population. The "tipo tall" style of consumption, also common in England, is cost-minimizing, since it does not require that the fish be either skinned or boned. In fact, processing requires only that the fish be deheaded, detailed, and gutted, an operation sufficiently simple to be totally automated by South African technology.

The international distribution channel thus established consisted of three types of firms: the South African producer-distributor consortium (Federal Marine), the Peruvian firm which acted as purchasing agent for the South Africans, and the Peruvian producers. The functions of the consortium were to set the product specifications, establish the quality control system which would govern production, and place the orders through the agent. The functions of the agent were to transmit orders to the producers, supervise production through a subsidiary inspection company, accept delivery of the orders, and arrange shipping. The function of the producer was to produce to specifications and to schedule.

This South African connection became a major part of the canned pilchard export boom of the late 1970s. The first such exports to South Africa were shipped only in 1977, but by 1981, the peak year of the boom, South Africa accounted for 32 percent of Peru's canned pilchard exports.

Nevertheless, the South African export trade disappeared as quickly as did the tuna substitute trade in the United States, at the same time but for different reasons.

The first blow came in 1982. A balance of payments crisis in South Africa caused the government of that country to impose exchange controls, which sharply limited canned fish imports. Several new Peruvian factories built with South African technology had just come on line and, producing in anticipation of orders which never materialized, had accumulated an unsold inventory of a million cases by the end of 1982. Thus much of the canning industry was in crisis even before El Niño wiped out a year's production in 1983.

---

[26]Another pilchard fishery which acquired literary fame was also ruined by the disappearance of the fish. It was the industry located in Monterrey, California, and made famous by John Steinbecks's *Cannery Row*. The first Peruvian canning plants had been dismantled in Monterrey and shipped to Peru in the 1940s.

Both fish supplies and the South African economy returned to normal in 1984, but for Peruvian producers most of the South African business had been lost permanently, partly because Namibian fish supplies had recovered, partly because South Africans had invested heavily in Chile and preferred to import from their facilities there. Peru has become a third-ranked supply source, exporting to South Africa in recent years less than a tenth of the peak volume of 1981.

What can be said of the marketing effort of Peruvian producers in these exporting experiences with the United States and South Africa? It should be remembered that the effort required of them was "merely" to produce a quality product on schedule. The assessment of importer-wholesalers after the fact was that some did and some did not, but that those who did not or could not were cut out of the export business fairly quickly. Those who proved themselves capable of supplying acceptable quality on an acceptable schedule were able to meet demand, at least until the return of El Niño in 1983.

Market positioning is to some extent a trial and error process. Effective marketing strategy minimizes the costs of the process, but meanwhile margins need to remain favorable, in order to encourage continuation of the learning experience represented by the trials and errors. In the United States, there was hardly time for much learning before tuna prices collapsed. To my knowledge, importer-wholesalers never acquired more than the vaguest of ideas regarding the relation between the size of price discount from tuna and the degree of market penetration.

Some learning was however accomplished with respect to the identification of promising submarkets. The Hispanic market in the U.S. continues to take a small but steady supply of pilchards in the 15–oz. oval can, packed in tomato sauce. Also, one company is well established among poor people in the Southeastern U.S. with a product similar to South Africa's "tipo tall," but packed in water rather than tomato sauce.[27] These examples emphasize the extent to which different importer-wholesalers had differential success with their marketing strategies, with consequent good or ill fortune for their dependent producers.

After over 10 years of various experimental strategies for marketing canned pilchards in the United States, can it be said that all potential submarkets have been well explored? Recent experience in countertrade suggests that the answer is no. A case in point is the so-called institutional market, i.e., hospitals, prisons, etc., where bulk purchases are made by price-conscious buyers. Whereas the retail can is one of 7 oz., the institutional can is a four-pounder.

---

[27]The brand is "Eatwell," marketed by Starkist.

The institutional market was explored with varying success by a number of importer-wholesalers during the boom period. But recently one such importer-wholesaler has returned to this market with considerable success, as part of the countertrade commitments of Eastman Kodak Co. Kodak quite rightly recognized its lack of expertise in the marketing of fish products. It was however able to provide elements to the marketing mix which had been largely absent before, viz., finance, especially for the purchase of high quality cans from Chile, and the good reputation associated with brand recognition.[28] Recent marketing successes in this area suggest that consumer (or supermarket) resistance to a relatively unknown product has been compounded by the fact that some of the most entrepreneurial importer-wholesalers have also been relatively unknown, as well as underfinanced.

Exporting within Latin America

The competitive position of pilchard exports in neighboring Latin American countries also merits examination. Brazil, Venezuela, and Colombia may be taken as examples.

Brazil has been a major destination for Peruvian canned fish exports ever since the 1940s, when the market was developed at the initiative of the now-defunct Compania Pesquera Coishco. The product was tuna in the early years, then bonito in the 1960s, and finally pilchards in the 1970s and the 1980s but always in a tuna-sized can and mostly with the CPC label. This label is now owned by another company and presently worth a 15 percent price premium in Brazil from brand recognition.

The key figures on the Brazilian side of this trade have been Brazilian sales agents, who visit supermarkets to secure orders and handle customs and other importing chores. Often they also recommend appropriate price discounts to wholesalers and retailers, depending on judgements regarding the competitive position of the Peruvian product, and report to the Peruvian exporter on market conditions generally. In this Brazilian distributive arrangement, the agent serves the Peruvian exporter, whereas in the U.S. market the Peruvian producer served the North American importer-wholesaler. The locus of decision making regarding marketing strategy is in Peru rather than in the importing country.

Two consequences arise from this more active marketing role assumed by the Peruvian exporter. First, the contracts with Brazilian agents generally require a modicum of exclusivity. That is, a Brazilian agent may deal in other food products, and even other fish products, but not in other Peruvian fish products. Second, the Peruvian exporter

---

[28]The brand recognition was exploited at food fairs, not on the label.

becomes obliged to develop some means of assessing distributor performance. In one case, neither sales growth targets nor other quantitative performance measures were thought to be meaningful, given the many exogenous shocks to which this export trade had been subjected, in both Peru and Brazil. Instead, effort and effectiveness were assessed more impressionistically but also more directly, simply by periodic visits to wholesalers and retailers to inquire about a given agent's performance.

The firm which was exercising such vigilance over its distributive network in Brazil was at the same time exporting to South Africa under the tight instructions of the South African consortium. The greater control over marketing activity in the case of Brazil may be attributed partly to the exporter's experience, specific to the market in question, and partly to the differential degree of control exercised by importing firms in different countries.[29]

The distribution system in Venezuela contained a mixture of the characteristics previously noted in the United States and Brazil. As in the case of both those other markets, the Peruvian product was pilchard packed as a tuna substitute. Exporting to Venezuela began in the late 1970s on the initiative of one particular Venezuelan importer-wholesaler, who made a trip to Peru, visited various Lima supermarkets, looked at the prices and qualities of the products displayed, and estimated which might prove competitive in Venezuela. From that visit, he established contacts with producers and ultimately became an importer of Peruvian canned fish, canned asparagus, and flashlight batteries.

On the initiative of the importer-wholesaler, Venezuelan marketing arrangements resembled those of the United States. But the variety of products ultimately acquired indicates the way in which the Venezuelan market more closely resembled that of Brazil. Handling a diversified line of food products plus a few other items also sold in supermakets, the Venezuelan importer-wholesaler was as diversified as his Brazilian counterpart. Thus he was not sufficiently specialized in fish products to attempt persuading the Peruvian exporter to redesign his product, in line with the needs of the Venezuelan market. Rather, he ordered from

---

[29]It was not clear from interviews why a tuna-substitute type business was retained in Brazil while it was lost in the United States. Four possibilities may be suggested. First, tuna prices may have been kept high in Brazil, either by protectionism or market failure. Second, Brazilian consumers, long accustomed to canned bonito, may have been more positively inclined toward other tuna substitutes as well, requiring less of a price discount. Third, canned pilchards were introduced into Brazil under a recognized label, not the unrecognized labels used in the United States. This too should have reduced the price discount substantially. And finally, canned bonito may be imported into Brazil duty-free under an ALALC (ALADI) provision. It has been suggested that a certain amount of canned pilchard exports to Brazil have been labeled as bonito.

already-produced stocks, accepting the quality normally produced by the Peruvians for their domestic market, often accepting the same label as that used in Peru. The quality demands of the Venezuelan market were satisfied largely by importing the solid pack pilchard and avoiding the grated. In this respect the pattern of exports to Venezuela differed from both Brazil and the United States, where the grated product assumed greater relative importance. This difference perhaps reflected distinctive preferences of the Venezuelan consumer, but it probably also reflected a tendency of the Venezuelan importer-wholesaler to specialize in serving supermarkets in middle-class areas.

On the canned fish shelves of Caracas supermarkets (in June 1982), most of the space was devoted to Venezuelan tuna, with the import competition coming from Ecuadorean tuna and Ecuadorean and Peruvian "sardinas." Although the Peruvian product seemed to have no particular price advantage over the Venezuelan competition, it was said that supermarkets earned higher margins on the Peruvian product, and therefore promoted it in various ways. While the Peruvian competitive position in Venezuela therefore seemed quite solid, protectionist pressures were building up. At that time, the Venezuelan canning industry was said to be on the verge of collapse because of the strength of foreign competition.

At the same time, June 1982, the Peruvian competitive position seemed substantially weaker in Bogota, where Ecuadorean tuna dominated the supermarket shelves. The dominance was explained partly by the tariff preferences given to Ecuador as a less developed country within the Andean Group, and partly by the fact that the Ecuadorean product is in general superior, being solid-pack tuna in a clean can with a label of good quality. In many cases the cans carried well-known multinational brand names, such as Van Camps, Bumble Bee, and Isabel (a Spanish label). Yet these factors should also have held with equal strength in the Venezuelan market, where the Peruvian product seemed in a much better competitive position. The additional factor tipping the balance toward Ecuador in Bogota was imply the proximity of Colombia, which caused truck transportation to be less expensive than ocean freight, and therefore made the shipping cost of the Peruvian product substantially higher than that of the Ecuadorean.[30]

The Colombian importer was generally a broker who arranged sales from inventory, sometimes with producer labels sometimes with a special label added for the Colombian market. Peruvian canned fish seemed at best a marginal business in Colombia. This impression derived partly

---

[30]Ecuadorean advantage in transportation cost by truck is heightened by the regulation that all freight trans-shipments through Ecuador have to be reloaded onto Ecuadorean trucks. This policy is attributed to the political power of Ecuador's truck drivers union.

Table IV-12. Andean Group Trade in Canned Fish (16.04), 1979
(Thousand of dollars)

Importing Country	Exporting Country					
	Bolivia	Colombia	Ecuador	Peru	Venezuela	Rest of World
Bolivia	—	0	58 (42)	2,979 (8,831)	0	516
Colombia	0	—	18,279 (17,627)	447 (778)	0	607
Ecuador	n.a.	n.a.	—	n.a. (1,353)	n.a.	n.a.
Peru	n.a.	n.a.	n.a. (0)	—	n.a.	n.a.
Venezuela	0	326	3,578 (3,009)	1,335 (1,455)	—	7,183
Rest of World	n.a.	n.a.	n.a.	n.a.	n.a.	—

Peru's share of total 16.04 imports in:
Bolivia   84%
Colombia   2%
Ecuador   n.a.
Venezuela   11%

Note: Figures in parentheses are export statistics. Other figures are import statistics.
Source: Junta del Acuerdo de Cartagena (JUNAC).
Comercio Exterior 1970–1980 (Lima: JUNAC, 1982).

from the limited or non-existent shelf space of Peruvian products in the supermarkets visited, partly from the minuscule size of operation of the one importer visited (the company essentially operated out of somebody's house), and also because of questionable labeling in some instances, where pilchards were made to look like tuna.[31]

This impression of Peru's superior competitive position in Venezuela as compared to Colombia is borne out in Andean Group trade statistics, reproduced in Table IV-12. The table gives data for 1979, one of the boom years, and shows Peruvian dominance of the Bolivian market, Ecuadorean dominance of the much larger Colombian market, and wide-open competition in Venezuela.

After 1983, however, Peruvian pilchards disappeared from both Colombian and Venezuelan markets. There was no fish to be exported during the reign of El Niño in 1983, and by 1984 both countries had been largely closed to fish imports as a part of government response to the debt crisis. The Venezuelan bolivar was devalued drastically in 1984,

---

[31]Some cans contained the word "ATUN" in large letters followed by "tipo" in exceedingly small letters. Being from the family of fish, pilchards could be said to be tuna-type fish. A different Peruvian product in a tuna-size can was labelled "BOCADITOS" (snacks), followed by the microscopic tag line "tipo atun".

thus saving many domestic industries while also confirming the sense of foreboding held by those selling Peruvian products in Venezuela when they were interviewed in 1982.

Quality Improvement and Quality Control

The major importers from the United States and South Africa were not content simply to buy from Peru. They worked actively to improve product quality. This was done largely for reasons of competition rather than to meet government-enforced standards. The basic government standard in Peru and elsewhere has been that the food must be safe, the fish not spoiled. Peruvian producers have with a few exceptions satisfied that requirement.[32] Successful exporting, however, requires more in the way of quality. The external appearance of the can must be sufficiently attractive to persuade the consumer to make the first purchase. The contents of the can must also be attractive enough to persuade that consumer to make subsequent purchases.

To ensure this higher quality, testing takes place both in Peru and in the importing countries. The testing criteria are qualitative and not easily reduced to measurement, but are nevertheless understood by people experienced in the field. In these tests, cans are opened and the contents cut and examined for texture, color, odor and taste. In addition, the tightness of pack, the adequacy of the sauce and the net weight in the can are also considered.

In their quest of a product that will pass muster by those standards, importers prefer to deal with producers whose plants are clean and orderly. One importer expressed the fundamental rule as "know your packer." Even when working with a reputable producer, however, the importer or his broker will often maintain tight control over many dimensions of the production process, such as size of fish, time out of water, use of ice on the boats, cooking time before filleting, time delay in cooling, filleting, and getting the fish into the can, as well as the time in the retort where the fish is cooked again after sealing for purposes of sterilization.

The zeal with which various importer-wholesalers pursue these quality requirements can be quite variable. Some have inspectors in the factories during the whole course of production, while others merely have inspectors examine the product at the end of the process. Through one check or another, products are rejected periodically. In those cases, they will be sold in the local market or "por fronteras," i.e., to Bolivia, Ecuador or Colombia.

---

[32]The only published report of an unsafe product concerned a small shipment to Canada which was seized by the Canadian authorities in 1981. The producing company was small and not well known even in Peru. See *Andean Report*, December 1981, p. 233.

Perhaps the greatest concern about quality lies not with the fish but with the container. The steel sheets used for tin plate are imported exclusively by Siderperu, the government steel company, which then does the plating and sells the product to the two companies which make the cans. The result of duopoly erected on top of monopoly is a product of high price and low quality. The canning companies pay substantially more for cans than they do for fish. Yet they are able to import cans only when domestic cans are not available.

The basic quality problem with Peruvian tin cans is that they rust rapidly, particularly if held in inventory for any length of time in the humid warehouses of Peruvian ports. In a word, the plating process of Siderperu is deficient.

This condition was dramatized by the executive of one canning company through a display of Peruvian and U.S. cans in his office, available for casual inspection by the visitor. After having sat for six months to a year in the executive's Miraflores office, the Peruvian cans did indeed look terrible. Speaking of food products in general (in 1982), the Venezuelan importer-wholesaler remarked, "The Peruvians cannot produce a first-rate product because, unlike the Chileans, they do not have access to first-rate containers.

Learning by Exporting

It has been suggested that as firms acquire exporting experience they assume greater control over both product design and marketing functions, thus increasing the value added in exporting.[33] We might expect that learning by exporting is a version of learning by doing made particularly educational by the stiffer winds of competition in foreign markets and by the explicit pressures of importer-wholesalers.

Two complementary types of learning may be envisaged. First, there is a learning related to improved organization of production, involving both improved quality of product and cost reduction. The second type of learning is related to marketing and involves the producer's slowly shedding his passivity, to become both participant in and evaluator of the marketing process.

In the case of Peru's canning industry, however, little evidence of such progress can be discerned. To the extent that the industry has even survived after the battering it took in 1982–83, it has limped up to the present exporting essentially the same product with the same marketing arrangements as at the beginning of the pilchard boom in the mid-1970s. Product design and marketing arrangements have varied greatly among importing countries, but not over time.

---

[33]L. H. Wortzel and H.V. Wortzel, "Export Marketing Strategies for NIC- and LDC-Based Firms," *Columbia Journal of World Business*, Spring 1981.

Why is this so? Why has this Peruvian experience been so different from the East Asian experience analyzed by Wortzels? Cultural differences might be at work, but the more plausible explanation is simply that the Peruvian fishing industry has been too unstable. The model of design and marketing stages presumes that firms first focus on production problems, and that, when those problems become resolved and production becomes routinized, management is ready for new challenges, and finds these challenges in the areas of design improvement and international marketing.

This sequence is built on a number of necessary conditions: First, that the production problems are in fact overcome. Second, that design improvement and forward integration in marketing promise satisfactory returns on the investment of capital and management time. And third, that the export business is not so risky as to suggest that management should follow a more diversified investment strategy.

The Peruvian canning industry has not satisfied these conditions. Three production problems remain unresolved. The first is an adequate and assured fish supply. The industry was resilient enough to outlast El Niño in 1983, but longer-run changes in fish supplies are working against the industry. As coastal waters have cooled in recent years, most of the biomass of Pacific sardines has moved farther offshore and out of reach of the available fishing fleet. This is a problem for canners only because the fleet has not been re-equipped with larger boats. The fleet has, in fact, deteriorated notably ever since nationalization in the early 1970s.

The second unresolved production problem, already discussed, concerns the cost and quality of available tin cans. A third and related problem concerns costs and profits: In recent years, canning has been at best a marginal business. More money is to be made in fishmeal than in canning. but the major part of the fishmeal industry has been nationalized. Private companies are allowed to produce fishmeal only as a by-product of canning, a minimum canning output being required per unit volume of fish delivered to the factory. Thus canning has become a loss leader necessary to legitimize profitable fishmeal operations.

The weakness of the industry's position could of course change, through significant and lasting improvement in the sector's real exchange rate combined with a change in government investment policy regarding the nation's fishing fleet. But until such changes occur, the industry can best be described as hanging on rather than progressing to new stages.

This is not to say, however, that the industry's fate lies entirely in the macroeconomic aggregates with no role for initiatives from the industry itself. The sectoral real exchange rate depends largely on factors exogenous to the industry such as the government's exchange rate policy, the price of tuna and the question as to whether or not Venezuela devalues. But it also depends in part on the acumen of exporters and importer-wholesalers in seeking out market niches for Peruvian products. Unfortunately it remains true that the cleverest effort at finding niches can be steamrollered by adverse government policy.

Machinery and Fabricated Metal Products

The machinery and metalworking or *metalmecánica* industries have held special importance in Latin American industrialization strategies. The products of the sector consist largely of capital goods, and the limited production of capital goods has been identified by many observers as a key obstacle to long-run economic growth.[34] Thus the expansion of the sector has been seen to bring special benefits to a society: through the upgrading of worker skills, through the learning that comes from managing sophisticated technologies, and through the lessening of external economic and political constraints on national development. It is little wonder, therefore, that this sector has been the favored child of industrialization policy.

A country of recent industrialization, Peru has a machinery and metalworking sector of modest proportions. The modesty is seen in export statistics, where the sector's exports accounted for only $64.5 million or 8 percent of nontraditional exports in 1979, and therefore for less than 2 percent of total exports. While this figure was small in relative terms, it nevertheless represented an impressive variety of products and markets. This variety may be appreciated in Table IV-13, which orders the principal products of the sector by 1979 export value. Listed are those products which contributed $500,000 of exports in either 1979 or in the low year of 1983.

Two points can be made about the products listed. First, no single factor explains why Peru should be exporting these particular products. A few use natural resources which are relatively inexpensive in Peru, e.g., batteries and electrical cables. Others, which serve the mining and fishing industries as inputs or capital goods, are related to natural resource production. Fishing boats, pumps, electric motors, and drilling bits all fall into this category. Still others, representing import substitution at the final stage of production, give no indication of possible comparative advantage and undoubtedly entered into exporting either

---

[34]Fernando Henrique Cardoso and Enzo Faletto, *Dependencia y Desarrollo en América Latina* (Mexico: Siglo XXI, 1969), translated as *Dependence and Development in Latin America* (Berkeley: University of California Press, 1979); Guillermo O'Donnell, "Reflections on the Patterns of Change in the Bureaucratic-Authoritarian State," *Latin American Research Review*, no. 1, 1978, pp. 3–38; Albert Hirschman, "The Turn to Authoritarianism in Latin America and the Search for its Economic Determinants," in David Collier, ed., *The New Authoritarianism in Latin America* (Princeton: Princeton University Press, 1979, pp. 61–98).

Table IV-13. Peru: Exports of Machinery and Fabricated Metal Products
(Thousand of dollars)

Nabandina Code	Principal Products	Value of Exports 1979	1983
89.01	Fishing boats	20,133	7,115
85.03	Batteries	6,099	245
87.02	Trucks	4,666	9
84.01	Pumps	4,452	2,424
84.15	Refrigerators	4,328	0
85.01	Electric motors, transformers	3,333	1,255
84.61	Faucets, valves	2,763	443
73.36	Stoves	2,653	46
85.23	Electrical cables	2,465	0
87.06	Automotive parts	1,519	2,223
84.22	Pulleys	1,512	3,001
87.10	Bicycles	1,281	0
87.09	Motorcycles	1,125	0
84.59	Machinery n.e.c.	1,034	659
85.19	Plugs, switches, control panels	696	77
84.18	Filters, esp. auto air filters	594	43
84.45	Lathes, drills, presses	566	10
84.56	Miscellaneous machinery	535	867
73.38	Kitchen appliances	521	61
84.37	Knitting machines	300	791
84.06	Internal combustion motors	230	1,287
82.05	Drilling bits	172	668
85.04	Accumulators, and parts thereof	130	740
84.65	Piston rings	42	537
———	Other categories	3,553	3,639
Total exports, machinery and appliances		64,502	26,140

Note: Nabandina Code is the Brussels Tariff Nomenclature as modified by the Andean Group through its secretariat, the Junta del Acuerdo de Cartagena (JUNAC).
Sources: 1979: Computer tabulations of export authorizations.
1983: OFINE computer tabulations.

because of substantial excess capacity or because of compensatory export commitments which were a condition to their initial installation in Peru. Automotive products and home appliances are the prototypical products of this category. Finally, one of two may find exporting profitable for the most traditional of reasons: they use labor-intensive processes. Accumulators, which require hand-winding of the armatures, would fall in this category.[35]

The second point to note is that most of these sectors lost most of their export business during the economic crisis which has spread throughout Latin America since 1982. This may be attributed in part to the vulnerability of capital goods producers to recession, and in part to the weak competitive position of many of these exporters even in the best of times.

---

[35]In addition, much of the miscellaneous machinery of sectors 84.56 and 84.59 is likely to be re-exported used machinery.

Table IV-14. Peru: Exports of Machinery and Metal Products by Country of Destination, 1979
(Percentages)

Nabandina Code	Country of Destination								
	Ecu	Bol	Col	Ven	Chi	Other Lat Amer	Eur	USA	ROW*
89.01	8	—	40	6	8	33	—	—	5
85.03	33	32	10	22	0	2	—	—	0
87.02	3	3	57	—	36	0	0	2	—
84.10	78	1	0	—	5	1	8	2	4
84.15	2	3	0	95	0	0	—	—	—
85.01	29	17	17	31	4	1	—	0	0
84.61	2	0	1	85	1	4	3	4	—
73.36	22	7	—	70	0	0	—	—	—
85.23	30	4	—	2	1	0	—	63	—
87.06	3	1	1	1	0	8	—	85	—
84.22	67	4	15	0	6	7	—	0	—
87.10	—	—	—	99	1	—	—	—	—
87.09	—	1	66	—	3	30	—	—	—
84.59	24	4	12	—	2	58	—	—	—
85.19	59	29	2	1	3	4	—	1	—
84.18	30	16	14	0	5	3	—	33	—
84.45	22	7	55	0	—	6	6	4	1
84.56	41	54	—	4	1	1	—	—	—
73.38	5	70	6	1	18	—	—	—	—
84.37	2	62	31	—	4	0	—	—	—
84.06	0	44	1	—	14	—	12	3	25
82.05	24	14	—	2	—	47	13	—	—
85.04	28	—	30	41	—	—	—	—	0
84.65	88	8	0	—	4	1	—	—	—

*ROW = Rest of World.
Source: Computer tabulations of export authorizations.

Some insight into competitive position is gleaned from Table IV-14, which shows the distribution of 1979 exports by country and region of destination. What is to be noted particularly is that most exporters of manufactured metal products were able to establish their export business only in nearby countries: to those within the Andean Group, where they secured protection from third-country competitors, and to Chile, which is nearby and whose exchange rate was overvalued in 1979. The three sectors which directed a significant share of their exports to the United States (84.18, 85.23, 87.06) all showed significant participation by multinationals, much of whose exports derived from contractual commitments with the Peruvian government. The same factor explains the two cases of sectors directing more than 10 percent of their exports to Europe (82.05, 84.06). The only sectors *not* dominated by multinationals which directed a significant share of their exports beyond Peru's immediate neighbors were pumps (84.10, 15 percent of exports), lathes

Table IV-15. Peru: Exports of Machinery and Metal Products, Product Groups Arranged by Share Exported to Neighboring Countries

Nabandina Code	Principal Products	Share Exported to Andean Group & Chile, 1979 (percent)	Value of Exports ($000)	
			1979	1983
84.15	Refrigerators	100	4,328	0
73.36	Stoves	100	2,653	46
87.10	Bicycles	100	1,281	0
73.38	Kitchen appliances	100	521	61
84.37	Knitting machines	100	300	791
85.04	Accumulators, incl. parts	100	130	740
85.01	Electric motors, transformers	99	3,333	1,255
84.56	Miscellaneous machinery	99	535	867
84.65	Piston rings	99	42	537
85.03	Batteries	98	6,099	245
87.02	Trucks	98	4,666	9
85.19	Plugs, switches, control panels	95	696	77
84.22	Pulleys	93	1,512	3,001
84.61	Faucets, valves	89	2,763	443
84.10	Pumps	85	4,452	2,424
84.45	Lathes, drills, presses	83	566	10
87.09	Motorcycles	70	1,125	0
84.18	Filters	64	594	43
89.01	Fishing boats	62	20,133	7,115
84.06	Internal combustion motors	60	230	1,287
84.59	Machinery n.e.c.	42	1,034	659
82.05	Drilling bits	40	172	668
85.23	Electrical cables	37	2,465	0
87.06	Automotive parts	7	1,519	2,223

Source: See Table 13.

and drills (84.45, 17 percent), and fishing boats (89.01, 38 percent). Table IV-15 shows this relationship more clearly.[36]

Among the nearby countries, the variation in the relative importance of these subsectors in particular national markets is striking. A few producers, e.g., of stoves, refrigerators, faucets and bicycles, focused almost exclusively on the Venezuelan market. It is not entirely coincidental that they are among the industries virtually excluded from exporting by 1983. Other industries focused with nearly equal intensity on Ecuador and Colombia, but none on Chile or Bolivia, the latter simply because its market was so small.

With no more to go on than the data in Tables IV-14 and IV-15, only a few tentative conclusions are possible regarding the distribution of machinery and fabricated metal product exports by country of destination. First, for most products in this category Peruvian exporters can

---

[36]Excluded from consideration in this last point is Sector 84.59, Machinery n.e.c., which shows 58 percent of its exports going to countries other than Peru's immediate neighbors. This is mostly used machinery, however.

Table IV-16. Peru: Exports of Electric Motors and Transformers (85.01)
(Thousands of dollars)

	1965	1970	1975	1977	1979	1980	1981
Total Export Values	0	136	1,141	1,481	3,333	4,265	3,103
Distribution by Countries of Destination (percentage)							
Colombia	0	29	33	20	17	34	48
Venezuela	0	17	30	25	31	25	25
Bolivia	0	43	12	30	18	21	16

	1982	1983	1984	1985	1986	1987	1988
Total Export Values	3,087	1,262	1,708	1,231	1,168	1,289	2,204
Distribution by Countries of Destination (percentage)							
Colombia	17	44	24	55	72	47	13

Sources: 1965–77: Superintendencia General de Aduanas, *Estadística del Comercio Exterior*.
1979: Ministerio de Economía, computer tabulations of export authorizations.
1980–88: OFINE computer tabulations of actual exports.

find markets only in nearby countries. There they are protected from
the full force of world competition either by the external tariff of the
Andean Group or by the natural protection of higher transport and
communications costs sustained by competitors located in the distant
Northern Hemisphere. Second, the wide variation in relative importance

Table IV-17. Andean Group Trade in Electric Motors and Transformers (85.01), 1979
(Thousands of dollars)

Importing Country	Exporting Country					
	Bolivia	Colombia	Ecuador	Peru	Venezuela	Rest of World
Bolivia	—	14 (6)	0	230 (592)	0	9,921
Colombia	0	—	15	419 (575)	34	37,442
Ecuador	0	472 (376)	—	460 (796)	0	41,982
Peru	n.a.	n.a. (193)	n.a.	—	n.a.	n.a.
Venezuela	331	3,007 (860)	0	1,242 (997)	—	276,822
Rest of World	n.a.	n.a. (962)	n.a.	n.a. (188)	n.a.	—

Peru's share of imports from Andean Group countries in:
    Bolivia   94%
    Colombia 90%
    Ecuador   n.a.
    Venezuela 27%

Note: Figures in parentheses are export statistics. Other figures are import statistics.
Source: JUNAC, *Comercio Exterior 1970–1980* (Lima: JUNAC, 1982).

of markets within nearby countries suggests two possibilities. Either these regional markets have not yet been fully exploited, or the market positions thus far established are somewhat accidental, based on gaps in the import substitution process and/or accidentally high third-country tariffs in an economic integration process which has yet to achieve a common external tariff. More detailed investigation is required to establish which of these explanations is closest to the truth.

Selecting a few products as representative of so heterogeneous a sector is inevitably an exercise in arbitrariness. Nevertheless, the attempt must be made, and the products chosen for special examination are electric motors and transformers (85.01), pumps (84.10), and batteries (85.03). The first two are examples of relative success; they had developed a substantial export trade by 1979 and managed to hold on to it, albeit in reduced form, throughout the 1980s. Electric-motor producers did so with an export trade located almost entirely in neighboring countries, while the pump industry represents an unusual case of a machinery and metalworking industry which managed to extend a significant part of its export sales to more distant countries. Batteries, on the other hand, lost their export markets between 1979 and 1983.

Electric Motors and Transformers
Among the machinery and metalworking sectors described in Tables IV-13, IV-14, IV-15 and IV-16, electric motors (85.01) was one of the largest exporters in 1979 and one of the more successful in hanging on to its export markets in the early 1980s. As Table IV-15 shows, it was also one of the sectors whose export markets were confined almost exclusively to the Andean Group, Colombia and Venezuela being the most important.

Table IV-17 shows Peru and Colombia to be the only significant producing countries in the Andean Group and, judging from their market shares in third countries such as Venezuela and Ecuador, to be about equally competitive. Table IV-17 also seems to show, however, that intra-Andean trade in electric motors is trivial compared to imports from third countries. In fact, this impression comes from the heterogeneity of products included in the 85.01 category. Third-country imports are mostly alternators and generators for internal combustion engines, while those products are not prominent in intra-Andean trade.[37]

The electric motors and transformers produced by the major firms of this industry are not the familiar small articles for household use. Rather, they are large, heavy-duty products purchased for mines, fac-

---

[37]Peruvian 85.01 exports of $3,333,000 in 1979 divided as follows: Transformers, $1,906,000; polyphasic motors, $858,000; alternators, $258,000; generators, $76,000; other products $235,000.

tories, and, in the case of transformers, electric power companies. The major firms may be referred to as Alpha and Beta.

Company Alpha was the partially-owned subsidiary of a major European multinational with many years of experience in Peru. Having established sales representation in the 1930s and a repair shop in the 1950s, it opened a manufacturing plant in 1962 and began exporting in 1967. The exported share of total production was as high as 42 percent in 1976, because of domestic depression rather than export expansion, and 20 percent in 1982. The company produced transformers but not electric motors; however, its line of transformers ranged from relatively small models sold from inventory to very large designs produced to special specifications and sold through the awarding of public bids. The range of its exports was Central America, the Andean Group and Chile.

Company Beta was a wholly-owned Peruvian company which began producing in 1950 and exporting in 1970. For many years, it had operated under a licensing contract with an Italian producer, but more recently it was producing under its own Peruvian patents. Twelve to fifteen percent of its production was exported, all to the Andean group. Venezuela and Colombia were the most important foreign markets for its electric motors, Bolivia and Ecuador for its transformers. All its transformers were of relatively small size and sold from inventory.

Both electric motors and transformers may be described as standard products not on the cutting edge of industrial innovation. Nevertheless, they are both complex enough to the layman and clearly incorporate design features representing decades of accumulated engineering wisdom. Both companies had accumulated technical expertise sufficient not only to continue producing from old designs, but also to develop improved designs for the future. For Company Alpha, with its multinational connections, clearly this was no problem. It retained a technology contract with the parent under which it acquired the services of a design engineer and production chief. In addition, it regularly sent personnel to training programs in other parts of the multinational network.

Company Beta, while having no multinational network to fall back on, nevertheless pursued its own program of design improvement. This was focused not on a search for improvement to the standard motor, but rather the design of special motors for special uses. Some of the company's new motors offered additional protection or unusual voltages for fishing factories and mining camps. Other included a variable speed feature.

For purposes of competitiveness, product quality depends on two additional factors: service facilities and the consumer's perception of quality. Both of these factors present problems to Peruvian producers.

Minor repairs and adjustments are the responsibility of the local distributor. In this respect both companies had done well for themselves:

Company Alpha was able to work through the multinational's distribution network, while Company Beta seemed to have had good fortune in its choice of distributors, at least in Colombia, its principal export market, where its service record was said by one observer to be superior to that of Siemens, its principal competitor.

More substantial repairs were however a more substantial problem. Company Beta adjusted to this problem principally by exporting only its simplest, most trouble-free product line. Thus, paradoxically, the product directed to the domestic market was of higher quality, in terms of technological complexity, than was the exported product.

Company Alpha could not solve its repair problems so simply, because most of its transformers were large and complex and liable to major repairs. The magnitude of possible difficulty in this respect was demonstrated by a repair problem in Venezuela which had gone unattended for nine months. The delays had been caused first by customs difficulties with the shipment of repair parts, then by difficulties in obtaining visas for the technicians who would be sent to effect the repairs. At the time of interview the matter was still unresolved.[38]

Consumer perception, put quite simply, is that a Peruvian product is not as reliable as a European product. Thus sales effort tended to emphasize the European technological connection rather than the true Peruvian nature of the product. Unfortunately, such claims went beyond mere emphasis to deception when a distributor described Company Beta's product as "an Italian motor, assembled in Peru."

Both companies found it difficult to compete beyond the borders of the Andean Group. Company Alpha had made some sales in Central America, where the principal competition came from the United States. In Chile and the Andean Group, however, the principal competitors were local companies. This was also true for Company Beta, except in Bolivia, where the company claimed about 30 percent of the market for electric motors as compared to about 50 percent held by Brazilian producers. For both companies, however, their principal foreign market was Colombia where, in 1982, Peruvian motors and transformers paid a 10 percent tariff as compared to 60 percent for products from outside the Andean Group.

Company Beta's representative summed up his company's export prospects succinctly: They had tried Chile and Argentina without success, they found delivery times to be very long to Central American clients, and they found prices too low in the United States to consider

---

[38]The manager reported that he had been urged to visit the Venezuelan ambassador in order to have things straightened out. He had refused as a matter of principle, saying, "How can we pretend to be industrializing countries in a common market if one has to bother an ambassador every time something goes wrong?"

competing there. With the possible exception of Central America, their exports were confined to the Andean Group, and secured by Andean Group protection. While Company Alpha's experience in Central America and Chile was slightly more positive, they were less interested in pushing exports to new countries, because the multinational network of which they were part had essentially divided up the world, the Peruvian subsidiary being earmarked to serve the Andean Group and little more. In a ranking of products according to comparative advantage, therefore, evidently item 85.01 would rank rather low, although it cannot be said if the inefficiency lay with the motor and transformer industry itself or with its supplying industries.[39] Although the source of any such inefficiency can only be speculated upon, it seems likely that inability to exploit economies of scale would be determinant for industries of this sort.

The next question is how strong the competitive position of these companies was in the market to which their exports are restricted, namely the Andean Group. A partial answer is to be found in Colombia, the most important market.

In the case of Company Beta and its electric motors, the dominant producer was Siemens, a Colombian joint venture which used the prestigious name of its German partner. How well could Company Beta compete against such a formidable adversary? Company Beta's distributor, judged to be one of the best in the business, was able to point to some features of Beta's products which gave them an edge over Siemens, viz., the motor was bigger and had a more durable casing. A more impartial view, from a retailer who sold both Siemens and Beta motors, was less favorable to Beta. Although he considered that Beta actually had better service facilities, he also found that their motors tended to overheat and were therefore less reliable. Furthermore, he observed that they tended to require about 20 percent more horsepower than a Siemens motor to accomplish a given task. Finally, on the cosmetic level, he found them "ugly," with a rather crude exterior finish and unappealing colors. Nevertheless, he carried them in order to give his customers an alternative.

Faced with so unenthusiastic a recommendation from the manager of one of its principal outlets, the competitive strategy of Beta necessarily involved substantial price discounts as compared to Siemens. Officials in Lima admitted to a 5 percent discount, but this figure apparently referred to discounts from a list price already substantially lower than that of Siemens. Beta's list prices ranged from 22 to 30 percent lower

---

[39]Also, it cannot be said with certainty whether or not such industries generate positive externalities which would compensate for any current production inefficiency.

than those of Siemens motors of equivalent horsepower; with discounts included, the total price reduction was in the range of 30 to 35 percent.

Such price discounts run the danger of retaliation in an oligopoly, and apparently that was what happened in 1982. At that time, Siemens also began a program of price discounts, in response to a perceived decline in market share. This move was directed not so much at Company Beta as at Brazilian manufacturers, who had begun exporting parts to Colombia for final assembly there. Company Beta responded to Siemens' gambit by offering additional discounts to customers of the Brazilian product. The result was a mild price war destined to end in a reshuffling of market shares which left Siemens between 80 and 90 percent of the Colombian market, with Company Beta keeping 5 to 10 percent.

Despite many years of exporting experience and despite having been designated as an Andean enterprise under the Metalworking and Machinery Agreement of the Andean Pact, Company Beta's competitive position in its most important Andean market remained insecure. To be sure, it had a foot in the door and was better off than the newly arrived Brazilians. Nevertheless it was able to compete against a giant only with price discounts which squeezed profit margins substantially and made the export program vulnerable to any adverse change in the real effective exchange rate.

Company Alpha's position in the Colombian market was no stronger. By its own estimate, it had secured no more than 3 or 4 percent of transformer sales in that country. It too had to compete with Siemens,

Table IV-18. Peru: Exports of Pumps (84.10)
(Thousands of dollars)

	1965	1970	1975	1977	1979	1980	1981
Total Export Value	285	63	850	922	4,452	2,470	3,110
Distribution by Countries of Destination (percentage)							
Ecuador	0	27	28	43	78	69	49
Other Latin America	70	32	35	14	7	10	25
Western Europe	11	40	34	39	8	13	11
USA	0	0	2	3	2	3	9

	1982	1983	1984	1985	1986	1987	1988
Total Export Value	2,583	2,130	2,520	3,403	2,000	2,615	3,311
Distribution by Countries of Destination (percentage)							
Ecuador	42	36	57	45	35	38	38
Switzerland	1	6	3	9	25	24	26
USA	16	12	6	9	14	17	10

Sources: 1965–77: Superintendencia General de Aduanas, Estadística del Comercio Exterior.
1979: Ministerio de Economía, computer tabulations of export authorizations.
1980–88: OFINE computer tabulations of actual exports.

but it was able to do so with a multinational brand name of equal prestige. Having avoided one difficulty, however, it confronted another: most of the purchasers of large transformers were public enterprises with a buy-Colombian bias. Also, Company Alpha reported a substantial increase in the number of bidders for public contracts and therefore, in the early 1980s, saw competition intensifying.

In Colombia, therefore, it must be concluded that companies Alpha and Beta are not solidly entrenched. Rather, their precarious market position is maintained in part by the price umbrella of the leading oligopolist, and also in part by somewhat deceptive claims regarding the nation of origin. Colombia is, however, the home market of the most formidable competition in the Andean Group, and therefore a particularly difficult challenge. To the credit of Alpha and Beta, they have been able to continue exporting during the difficult 1980s. They will undoubtedly continue exporting for as long as there is an Andean Group. But for no longer than that.

Pumps

Looking back once again at Tables IV-13, IV-14 and IV-15, one is reminded that, among fabricated metal products, pumps (84.10) formed one of the largest export sectors in 1979 and one of the most successful in retaining their export markets in the 1980s. Moreover, the sector showed some success beyond the Andean Group, even though fully 78 percent of its export value went to Ecuador alone in 1979.

Table IV-18 explores pump exports more fully. It shows that a modest export trade was developed in the 1960s and that exports jumped sharply in the late 1970s. The countries of destination have varied over time, but the most enduring and important markets have been in Ecuador, Chile and Western Europe.

Nevertheless, Table IV-19 shows that competition within the Andean Group has been keen, from Colombian producers as well as from countries outside the group. These two tables suggest the paradoxical conclusion that the Peruvian pump industry is competitive world-wide but at the same time has had difficulty competing in its own market.

The paradox is resolved as follows: Peru's pump industry in fact consists of one firm, Hidrostal, which produces two distinctive product lines—solids pumps and water pumps. The solids pumps were developed for moving fish from boat to processing plant, and represent a response to the derived demand for capital goods that flourished during the fishmeal boom of the late 1950s and 1960s. Thus solids pumps are, indirectly, a natural-resource-based industrial product. In addition, they tended to be custom-made, with labor costs fully 35 percent of total production costs. Therefore they also reflect an efficient use of the factor endowments found in a less developed country.

Table IV-19. Andean Group Trade in Pumps (84.10), 1979
(Thousands of dollars)

Importing Country	Exporting Country					Rest of World
	Bolivia	Colombia	Ecuador	Peru	Venezuela	
Bolivia	—	252 (114)	0	52 (65)	0	5,261
Colombia	n.a.	—	n.a.	n.a.	n.a.	n.a.
Ecuador	0	558 (523)	—	665 (2,635)	0	20,974
Peru	0	65 (53)	0	—	2	14,829
Venezuela	n.a.	n.a. (47)	n.a.	n.a. (0)	—	n.a.
Rest of World	n.a.	n.a. (613)	n.a.	n.a. (670)	n.a.	—

Peru's share of imports from Andean Group countries in:
Bolivia   17%
Colombia   n.a.
Ecuador   54%
Venezuela   n.a.

Note: Figures in parentheses are export statistics. Other figures are import statistics.
Source: JUNAC, *Comercio Exterior 1970–1980* (Lima: JUNAC, 1982).

By contrast, water pumps are a standard product, requiring relatively little labor in production. They represent industrialization based on import substitution rather than comparative advantage derived from natural resource and labor intensity. Thus Hidrostal finds itself hard-pressed to compete in the Andean Group, where most sales are of water pumps, at the same time that its solids pumps find markets throughout the world.

The origins of Hidrostal go back to 1953, when an immigrant Swiss pumpmaker set up a small workshop in Lima. There the pumps were assembled and finished from parts whose casting and machining had been subcontracted elsewhere. This modest beginning put Hidrostal in the right place at the right time. Shortly thereafter, the fishmeal boom began, and the company grew with the fishing industry.

Hidrostal's innovative efforts have been directed exclusively to its solids pumps. The major breakthrough occurred some 30 years ago, when the founding owner invented and patented the screw impeller pump, whose interior vaguely resembles a giant corkscrew. This was the device which proved so successful in moving fish, and has subsequently been adapted to a myriad of other uses. It continues to undergo further improvements through the efforts of a technical department of seven or eight people, along with the continued active participation of the company's founder. The most recent major development is a new line of solids pumps which can simply be adjusted when parts become worn rather than having to be disassembled for worn parts to be replaced. Hidrostal does buy technology from two U.S. companies for specific pump designs, but it is also in the process of licensing technology sales to Japan.

Since the company has always been technologically oriented, exporting has not involved severe demands for product redesign and improved quality control. Nevertheless, some modifications have been required, particularly for exporting to the United States. For that market, each pump has to be tested before sale, its performance characteristics depicted by a series of graphs relating pumping performance to elevation and motor power, and the results certified to be within 5 percent of advertised performance characteristics in all circumstances. To meet these standards, some modifications in production have been undertaken. Water pumps have also been improved somewhat by the competitive demands of the Andean market, but the resulting performance improvement is said to be less than 10 percent.

Hidrostal's exports increased in the early 1970s, as the fishing boom peaked in Peru and further sales to that sector could come only from replacement demand. By the end of the 1970s, the export share of total production had risen to 20–30 percent. However, solids pumps represented a substantially larger share of exports than they did of total production. While solids pumps have been exported to all parts of the world, water pumps have been exported only to other counties of the Andean Group.[40]

Hidrostal's distribution network stretches across the globe, and includes representation in the Andean Group, Chile, Panama, the United States, Canada, South Africa, Australia, Mauritania, and ten countries in Europe. The company has benefited from a few special circumstances which have facilitated development of the network. Its Swiss origins made it relatively easy to establish contacts in Europe, and long association with multinational fishing companies in Peru has provided contacts in the fishing industry the world over. The greatest advantage, however, has simply consisted of having a quality product which is attractive to potential distributors. In fact, Hidrostal is one of the few Peruvian companies with enough market power overseas to be able to secure exclusive representation arrangements from its distributors.

Yet there are indications of unresolved difficulties in the distribution network. In some countries it has not been possible to secure exclusive representation. In others such representation was secured but failed to produce the desired results. These two cases represent Hidrostal's experience in Colombia and the United States, respectively.

---

[40]This information comes from interviews. Unfortunately export statistics do not differentiate effectively between these different products.

Hidrostal's initial entry into Colombia was through a distributor affiliated with a local pump producer, but the company soon changed the arrangement in favor of a number of unaffiliated regional distributors. That is, Hidrostal worked with only one distributor in each region of Colombia, but each distributor carried more than one line of pumps. The principal Hidrostal product marketed in Colombia was the company's line of water pumps, standardized and relatively undistinguished offerings compared to the solids pumps. Nevertheless, an experienced observer in Bogotá judged them to be equal or even perhaps slightly superior to those of the market leader, a U.S.-Colombian joint venture. Given this evaluation, it is curious that Hidrostal had captured only about 5 percent of the Colombian market, as compared to 90 percent for domestic production and 5 percent for other imports. This is no better than a market share in electric motors obtained by Company Beta with a product much less favorably evaluated vis-a-vis that of the dominant domestic supplier.

Hidrostal's exports to the United States have been solids pumps rather than water pumps. The export effort began in 1975, when the company set up display booths at engineering conventions as a means of recruiting distributors. A network of regional distributors, each with exclusive representation, resulted from this effort, but after a few years Hidrostal judged the sales results to be unsatisfactory and instead entrusted its U.S. distribution to Wemco, a California manufacturer. Wemco also produces solids pumps, but of a size and design such that the two lines complement each other nicely. Hidrostal pumps tend to be more vulnerable to abrasion but can move greater volumes and are clog-free. The random old rag, a nemesis of most pumps, passes through the screw impeller without difficulty.

With these qualities, the largest demand for Hidrostal pumps has come from municipalities, for pumping out storm water sewer systems. The pumps have, however, proven successful in a number of other unusual uses requiring care not to damage whatever is being pumped. Pulp used for making fine-quality paper requires such care, to ensure that the long fibers are not bent. So do cranberries, which are harvested by flooding the bogs, so that the berries float to the surface, and then pumping out the bogs. Perhaps the most unusual use comes from an electric power station which pumps water from a nearby river for cooling purposes with the assurance that any fish sucked into the pipes will be passed through the pumps unscathed and even untraumatized.

When asked what other companies might have competed with Hidrostal at the fish-friendly power plant, one observer replied, "There is no alternative supplier." Such is the distinctiveness of this remarkable Peruvian export. Its uniqueness has been preserved by patents, but even in recent years, as the major patents have expired, competitors have proven unable to replicate the screw impeller at competitive prices. This is because of the labor intensity of the production process and the high North American and European wages confronted by potential imitators.

Each distinctive use of the screw impeller pump requires the extensive adjustment and adaptation which fall under the rubric of sales engineering. Such efforts at the electric power plant were extraordinary, and included research subcontracted to a local university, a part of which involved analyzing videotapes of fish being sucked through transparent plastic pipes. Greater adaptability is achieved by exporting parts from Peru, so that the various pump components can be mixed and matched to the needs of each particular use. In recent years, parts exports predominate over assembled pump exports to both Europe and the United States.

Hidrostal's export growth, while higher than that of most Peruvian companies, has not been particularly robust by any international standard. This seems paradoxical, given that the company's water pumps are very respectable and its solids pumps unique. Part of the answer to this puzzle may come from the product-specific real exchange rate: domestic costs may have risen faster than exchange-rate-adjusted pump prices in foreign countries. It was not possible to assemble corroborating data, however. Furthermore, the plausibility of this explanatory factor must be greatly diminished in recent years as real wages have plummeted in Peru.

Another part of the answer seems to lie in marketing follow-through. Many of the unusual uses for solids pumps involve small market niches, each of which requires a significant sales engineering effort if each market's potential is to be realized. These efforts are more than a distributor alone can accomplish. The company itself also needs to participate. This is the point at which Hidrostal was faulted by one observer, who described the company as "weak on technical back up,. . . not good at customer follow-through."

Hidrostal is perhaps the most successful producer and exporter of engineering goods to be found in Peru. Its record of technological innovation and quality production should be envied by other Peruvian companies. Fortunately, its technological accomplishments have involved a product requiring labor-intensive production methods and facing, at an important time in its development, a large local market. All these factors have contributed to make this Peruvian product competitive enough to sell throughout the world. Hidrostal is in fact a success story whose generally promising future must perhaps be qualified by only two observations.

The first concerns marketing expertise. Hidrostal was created by an engineer, and the engineering side of the operation has always been the company's strong suit. Conversely, the marketing side, while certainly not weaker than that of other Peruvian companies, is not as impressive as the company's technology. So distinctive a product gives Hidrostal opportunities for market control to which other Peruvian companies could not possibly aspire. It is not evident that Hidrostal has grasped those opportunities.

The second qualification concerns the question of succession. Hidrostal has many capable executives and workers in its ranks, but its particular success has rested on the inventive genius of one person. That person is working his way out of the company, and it is not all clear what the company will be like without him. Perhaps the company can continue to thrive on the basis of minor future design modification without the need for innovative breakthroughs of the type which marked the company's initial expansion 30 years ago. But that is speculation. It remains true that the great challenge to the company's future success in exporting pumps will lie in its ability to institutionalize technological progressiveness after its founder is gone.

Dry Cell Batteries

Batteries provide a singular example of an export business which flourished for a few years, and then declined and died. Table IV-20 gives an outline of this unfortunate course of events. In 1979, the peak year, battery exports represented some 9 percent of total manufactured metal

Table IV-20. Peru: Exports of Batteries (85.03)
(Thousands of dollars)

	1965	1970	1975	1977	1979	1980	1981
Total Export Value	0	122	117	580	6,099	5,656	1,776
Distribution by Countries of Destination (percentage)							
Bolivia	0	0	4	0	32	21	61
Colombia	0	0	51	0	10	14	0
Venezuela	0	0	7	22	22	45	39
Ecuador	0	1	23	72	33	19	0
Other	0	98	14	6	2	2	0

	1982	1983	1984	1985	1986	1987	1988
Total Export Value	1,241	363	108	51	55	11	272
Distribution by Countries of Destination (percentage)							
Bolivia	60	38	99	100	43	100	0
Colombia	3	0	0	0	0	0	0
Venezuela	28	4	0	0	0	0	0
Ecuador	2	1	0	0	57	0	0
Other	7	56	0	0	0	0	100

Sources: 1965–77: Superintendencia General de Aduanas, Estadística del Comercio Exterior.
1979: Ministerio de Economía, computer tabulations of export authorizations.
1980–88: OFINE computer tabulations of actual exports.

exports.[41] These exports remained almost entirely within the Andean Group, with Venezuela and Bolivia the principal markets, and for the most part were accomplished by one small Peruvian company lacking any international affiliations.

While interesting for what it says about export possibilities, the company's experience in the battery business is perhaps more significant on the domestic front, since it expresses in microcosm the difficulties of national firms competing against multinational giants. These difficulties are particularly severe in brand-name consumer goods, where the multinational often possesses an enormous advantage in marketing expertise, in addition to the advantages in technology, product design, and production scale economies which it might have in any product.

In Latin America, batteries are an important consumer item for poor people, who use them mainly for operating ratios in homes lacking electrical outlets. As a result, battery advertising is massive, of an intensity which North American consumers would associate with beer, cigarettes or detergents.[42] Competition in the industry is so high-pressure that, as of 1982, only two national battery companies, using their own brands, remained in all of Latin America, one in Peru and the other in Paraguay.

The Peruvian company was the first battery producer in the country, having started operations in 1963. Over the years it marketed a variety of brands, but the best-known was "Lux, La Pila Chola." The company expanded production facilities in the late 1960s, just before two multinationals came into the Peruvian market. As a result, it suffered from excess capacity thenceforth.

The multinational entrants were Ray-O-Vac of the United States and Matsushita/Panasonic of Japan. Ray-O-Vac had become a household word in Peru decades earlier, having established a dominant market position through imports from its American factories. An even more formidable challenge came from the Japanese giant Matsushita, which entered Peru with a complete line of electrical products, all marketed under the same brand name: National. By 1982, these two multinational firms had gained nearly complete control of Peru's battery market. At that time, the manager of the Peruvian company estimated that his firm retained only 8 percent of the market, while Ray-O-Vac held about 35 percent and National the rest.[43]

---

[41]See Table 13.

[42]Battery makers in Peru have been known to buy pieces of the soccer field for local sports broadcasts, allowing the announcer to utter such exclamations as, "Corner kick from the Ray-O-Vac corner!"

[43]Some informal inquiries undertaken by the author around Lima suggested that this 8 percent figure was in fact too high.

Why did the multinationals win the marketplace struggle so resoundingly? The first and perhaps the most significant reason was product quality. The typical consumer tended to think of the Pila Chola as an inferior product. This was clear from the reaction of many acquaintances of this writer; it was also clear from the market surveys undertaken by the producing company.

One such survey, taken several years ago in Lima when the Pila Chola was still the market leader, established that brand recognition was very strong among consumers. When asked which brand name was the best, consumers generally replied with the name of the brand which they themselves had been purchasing. When asked which was the worst, however, the Pila Chola was the brand most frequently mentioned. When asked why they reached this judgement, it was generally because of a bad experience with the battery, but not an experience of the respondent himself. In other words, the survey was inconclusive as to whether the battery's bad reputation was based on solid consumer experience or on rumor and hearsay.

Despite this solid evidence of negative consumer reaction, it is not certain that the Pila Chola was in fact a bad battery. The company manager reported that tests conducted both in the company's lab and in a testing company in the United States indicated that the battery was in fact slightly superior to those of the competition. It met the norms of ITINTEC, the Peruvian standards-setting agency, with respect to charge, and it substantially exceeded established norms with respect to leakage.[44] Even more perplexing, the company reported that it had undertaken tests on batteries which had been returned from Venezuelan distributors with the complaint that they were defective, yet the tests found that these same batteries satisfied accepted performance standards.

This contradictory evidence might be explained by a number of factors. One such factor is excessive delay between the time of production and the time of final purchase by the consumer. Battery producers generally anticipate that their product will move slowly through distribution channels and may stay on the shelf for a long time before sale, but this delay could well have become excessive in the case of Pila Chola. Representatives of more than one battery company commented that wholesalers often fail to appreciate the importance of moving battery inventories on a first in, first out basis, and that failure to do so does

---

[44]The present writer examined copies of the charge test, which was based upon Venezuelan norms and required batteries to exceed a minimum voltage for a specified period of time after having been discharged by use in a flashlight. The leakage test required that the battery not leak for 12 days after having been discharged; the Pila Chola lasted some 40 days.

occasionally make batteries obsolete before sale. Faced with a declining market for other reasons, this shelf-time factor could have been particularly damaging to the quality of the Pila Chola at time of sale.

This factor would not explain, however, why batteries returned as defective would be found acceptable when tested by the producing company. A possible explanation for this was suggested by the manager of a multinational company, who reported that his company had regularly tested not only its own product, but also the products of all other battery producers in the entire Andean Group. With respect to the Pila Chola, he had concluded that the battery was not of generally poor but of variable quality.

The third possible explanation for the conflicting evidence regarding the quality of the Pila Chola is simply consumer prejudice. It should be noted that in both Venezuela and Peru, this was the only South American brand in the market. Except for a handful of low-priced batteries from the Far East, the rest of the competition consisted of the brands of major multinationals: Eveready (Union Carbide), Ray-O-Vac, National and Varta (a European brand). Beyond suffering from the visceral preference which the typical Latin American consumer holds for foreign as compared to local brands, the Pila Chola suffered from the additional liability of being identified with indigenous culture rather than the fashions of the upper classes. The brand was in fact developed during the Velasco regime, when the promotion of indigenous values seemed the wave of the future in Peru. Thus the producing company faced a dilemma: It had a product which enjoyed widespread brand recognition, but it also was a brand which people, at least middle-class people, looked on with some amusement and condescension. It is easy to imagine this attitude being turned into one of unjustified perception of poor quality. Thus the national and indigenous brand image of the Pila Chola was a second liability, independent of true product quality, which the producing company had to bear in its struggle against multinational competition.

In addition, a third factor added significantly to the advantages of the multinational: marketing experience. It had already been noted that this factor acquires particular significance for a product which is as heavily advertised as batteries are in Latin America. Ray-O-Vac's commercial slogan is one of the best known in Peru. Nevertheless, for intensity of advertising, the National effort seems, to the casual observer, to lie in a higher dimension. The National name, on billboards and store signs, is ubiquitous, as is its logo. Particular emphasis is given to television sets, but National (Panasonic) markets a full line of consumer electronic products, so the advertising effect is mutually reinforcing.

Faced with a declining market share and aggressive market strategies from its multinational competitors, the producers of the Pila Chola responded with a number of marketing strategies of their own, but generally without success. Bodegas were provided battery dispensers, but they only got in the way. An attempt was made to locate batteries near checkout counters in supermarkets, but sales did not go up, thereby demonstrating that batteries were not purchased on impulse. What did go up, however, was the theft rate. New packaging materials were introduced, based on petroleum-derived plastics, but their costs shot up with increasing petroleum prices in the 1970s. Attempts were made to bypass wholesalers by distributing direct to retailers through the company's own trucks, but costs were excessive. Finally, an advertising campaign on television reproduced a test showing the Pila Chola to be superior to other major brands. However, the ads had to be discontinued because of a regulation disallowing comparison advertising on Peruvian television. Follow-up inquiries established that viewers did not believe the tests anyway.

That so many unsuccessful marketing strategies were attempted is evidence of the great advantage multinational companies have through their accumulated knowledge of what works and what doesn't. The makers of the Pila Chola were finding everything out the hard way. The resulting course of competition was most dramatically shown in the jungle city of Iquitos. The Pila Chola was particularly well-established there; it had 90 percent of the market, in part, perhaps, because its casing proudly proclaimed it to be "tropicalizada." It also had established exclusive advertising arrangements with local radio stations, preventing other batteries from using that medium. Nevertheless, in the space of just a few years the Pila Chola's share of the market was reduced from 90 percent to 25 percent. National accomplished this by invading the Iquitos market with low prices and an advertising blitz that bypassed radios and focused on billboards and special promotional campaigns, such as offering free admission to a theater upon presentation of a used National battery.

The makers of the Pila Chola concluded, however, that the main explanation for their loss of the Iquitos market lay in the aggressive price competition of their major competitor. It was alleged, in fact, that batteries constituted a loss leader for National. An executive of another battery company stated that a National representative had once said to him, "We are prepared to lose a lot of money on batteries. How much are you prepared to lose?"

While this strategy was not confirmed from other sources, it was not inconsistent with the comment of a National representative that Matsushita Electric generally preferred to establish itself in a new market first through batteries, since they were particularly widely distributed and would serve to establish brand identification for other products introduced later. To the extent that batteries do serve as a loss leader, access to financial resources becomes the fourth and final factor explaining the disadvantages of national companies in competing against multinationals.

The four factors of disadvantage, therefore, were product quality, image, marketing experience, and access to financial resources.

Faced with such disadvantages, it seems surprising that the producers of the Pila Chola had developed any export business at all. One informant, however, described international trade in batteries as largely based on the seizure of transitory opportunities, pricing at what the market will bear, provided only that price is above marginal cost. This description probably explains the export trade to Venezuela that grew so quickly in the second half of the 1970s.[45] The opportunity arose because Venezuelan producers were beset by production problems which prevented them from fully supplying their own national market.

This opportunity was perceived by the producers of the Pila Chola simply because they also had a second export product which kept them in touch with Venezuelan battery producers. This product was the zinc calot, a specially shaped alloy disk which stamped to form battery cases. The company is the only calot producer in Latin America and enjoys a worldwide export business which includes Venezuela.

The Peruvian producer's strategy in this circumstance was to be rather unobtrusive and to take a small part of the market, so as not to draw retaliation from the Venezuelan producers. Because of cooperative relationships deriving from the zinc calot business, this plan regarding market shares was in some sense coordinated and agreed to.

As perceived by the producers of the Pila Chola, things got out of hand in two respects. First, the shortfall of national production was larger than expected, and distributors placed very large orders with the Peruvian producer.[46] The second difficulty was that batteries were price-controlled in Venezuela, and had to be sold for either 1.75 or 2.0 bolivares. The Pila Chola sold for 1.75, but this did not represent a sufficient price discount to offset the disadvantage of not being an internationally established brand. The Pila Chola could hope to survive in any market only by being priced substantially below the Ray-O-Vacs, Nationals, and Evereadys of this world. In Venezuela it was not possible. Thus when Venezuela's battery shortage attracted the attention of other major producers, the Pila Chola was vulnerable.

---

[45]Venezuelan battery imports (85.03) jumped from $1.0 million in 1974 to $2.3 million in 1976, $4.9 million in 1977, and $10.9 million in 1980. See JUNAC, *Comercio Exterior 1970–1980* (Lima, 1982), p. 689.

[46]It might be noted that the Peruvian producer manufactured the same battery under a number of different labels, the Pila Chola being by far the best known. It worked with several distributors in Venezuela, giving a different brand name to each distributor.

Table IV-21. Andean Group Trade in Batteries (85.03), 1979
(Thousands of dollars)

Importing Country	Bolivia	Colombia	Ecuador	Peru	Venezuela	Rest of World
				Exporting Country		
Bolivia	—	0	0	71 (1,877)	1	547
Colombia	n.a.	—	318	277 (490)	0	840
Ecuador	0	493 (266)	—	540 (1,867)	0	452
Peru	0	n.a. (0)	n.a.	—	n.a.	n.a.
Venezuela	n.a.	493 (474)	0	1,822 (1,553)	—	6,192
Rest of World	n.a.	n.a.	n.a.	n.a. (52)	n.a. (107)	—

Peru's share of total imports of batteries in:
  Bolivia   11%
  Colombia   16%
  Ecuador   36%
  Venezuela   21%

Note: Figures in parentheses are export statistics. Other figures are import statistics.
Source: JUNAC, *Comercio Exterior 1970–1980* (Lima: JUNAC, 1982).

Table IV-21 gives an indication of the market position of the Pila Chola as of 1979, while the Venezuelan business was at its best. Peruvian batteries, nearly all Pila Chola, accounted for only 20 percent of Venezuela's battery imports, but 79 percent of battery imports from Andean countries.

Or course, another possible reason for the decline of the Pila Chola in Venezuela is the same one which bedeviled it in Peru: a perception of poor quality on the part of the consumer, perhaps based on reality, perhaps not.

Cotton Textiles

Cotton textile producers form the oldest and most solidly established industry in Peru. Many textile firms date from the dawn of modern manufacturing, at the turn of the century.[47] Many have exported sporadically over the decades, but the industry had returned exclusively to

---

[47]J. Fred Rippy, "The Dawn of Peruvian Manufacturing," *Pacific Historical Review*, (1946), pp. 147–157. See also Rosemary Thorp and Geoffrey Bertram, *Peru 1980–1977. Growth and Policy in an Open Economy* (New York: Columbia University Press, 1978); David Chaplin, *The Peruvian Industrial Labor Force* (Princeton: Princeton University Press, 1967).

Table IV-22. Peru: Exports of Cotton Yarns (55.05) and Fabrics (55.09)
(Thousands of dollars)

	1965	1970	1975	1977	1979	1980	1981
Total Export Value							
Yarns	1	50	245	9,682	33,344	52,536	34,955
Fabrics	0	565	1,524	13,380	46,734	42,038	51,889
Distribution by Countries of Destination (percentage)							
Yarns							
USA	0	100	0	1	6	3	20
Italy	0	0	69	31	15	n.a.	8
Other W. Europe	0	0	13	59	67	n.a.	54
Latin America	100	0	17	3	4	n.a.	13
Fabrics							
USA	0	99	46	54	66	77	79
Italy	0	0	24	16	7	9	5
Other W. Europe	0	0	20	19	10	7	4
Latin America	0	1	5	7	16	5	9

	1982	1983	1984	1985	1986	1987	1988
Total Export Value							
Fabrics	38,443	34,394	43,027	45,277	42,106	39,394	29,869
Distribution by Countries of Destination (percentage)							
Fabrics							
USA	78	70	69	43	37	46	42
Italy	8	10	6	9	7	10	9
USSR	0	0	0	26	33	11	2

Sources: 1965–77: Superintendencia General de Aduanas, *Estadística del Comercio Exterior*.
1979: Ministerio de Economía, computer tabulations of export authorizations.
1980–88: OFINE computer tabulations of actual exports.

the domestic market when exporting acquired renewed profitability during the 1970s. As Table IV-22 indicates, the exporting effort was in-
consequential until 1976–77, but then most firms began or resumed
exporting with unprecedented intensity. By the late 1970s and early
1980s, major firms in the industry were generally exporting upwards of
half their total output.

Since most Latin American countries give strong protection to their
own cotton textile industries, export opportunities within the region are
limited. Successful exporting therefore requires successful invasion of
the markets of Europe and the United States. That is what was accomplished, but in very different proportions: about 75 percent of yarn
exports were directed to Europe, and 75 percent of cotton fabrics to
the United States.

Table IV-22 shows that cotton yarn and fabric exports leveled off
at $80–90 million annually during 1979–1981. This represented about
half of total textile exports, which also include wearing apparel, alpaca
yarns and fabric, and other specialty items. During this period, there-

fore, cotton yarns and fabrics represented about 11 percent of total nontraditional exports and 2.5 percent of total exports.[48]

This export expansion was facilitated greatly by the recognized quality of the Peruvian product. Its reputation is based first and foremost on the exceptional quality of Peruvian cotton, whose principal varieties are either long staple or extra-long staple. That factor aside, however, the quality of Peruvian workmanship is also recognized. One Venezuelan textile buyer, for example, spoke admiringly of the Peruvian product as "of European quality."

It was recognized by the Peruvian producers, however, that their quality would not have been up to the standards required for exporting had it not been for major investments in new machinery undertaken during the early 1970s, when low-cost credit and an overvalued exchange rate made such investments attractive. When export opportunity came in the years subsequent to 1976, Peruvian producers had the machinery as well as the cotton required to meet the quality standards of the North American and European markets.[49]

Neither does there seem to have been great difficulty in establishing contacts with overseas buyers. In the case of textile shipments to the United States, the first initiatives generally came from importer-wholesaler firms located in New York. These firms have long been accustomed to scanning the world in search of lowest-cost production sources. While most of their import business comes from the Far East, they also keep up-to-date on developments affecting national textile industries in all Latin American countries. The massive devaluation and increase of export subsidies undertaken by the Peruvian government in 1975–76 did not escape their attention. Neither did it escape the attention of European brokers, who began the flow of yarn exports by visiting Lima and making purchases for their own account.

Thus the product was of acceptable quality and the distribution channels materialized almost without effort. Nevertheless, even in its most prosperous moments, textile exporting has been faced with severe limitations. In the first place, the business has involved only standard products: yarns and cotton gray goods (tocuyos).[50] This contrasts with production for the domestic market, which involves a full range of products including dyed and stamped fabrics in various blends of cotton and

---

[48]Banco Central de Reserva, *Memoria 1984*, p. 145.

[49]One quality problem did however bedevil the industry for a period. It derived from the use of polypropelene sacks for the cotton harvest. A few fibers from the sacks, when mixed with the cotton fibers, would pass undetected until the cotton was spun, woven, and dyed, at which time the polypropelene fibers would respond differently to the dyes and suddenly be revealed as imperfections. These sacks are not longer used in Peru, but the damage to Peruvian products caused great concern for a few years.

[50]The USSR had however purchased finished goods under recent commercial agreements.

synthetic fibers. Furthermore, the gray goods are restricted to heavy fabrics used for products such as curtains, hospital gowns, and sheeting. In other words, the products tend to be raw-material-intensive and require little quality workmanship.

Even in this limited range of products where Peru's competitive position is strongest, market price has in most cases covered only variable costs, with little left over to contribute to fixed costs. It should not be inferred from this, however, that Peruvian companies have been indifferent about such exports. This is because labor costs are by custom included in variable costs but may in fact be fixed by custom, union contracts, or legislation. If such exports fail to contribute to the covering of fixed costs, traditionally defined, at least they have served to buy labor peace.[51]

With the routinizing of textile exports in the years since 1976, some Peruvian exporters have assumed a more active marketing role in the exportation of yarn to Europe. This has meant bypassing the broker-importers in order to sell directly to European mills. One major exporter established a network of representatives whose only business was to sell Peruvian yarns. These representatives were, by and large, Europeans already established as textile merchants. Despite the excellence of this distributor network, it still remained necessary to convince European knitting mills that a Peruvian supplier could be a reliable supplier. The Italian origins of the Peruvian company undoubtedly assisted in the process.

In contrast to this, however, no such evolution can be seen with respect to the marketing of cotton fabrics in the United States. Such exports continue to involve dealing only with the importer-wholesaler, the Peruvian exporter having contact with neither manufacturers nor retailers. The importer-wholesaler sets the specifications in great detail: number of threads per square inch, size of thread, width of cloth, type of cotton. The product is so standardized that the market essentially sets the price, the latitude for bargaining being no more that 1 percent.

The fact that Peruvian exporters have remained so passive with respect to marketing effort was explained by different commentators in two quite different ways. On the one hand, it was argued that the New York importer-wholesaler firms had a particularly tight market control, and could threaten retribution against any exporter attempting to bypass them. Others, however, argued that Peruvian exporters simply had not

---

[51]It should be remembered that the countervailing duties imposed in 1982 by the United States on Peruvian shipments of cotton textiles, both cloth and yarn, came about as the result of complaints lodged by affected domestic producers in response to significant price cuts on some Peruvian textile products. That the Peruvian exporters were able to implement such price cuts suggests that some of them, at least, had been capable of earning returns in excess of marginal costs.

exerted themselves sufficiently. It might be added that additional marketing effort is expected to yield low returns when the product is so standardized.[52]

It was observed that export opportunity was more easily grasped by Peruvian producers because product quality was reasonably well assured by the quality of Peruvian cotton and of recently acquired machinery. Nevertheless, export markets have generally demanded of producers quality standards higher than the customary standards of the domestic market. One producer neatly illustrated the difference in standards by pointing out that his firm met most of the fabric needs of the domestic mattress industry with export rejects.

Not all producers have been able or willing to adjust to the higher standards of exporting. One informant enumerated the factors causing some companies to be unsuccessful exporters as: old machinery, lack of quality control, and, a more general indictment, "lack of seriousness" or "lack of professionalism."

Cotton weaving mills have been hard hit in recent years. Exports have slumped, as Table IV-22 shows, partly because of countervailing duties in the United States, partly because of intensified competition in gray goods from mainland China. In addition, the domestic market has virtually disappeared because of the current recession in Peru.

Nevertheless, producers have not had great success diversifying into other export lines. The main obstacle, apparently, is the high cost of inputs, especially dyes and synthetic fibers. By sticking with gray goods, fabric exporters confine their input demand to cotton, the only input available to them at what is by international standards a reasonable price. This is not to say that complaints are not voiced about domestic cotton prices, since they have been held above FOB prices. Nevertheless, other input prices are by international standards substantially higher.

Industrial Chemicals

Peru is a net importer of chemicals, but exports a limited number of inorganic chemicals. The value of these exports ranged between $10 and $15 million annually during 1978–81, but fell below $10 million in subsequent years. Table IV-23 shows their variety and relative importance.

---

[52]This comment does not, however, explain the differential marketing effort as between yarn exporters to Europe and gray goods exporters to the United States. Among possible explanations, in addition to the two points made with reference to the New York importer-wholesalers, are: (1) European brokers may have been charging higher margins; (2) long staple yarn may be considered a more distinctive product than cotton gray goods, and therefore worthy of greater marketing effort; and (3) exports to Europe are more often affected by quota limitations, which encourage producers to seek means of raising value added per unit exported.

Table IV-23. Peru: Exports of Inorganic Chemicals; Detail for 1979

Customs Code	Product	Value ($000)	% of Total Inorganic Chemical Exports
1) 28380110	Copper sulphate	2,525	21.1
2) 28270001	Lead protoxide (litharge)	2,213	18.4
3) 28280205	Copper oxides	1,011	8.4
4) 28270002	Lead oxides (minium)	702	5.8
5) 28190100	Zinc oxides	661	5.5
6) 28110001	Arsenic trioxide	566	4.7
7) 28010002	Chlorine	545	4.5
8) 28450001	Sodium silicates	537	4.5
9) 28380106	Aluminum sulphate	482	4.0
10) 28170199	Caustic soda	418	3.5
11) 28300202	Copper oxychloride	418	3.5
12) 28310201	Sodium hypochloride	377	3.1
13) 28560001	Calcium carbide	373	3.1
14) 28410205	Arsenate of lead	296	2.5
15) 28040100	Oxygen	172	1.4
16) 28060100	Hydrochloric acid	166	1.4
		11,461	95.4
	Other products	548	4.6
		12,008	100

Source: Computer tabulations of export authorizations.

Table IV-24. Peru: Exports of Inorganic Chemicals by Countries of Destination, 1979
(Percentage distributions)

Customs Code	Bolivia	Colombia	Ecuador	Venezuela	Brazil	Other Latin America	USA	Rest of World
1) 28380110	11	1	3	2	68	9	3	2
2) 28270001	0	65	2	26	0	6	0	1
3) 28280205	0	2	2	8	51	0	22	16
4) 28270002	1	22	8	22	0	46[1]	0	0
5) 28190100	1	11	35	0	0	27	4	23
6) 28110001	0	0	0	0	7	67[2]	26	0
7) 28010002	5	44	50	0	0	0	1	0
8) 28450001	12	0	88	0	0	0	0	0
9) 28380106	12	0	88	0	0	0	0	0
10) 28170199	0	0	0	100	0	0	0	0
11) 28300202	0	34	1	13	0	0	0	52
12) 28310201	0	0	100	0	0	0	0	0
13) 28560001	65	3	28	3	0	1	0	0
14) 28410205	0	0	0	0	0	93[3]	0	7
15) 28040100	0	0	98	0	0	0	2	0
16) 28060100	8	0	78	13	0	0	0	0

[1]Argentina, Uruguay, Costa Rica, Chile.
[2]Chile.
[3]Costa Rica, Guatemala, El Salvador.
Source: Computer tabulations of export authorizations.

Many but not all are compounds based on the nonferrous metals which Peru produces in abundance. Thus part of this export is natural-resource based, but another part derives from import substitution.

The significance of this division is brought out in Table IV-24, which shows the geographical distribution of exports for the same products as in Table IV-23. The following pattern emerges from the apparent confusion of different destinations:

(i) More than 90 percent of exports directed to Andean Group countries:

(2)	Lead protoxides	(93%)
(7)	Chlorine	(99%)
(8)	Sodium silicate	(100%)
(9)	Aluminum sulfate	(100%)
(10)	Caustic soda	(100%)
(12)	Sodium hypochloride	(100%)
(13)	Calcium carbide	(99%)
(15)	Oxygen	(98%)
(16)	Hydrochloric acid	(100%)

(ii) Less than 55 percent of exports directed to Andean Group countries:

(1)	Copper sulfate	(17%)
(3)	Copper oxides	(12%)
(4)	Lead oxides (minimum)	(53%)
(5)	Zinc oxides	(47%)
(6)	Arsenic trioxide	(0%)
(11)	Copper oxychloride	(48%)
(14)	Arsenate of lead	(0%)

Thus these chemical exports are quite dichotomized according to the geographical pattern of their destinations. Among the 16 products considered, either more than 93 percent or less than 53 percent of their exports were directed to the Andean Group. Furthermore, only one of the nine products directed largely to the Andean Group was a derivative of Peruvian-produced metals. That product was lead protoxide (litharge). On the other hand, *all* of the seven products with substantial markets beyond the Andean Group were derivatives of Peruvian metals: copper, lead, zinc, and arsenic. The natural-resource-based products therefore had market possibilities encompassing all of Latin America and in many cases beyond that to such esoteric destinations as Thailand, Greece, and Lebanon. Other products not based on these natural resource endowments had to stay close to home.

Those products confined to the Andean Group are not without potential for further market development. If, as Table IV-24 indicates,

100 percent of one product's exports go to Ecuador, 100 percent of another's to Venezuela and 65 percent of a third to Colombia, this at least suggests the existence of untapped markets in other Andean countries.

Table IV-25 gives further evidence of the strength of Peru's market position in the Andean Group. As far as intra-Andean trade is concerned, it shows that Colombia and Venezuela export a few inorganic chemical products, but not the same ones as Peru. Within the Andean Group, Peru is essentially a monopolist as regards most of the chemical products it exports.

From this variety of inorganic chemicals, we choose two for closer examination: oxides of lead and sulfates of copper. They encompass products no. 1, 2, and 4 on Table IV-24 and approximate nos. 28.27 and 28.38 in the 4–digit customs code. The most significant chemicals in this category are high metallic lead oxide (plomo verde), used in batteries; minium (red oxide of lead) and litharge (lead monoxide), used in batteries, paints, and glass; and copper sulfate, used primarily as fungicide.

The production processes involved are relatively simple and the factories producing these chemicals appear modest with respect to both scale and technological complexity. In fact, the industry adds a relatively small increment of industrial value added to what remains basically a mineral product. Raw material purchases amount to about 80 percent of the value of output, leaving about 20 percent as the industrial value added share.[53]

By international standards, the principal inputs are relatively inexpensive, since input costs are similar to FOB export prices. This advantage is somewhat neutralized, however, by two other factors. The first concerns the difficulty of obtaining commercial credit for purchases from state-owned mineral companies. In the absence of such trade credits, chemicals producers have been hard-pressed to secure sufficient bank credit to enable them to extend competitive financing terms when they export. The second factor concerns transportation. Metals are shipped in bulk but chemicals are shipped in bags or drums and thus incur higher transport costs. This factor alone suggests that the industry would tend to locate near markets rather than supply sources.

Table IV-26 shows the evolution over time of oxide and sulfate exports. It shows that, after only sporadic export efforts in the 1960s and early 1970s, systematic exporting began in the mid-1970s and grew to a peak in 1979–80. The table also shows unusual stability in the geographical distribution of exports, with Brazil the most important

---

[53]By the figures of an informant in the U.S., lead cost 18–19 cents/lb., and production of oxides added 5–6 cents/lb. additional value, but only 2–3 cents/lb. for some products.

Table IV-25. Inorganic Chemical Exports Within Andean Group, 1979
(Thousands of dollars)

Exporting Country	Peru		Colombia		Venezuela	
Importing Region	Andean Group	Rest of World	Andean Group	Rest of World	Andean Group	Rest of World
28.01 Halogens	496	0	—	—	—	—
28.03 Carbon Black[1]	—	—	344	1,148	381	566
28.16 Liquid Ammonia	—	—	—	—	3,525	11,814
28.17 Hydroxides	421	0	—	—	—	—
28.19 Zinc Oxides	308	401	—	—	—	—
28.27 Lead Oxides	2,074	516	—	—	—	—
28.30 Chlorides and Oxychlorides	195	234	—	—	—	—
28.38 Sulfates	1,007	2,701	—	—	—	—
28.41 Arsenates	0	294	—	—	—	—
28.42 Carbonates	—	—	1,252	2,060	—	—
28.45 Silicates	476	0	323	8	—	—
28.56 Carbides	319	5	—	—	—	—
Total	5,296	4,151	1,919	3,216	3,906	12,380

[1]Negro de hume.
Source: JUNAC, Comercio Exterior 1970–1980 (Lima: JUNAC, 1982), pp. 476, 525–27, 550.

Table IV-26. Peru: Exports of Oxides (28.27) and Sulfates (28.38)
(Thousands of dollars)

	1965	1970	1975	1977	1979	1980	1981
Total Export Value							
Oxides (28.27)	81	0	311	773	2,915	2,421	2,015
Sulfates (28.38)	0	537	465	1,695	3,130	3,199	1,882
Distribution by Country of Destination (percentage)							
Oxides							
Andean Group*	100	0	65	86	86	87	90
(Colombia)						(40)	(60)
(Venezuela)						(36)	(25)
Other Lat. Amer.	0	0	35	13	13	13	10
Sulfates							
Andean Group[a]	0	10	84	32	31	36	42
Brazil	0	82	4	51	55	56	46
USA	0	0	0	12	4	4	5

	1982	1983	1984	1985	1986	1987	1988
Total Export Value							
Oxides (28.27)	1,220	770	1,549		1,542	3,495	2,436
Sulfates (28.38)	1,671	1,349	1,338		1,540	2,050	1,743
Distribution by Country of Destination (percentage)							
Oxides							
Colombia	53	70	77		43	54	12
Venezuela	27	5	10		21	19	53
Sulfates							
Brazil	57	52	40		39	53	37
USA	12	20	9		29	24	51

[a]Includes Chile
Sources: 1965–77: Superintendencia General de Aduanas, Estadística del Comercio Exterior
1979: Ministerio de Economía, computer tabulations of export authorizations.
1980–88: OFINE computer tabulations of actual exports.

market for sulfates and Colombia, and to a lesser extent Venezuela, the key markets for oxides.

For the oldest of the three chemical firms interviewed, production and exporting both began as far back as 1959. In 1982, the two largest of these firms each exported about half of their total production.

The competitive position of the oxide exporters was examined in their major markets, Colombia and Venezuela. Marketing mechanisms differed somewhat in these two countries. In Venezuela, chemicals occupy the exclusive attention of a few large importing firms. One such company had exclusive contracts with some 60 to 70 foreign chemical producers, of which five were Peruvian companies. Exclusivity in this instance was granted by the exporter, not by the importer. That is, the Peruvian exporter could deal with only one Venezuelan importer, but the Venezuelan importer could obtain the same chemical product from more than one source. A second Venezuelan chemical importer also reported the same kind of contract, but in addition it employed medium-term purchase contracts of six months to a year for buying copper and zinc from Centromin, and also made occasional spot purchases.

These trading relationships were first established in the early to mid-1970s, with initiatives taken by both sides. Given that both exporting and importing firms were completely specialized in industrial chemicals, initial contacts were not difficult to establish.

Industrial chemicals are perhaps the quintessential standardized product. Brand names are of minimal importance: rather, each product is generic, defined by a chemical formula. Nevertheless, important quality differences do exist, and have their influence on buying decisions and market structure. The most obvious such quality dimension is measured by the percentage of impurities and by the producer's ability to hold to the declared maximum impurity level. In some cases, buyers issue specifications and call for the delivery of samples satisfying those specifications. A producer sample having been delivered and certified through testing, the producer is placed on the buyer's list of approved suppliers and can receive orders. In other instances, however, the buyer simply buys on the basis of the specifications advertised by the producer. In any case, buyers generally perform tests on every shipment received, and producers retain samples of each shipment, for subsequent testing in the event that the buyer should complain about quality.

In general, Venezuelan importers were satisfied with the quality of industrial chemicals purchased from Peru. In some instances, however, Peruvian exporters were not able to secure contracts because their product was not up to the standards of particular Venezuelan buyers. Thus one Peruvian company was able to produce 93 percent pure acetic acid, but Venezuelan buyers wanted a 99 percent pure product. In another case, Peruvian litharge, being only 99.5 percent pure, could not secure buyer approval. In the assessment of one importer, the sub-standard nature of those products was caused by deficiencies in production procedures rather than obsolescence of machinery. In the case of litharge, however, the Peruvian producer was working to deliver a higher-quality product at the time of the interview.

Impurity levels were, however, a relatively unimportant quality problem compared to the problem of punctuality of delivery. This did not represent a shortcoming of the Peruvian producer so much as a reflection of the gross deficiencies in mail service, telephone service, and shipping service between Lima and Caracas. Road transportation is exorbitant, particularly since Ecuador requires all through shipments to be reloaded at both borders. Ocean transport is highly irregular, simply because there is not enough trade between Peru and Venezuela to justify more frequent service. However, in the early 1980s the burgeoning trade of the Andean Group caused this situation to improve, in the words of one importer, from "very bad" to "fair."

No similar improvement in mail service could be discerned. One importer's most heated comments were reserved for the postal system, two of his complaints being that checks cleared very slowly and shipping documents often arrived after the shipment, causing imports to run up warehousing charges while held in customs. As for the telephone service, another importer summed it up with, "It's easier to call Sweden than Peru."

The Peruvian producer did not get off scot-free in the importer's assessment of punctuality problems. One major importer noted occasional delays in delivery arising from lags in production, despite the fact that chemicals are generally standard products sold from inventory. That same importer noted, however, that Peruvian producers earned higher marks than their Mexican competitors on questions of punctuality.

A final quality problem concerned packaging. Through the insistence of some buyers, Peruvian exporters were shifting from bags to drums, in order to reduce health hazards in materials handling and to minimize risk of water penetration during sea voyages.

Thus it can be said that Peruvian exporters had a basically satisfactory product whose quality had been improved slightly, mostly as a result of better packaging and more frequent shipping service. In addition, the Peruvian product had become increasingly price-competitive in the early 1980s through the process of tariff reduction within the Andean Group. This was significant because Peru's competitors lay almost entirely outside the Group. Venezuelan tariffs on chemicals were not insubstantial: 10 percent for copper sulfate, 30 percent for minium, litharge, and acetic acid, and 60 percent for high metallic lead oxide (plomo verde), the only one of these products produced locally. By contrast, by 1982 the intra-Andean tariff had fallen to 2 percent for minium and litharge.

Given the significant competitive advantage represented by these tariff differentials, it is not surprising that Peruvian exporters were expanding their market shares in Venezuela in the early 1980s. The 'plomo verde' market, formerly shared between Mexico and Peru, was lost to Venezuelan producers. However, at the same time Peru's share for the litharge market rose from less than half to nearly all of it, at the expense of U.S. competitors. Its share of the minium market was about 80 percent, the remainder coming from Mexico. The market share of other chemicals was also being expanded at the expense of competitors in the U.S., U.K., and continental Europe.

Despite these promising trends, subsequent developments revealed that Peruvian producers were unable to consolidate their market position. Supply problems became acute during Peru's 1983 economic crisis, and turbulence in the Venezuelan economy reduced Peru's export trade in later years. As Table IV-26 indicates, only in 1987 and 1988 did Peruvian chemical exporters regain the position in the Venezuelan market which they had first acquired in the early 1980s.

The marketing system used in Colombia was essentially the same as in Venezuela, except that the distributors tended to be smaller firms devoted more exclusively to their Peruvian exporter clients. As in Venezuela, the early 1980s were a time when Peruvian exporters were expanding their market shares. This was particularly the case with lead oxides used in automobile batteries. The largest producer, the subsidiary of a multinational, shifted the major part of its lead oxide purchases from Mexico to Peru. The final decision occurred at the end of a testing period which had stretched over a number of years, involving the home office as well as the Colombian subsidiary. Final approval had taken so long partly because some of the Peruvian samples had failed certain tests. In the end, however, the Peruvian product was certified as acceptable.

With that certification, the principal Peruvian exporter was able to defeat the Mexican competition on the basis of both price and punctuality. This was possible even though relevant Colombian tariffs were so low as to make insignificant the differential between intra-Andean and external tariffs. For Colombia, however, truck transportation from Peru was cost-effective, despite Ecuadorean trans-shipment requirements. Trucks also liberated Peruvian exporters from the tyranny of erratic shipping schedules, thereby guaranteeing greater punctuality of delivery.

This competitive shift is reflected in import data, which show Peru's share of Colombian lead oxide imports to have risen from 16 percent in 1975–77 to 56 percent in 1979–80.[54] As in the case of Venezuela,

---

[54]JUNAC, *Comercio Exterior 1970–1980* (Lima, 1982), pp. 526, 589.

however, the gains of the early 1980s were not maintained after 1983. Exports collapsed in Peru's crisis year of 1983 and have been erratic ever since.

Yet among Peru's industrial exporters, chemical producers have been relatively successful in the 1980s. Whereas many other sectors have seen their export markets shrink, oxides and sulfates have rebounded to the point where 1987–88 figures are about equal to the peak years of 1979–80. Moreover, this was accomplished despite the serious economic difficulties which overtook the principal countries of destination during the 1980s.

Peruvian oxide producers have acquired a degree of market control throughout the Andean Group enjoyed by very few Peruvian industrial sectors. At the same time, these producers have had no success in penetrating the U.S. market. The situation has been quite the opposite for copper sulfate exporters: little success in the Andean Group, but solid market entry farther afield. Among Andean countries, an entrenched market position was established only in Bolivia, based largely on sales to mining companies for purposes of ore treatment, but that business disappeared with the paralysis of tin mining in the past few years. In Colombia, meanwhile, local producers have proven able to control the market and keep Peruvian competitors out. The Brazilian market, however, remained reliable even through the vicissitudes of the 1980s, with minimal competition from local producers. And, as Table IV-26 indicates, since 1986 copper sulfate has become one of the few Peruvian chemical products to make even modest inroads into the U.S. market.

Sulfate production seems even simpler than oxide production. Impurity levels present no great problem. The product is therefore highly standardized and sales can be made on a spot basis, with bids secured by telex. Product quality adjustment to a new market involves only bag design and crystal size, as determined by the fineness of wire screens. Thus it seems that marketing success in various foreign countries has depended on an almost random distribution of local competition—e.g., too much in Colombia, hardly any in Brazil—and also on price competitiveness which, in this particular case, puts the U.S. market within reach.

Constraints on Export Expansion

Products and Destinations

From a sample of Peruvian industrial products, this study has reviewed experiences as varied as those of exporting canned fish (tipo tall) to

South Africa, cotton yarn to Europe, solids pumps to the United States, lead oxides to Venezuela, and canned fish (grated) to Brazil. From these examples, what general patterns can be discerned regarding type of product exported, destination, and competitive position?

Taking the last point first, the general impression gathered by this survey is one of a weak competitive position. Some exports have diminished greatly during the 1980s (e.g., canned fish), while others have been extinguished altogether (e.g., batteries). Other exports show a certain resilience (e.g., electric motors, water pumps, cotton fabrics), but that resilience could also be described as hanging on, highly vulnerable to any change which would adversely affect an already squeezed profit position. The field work of this study began with surveys and interviews in other sectors which in the end were not included in the study, but these other sectors (e.g., cement, fishing boats, lumber) also showed evidence of pervasive weakness in their export markets.

To be sure, a few areas of market strength also came to light (e.g., industrial chemicals, solids pumps, canned fish in Brazil). Moreover, the sample failed to include any of those few sectors which have shown substantial export growth over the 1980s (e.g., knitwear, asparagus, mangos, frozen shrimp), simply because they were virtually invisible at the time the study was begun. These last four products are however about the only bright spots among the scores of nontraditional products exported by Peru in the 1980s. The decade has been a hard time for all sectors of the Peruvian economy, exports included.

What might explain this pattern of exports, by type of product and by country of destination? First, it should be noted that all these products are natural-resource-related. Either they use natural resources as inputs or they are inputs in natural resource production. Their relationship to natural resources bestows some type of cost advantage which makes such products competitive in foreign markets, at least relative to other products which are not exported at all.

The cost advantage for an input to natural resource production is limited, however. This status implies the saving of some transport costs, the economies of scale from having a larger market, and, in a few cases, the opportunity to develop superior product designs as a result of proximity to the customer, in the manner of the product cycle theory. But the industries which have flourished through producing inputs for mining and fishing (e.g., pumps, motors, boats, nets, etc.) have in general not been able to project export sales beyond the limits of the Andean Group. In most cases, moreover, the market share they have been able to capture in other Andean countries has been extremely limited.

The natural resource base for the other exports is varied: the oceans for canned fish, irrigated farmland for cotton textiles, rain forests for plywood, limestone for cement, and copper, lead and zinc mines for industrial chemicals, structural shapes, alloys, and, at a more elaborated level, copper cables and zinc-based batteries. Yet while the advantage of a low-cost resource input makes these products prime candidates for import substitution, foreign markets are found only with some difficulty. A natural-resource base gives a clear opportunity for exporting only if that same resource is lacking in other countries. Within the Andean Group, textiles and clothing are produced everywhere and excluded from internal tariff concessions. The canning industries of Ecuador and Venezuela have proved impenetrable, leaving only Bolivia as a secure market for Peruvian fish products. Cement and plywood production is widespread. The only products in which Peru has the potential for clear market dominance in the Andean Group are those derived from nonferrous metals, viz., industrial chemicals, alloys, etc.

Regarding exports to the rest of the world, the natural resource advantage must be particularly strong to make Peruvian products competitive in distant, relatively unprotected markets. That is, the resource must be of particularly high quality or low cost. Hidrostal's solids pump is perhaps the only item which has managed to flout this generalization and enjoy some success in distant markets.

It must be remembered, however, that a given composition of exports does not arise simply from the natural workings of comparative advantage. Government policy also intervenes, in two important respects. First, the export subsidy to nontraditional exports (Certex) has been incompletely adjusted to allow for different degrees of industrial value added, with the result that the effective rate of protection for exports has been particularly high for some natural-resource-intensive products. Second, the real exchange rate has remained persistently overvalued, with the result being that Peru has continued to rely mostly on foreign exchange earnings from primary products, with relatively little room for maneuver available for industrial goods further down the scale of comparative advantage. That the exchange rate has been overvalued derives directly from the presence of at least one of two phenomena at all moments of Peru's recent past. The first is the reality of exchange control. The second is that national income levels and rates of capacity utilization are constrained by the availability of foreign exchange.[55] The situation is perpetuated by the apparent inability of government to design a politically viable devaluation package.

In sum, the pattern of industrial exports is explained in part by natural-resource intensity, which seems the most important determinant of comparative advantage, and to a lesser extent by economies of scale and other cost-reducing factors associated with producing inputs for

---

[55]For further elaboration see Schydlowsky, Hunt and Mezzera, *La promoción de exportaciones no tradicionales*, passim.

natural-resource-extracting industries. Such factors are determinants of exports only to the extent that Peru's natural resource endowment differs from that of its trading partners, and that such trade advantages are preserved despite government policy measures which might discourage exports through differential export subsidies and exchange rate over-valuation.

However, the principal concern of this study is not current structure: it is the identification of constraints on future export expansion. Three are considered: product quality, marketing know-how, and cost struc-ture. They will be discussed in turn.

Product Quality

The problem of product quality as a constraint on export expansion can be divided into the objective and the subjective. We ask, on the objective side, how good are Peruvian products, as compared to those of the competition, and what prospects exist for product improvement? On the subjective side, to what extent are consumers prejudiced against Peruvian products, perceiving a lower quality than that which actually exists, and to what extent can those attitudes be overcome?

In the gamut of industrial products spewed forth by the factories of today's world, the Peruvian industrial exports of our sample are relatively uncomplicated. Although some incorporate special design fea-tures, they tend to be standardized products. In this context, a general assessment of product quality is that the standardized products are up to standard (e.g., cotton fabrics, cotton yarn, industrial chemicals) and that the more distinctive products range broadly in quality, but with more below than above the standard of the competition. A rough cat-egorization of this latter group would be:

Above standard:	Pumps (USA, Colombia)
At standard:	Transformers (Colombia)
	Canned fish (Brazil)
Slightly below standard:	Canned fish (Venezuela, USA)
	Electric motors (Colombia)
Below standard:	Batteries (Venezuela)

In some of these lines, the product is perhaps inevitably inferior and the export business must be based on compensatory price differ-entials as a permanent condition. Pilchard must always be priced below tuna, for example. Despite this caveat, a review of the above list suggests strongly that product quality is a problem not yet satisfactorily resolved for many Peruvian exporters. For the country, it is perhaps an even greater problem in those sectors which have not been able to export at all.

With regard to improvements in actual quality, the prospects for the future can best be assessed by indicating the extent of accomplishments in the past. To what extent have products actually been redesigned for export?

A first response to the question must differentiate between countries of destination. Pressures for product redesign are very slight if the product is exported to other countries of the Andean Group or elsewhere in Latin America.[56] The only cases which came to light in our sample were those of industrial chemicals to Venezuela and Colombia, and water pumps to Colombia. In both cases however the quality improvements were small.

Exporting to the United States or Europe, however, is quite a different challenge. In a variety of cases, and a variety of ways, pressure for quality adjustment can be substantial. The clearest case in the sample was that of canned fish, where the importer-wholesaler often imposed a series of quality standards relating to all stages of the production process. The resulting quality improvement involved the label, the can and the fish inside.

A variant of this case involves a change in the design of the product, not simply to improve its quality, but to adjust its character to the pattern of existing demand. In the fishing industry, the experience with "tipo tall" in the South African market is illustrative. A similar situation with respect to norms exists for many other products. Virtually every product is affected by a number of norms and quality standards which govern buying decisions. For example, even so apparently homogeneous a product as plywood actually has 32 quality classes which give structure to the plywood market in the United States. It has been commented that Latin American plywood producers, in Peru and elsewhere, do not produce to U.S. quality standards. By these standards, the Latin American product is not inferior; it is simply undifferentiated. But in that undifferentiated condition, it has virtually no market prospects in the United States.[57]

Although this study chose a variety of industrial exports for special examination, in the end very few products were identified as having introduced substantial quality improvements under the pressures of export competition. The paucity of such examples stands in contrast to the results of Morawetz and Keesing, who found substantial pressure for quality improvement, and who differentiated between successful and unsuccessful export experience according to the effectiveness of the exporter's response to those pressures.[58]

---

[56]This finding is consistent with the work of Morawetz, who reported that Colombian clothing producers marketed their traditional lines in Venezuela with the same success they had always achieved in Colombia. See Morawetz, *The Emperor's New Clothes*, pp. 30–34.

[57]Personal communication with representative of American Plywood Association.

[58]Morawetz, *The Emperor's New Clothes* and Keesing, "Exporting Manufactured Consumer Goods."

This apparent paradox may be resolved as follows: Morawetz and Keesing focused on product lines in which (a) quality is important, and (b) developing countries have substantial cost advantages in production. This means that (c) importer-wholesalers in the United States find it worth their while to make substantial efforts to push LDC exporters into quality improvements. There are many other products lacking the characteristics just described but still possessing some export potential. Some are so standardized as to present little difficulty in satisfying quality requirements. In such cases that quality was already embodied in the product destined for the domestic market. In other cases no importer-wholesaler has taken the products in hand to reshape them and push them in major markets of the Northern Hemisphere. This could be because such products simply do not possess the cost advantages which will make such efforts worthwhile. Alternatively, these products (such as plywood perhaps) are still awaiting discovery.

We now come to the subjective problem: consumer attitudes which credit the product with a lower quality than it actually possesses. Latin American industrial products generally confront an image problem, at home as well as abroad. This is in part the product of cultural stereo-typing, but it also has foundation in fact. Among the characteristics of the dominant culture in Latin America, attention to detail has never been noted to play a particularly prominent role. Faced with consumer skepticism based on sometimes bitter experience, the Latin American industrial exporter is restricted to two types of products. On the one hand, he can sell products so highly standardized that quality is easily assessed. On the other hand, he can sell to specialized purchasers who are particularly knowledgeable in assessing product quality. Ruled out, therefore, are products for which the final consumer has difficulty in assessing quality.

It takes many decades for industrial exporters from a given country to develop a reputation for product quality. That attitudes can be changed is effectively demonstrated by the extent to which U.S. attitudes about Japanese products have changed from the contempt of the 1930s to the envy of the 1980s.[59] Popular attitudes of those two points in time are perhaps an exaggeration of the respective realities, in opposite directions, but clearly the major factor in changing attitudes was the actual change in product quality. Since nation of origin influences the consumer's perception of product quality, it follows that the consumer's assessment is based partly on the actual quality of the product in question and partly on an average quality of products from the country in ques-

---

[59]The even more rapid emergence to respectability of Korea may be noted in recent television ads for the Hyundai which describe it as produced by "The Master Builders of Asia."

tion. Two conclusions derive from this point. First, attitudes about Peruvian industrial products will be improved only if the products themselves actually improve. Second, any product of poor quality which is exported or even sold on the domestic market transmits an image of poor quality which is damaging to all other Peruvian producers.

Deceptive claims are one aspect of poor product quality which came to the author's attention a number of times during the course of interviews. The most frequently noted deception involved misrepresentation regarding the country of origin, pretending that Peruvian products were in fact from somewhere else. The cases are worth counting. A distributor claimed that his Peruvian pumps were Swiss and that his Peruvian electric motors were Italian. A clothing producer, while correctly labeling the country of origin for his exports to the United States, labeled his sales to the domestic market as made in Italy. A manufacturer of personal care items, largely for the domestic market, sold two principal lines, one with an aristocratic Italian name to which was affixed on the product the word "Roma," and one with an aristocratic German name to which was added the word "Germany" (in English). His principal competitor, he reported, marketed two lines entitled "Cuzco" and "Sacsahuaman," with disastrous results. His conclusion that the typical Peruvian consumer would prefer to project the image of an Italian rather than of one hailing from the Peruvian provinces seemed reasonable enough.

Other instances of deceptive labeling noted in this survey concerned canned pilchards, which were labeled as tuna on the shelves of a Colombian supermarket, and, allegedly, as bonito in some exports to Brazil. Perhaps more immediately damaging to Peruvian exporters was a different experience of that same Colombian supermarket, which reported having purchased Peruvian garlic only to find that it had spoiled during shipment. The buyer for the supermarket stated that the Peruvian exporter had not made good on the matter. Furthermore, from this experience, the buyer declared his unwillingness to make further purchases of any product from Peru.

Probably the most scandalous case of quality deficiency in a Peruvian export in fact created very little scandal in Peru. The product was highly nontraditional: sterilized fruit flies. The buyer was the State of California, which in 1981 was experiencing an infestation of the Mediterranean fruit fly, severely threatening the state's fruit producers. Seeking to avoid the environmental damage which might be caused by aerial spraying of pesticides, state officials instead chose to eliminate the flies by introducing a population of sterilized flies so large as to cause the probability of mating between two fertile flies to be reduced to zero. Sterilized flies were imported from a number of sources, including Peru, and the problem was on the verge of solution when the fruit fly population in one area skyrocketed. That area was where the Peruvian flies had been released, and it turned out that the Peruvian flies had not been sterile after all. In the words of one state official, "We got burned on a shipment from Peru."[60]

It is worth noting that Colombian and Venezuelan importers, when expressing satisfaction with a Peruvian product and its producer, were often quick to mention the Peruvian exporter's cooperativeness in making good for any shipment which turned out to be below agreed-upon standards. Such an attitude is an essential element of product quality.[61]

In the foreseeable future, Peru cannot hope to compete with the Japanese and Koreans in the minds of the American consumer. But it can aspire to improve its reputation with specialized buyers such as importer-wholesalers of consumer products. Such buyers should be expected to be able to see beyond the negative publicity of drugs and guerrillas, changing their perceptions rapidly as actual products change. It therefore remains for the Peruvian nation, i.e., either the government or the exporters themselves, to give greater impetus to a national system for quality upgrading.

Marketing

The marketing questions posed at the beginning of this study were these: Do Peruvian exporters have effective market development strategies in given countries of destination? And are they effective in seeking out new markets? The answer to these complex questions must of course be a qualified one: it depends, on both the product and the country.

Export marketing strategies may be divided into two types which have been called "stay-at-home" and "go-abroad" marketing.[62] An exporting firm practicing stay-at-home marketing responds to importer initiatives and concerns itself simply with meeting importer orders sat-

---

[60]*New York Times*, August 29, 1981, p. 8.

[61]The importance of quality guarantees based on the mutual confidence developed through long-term business relationships can best be illustrated with a non-Peruvian example. During interviews in the United States, the principal buyer for a large shoe retailing firm was asked if he had considered sourcing in Latin American countries other than Brazil, the only such country from which he was making regular purchases. He proceeded to recount a series of abortive sourcing efforts in Uruguay, Argentina, Chile, Peru, and Colombia. His most serious efforts had been in Uruguay, Argentina, and Chile, where although exchange rate overvaluation and export subsidy cutbacks played an important role in undermining sourcing agreements, the negative point which he emphasized time and again was that he considered exporters in those countries to be unreliable. By contrast, his experience in Brazil had convinced him that exporters there were reliable: they stuck to the terms of the contract, and delivered what they promised.

[62]Shane Hunt, "Marketing Requirements for Successful Exporting: Some Peruvian Examples," CLADS Discussion Paper no. 88, Boston University, June 1989. These strategies correspond approximately to Stages I-II and III-IV respectively in the scheme presented in Wortzel and Wortzel, "Export Marketing Strategies for NIC- and LDC-Based Firms."

isfactorily in respect to product quality, packaging and delivery. Stay-at-home marketing essentially foreswears an export marketing strategy in order to concentrate on production problems. The effectiveness of the strategy depends on the enterprise of importer-wholesalers, and on the wisdom of their marketing decisions. In East Asia and to a lesser extent in Brazil, stay-at-home marketing has been seen as a learning stage which prepares exporting firms for more aggressive marketing efforts subsequently. This evolution has not, however, occurred in Peru. Stay-at-home marketers have all remained at home, as in the cases of canned fish to the U.S. and South Africa, cotton textiles to the U.S. and industrial chemicals to Venezuela.

The exporter who has opted for go-abroad marketing must do just that: go abroad, set up distribution channels, and in some way manage those channels. Among the examples of such activity noted in this survey were canned fish in Brazil, motors, pumps and chemicals in Colombia, cotton yarns in Europe and pumps in the United States.

In textbook presentations, marketing strategy is said to consist of four components: product quality, price, promotional effort, and choice of distribution channels. By this broad definition, it must be concluded that the go-abroad marketing strategies reviewed in this study have not been effective, for the business pursuing them did not prosper. The failures were not for not trying: interviews disclosed various cases in which exporters exercised administrative control over distributors, at times even changing the distribution system completely when past sales results seemed unsatisfactory (e.g., pumps in the U.S., batteries in Colombia).

As to seeking out new markets, most interviews established that exporters had indeed looked carefully at a wide range of potential countries of destination. In a few cases, Peruvian exporters have indeed established market representation in a surprisingly wide variety of foreign countries. Canned fish and solids pumps were particularly impressive in this respect.[63] In other cases, exporters had explored a number of possible destinations without being able to establish footholds (e.g., electric motors).

The effectiveness of control over distribution channels, and also the quality of distributors, is not independent of the price and product quality variables. With a better product and lower price, exporters can attract better distributors and exercise greater control over them. In the case of stay-at-home marketing, lower costs lead to greater efforts by

---

[63]The most far-flung export business brought to light in interviews was however that of zinc calots. This is a disc of a particular alloy from which flashlight battery cases are made by a stamping process. The Peruvian manufacturer exports to about 50 countries, including such esoteric destinations (from the Peruvian perspective) as Finland, Sudan, and Bangladesh.

importer-wholesalers toward improving product quality. Thus the long-run success of the marketing program is intimately related to cost factors, to which we next turn.

Costs

Costs are a constraint on exports only in their relation to price. Export expansion requires price-cost margins adequate to cover marginal costs in the short run and to attract new investment in the long run. To speak of costs as a constraint on export expansion is therefore to speak of the importance of the real effective exchange rate.

Although this study was intended to focus attention on constraints on export expansion other than those of price and cost, the ultimate emphasis is once more upon these more traditional variables. This is because the less traditional variables such as product quality and marketing know-how are to some extent dependent on the real effective exchange rate. That is, favorable price-cost margins do more than directly encourage greater quantities to be exported, in the manner suggested by export supply functions. They also encourage greater effort at whatever it takes to succeed in exporting. If the product's quality needs to be improved, this will be done. If market penetration techniques need to be learned, this too will be done. And if it is not done by the exporters, importer-wholesalers from various foreign countries will take the initiative and do it for them.

Among the products examined in this study, that process was perhaps best exemplified in the fish-canning industry. The price-cost margins having become favorable, importers arrived, from the United States, from South Africa, from Venezuela. They cajoled producers into various product quality changes and they developed marketing strategies which had varying degrees of success. Had price-cost margins continued to remain favorable, one can imagine that ineffective marketing strategies would have been dropped and the more successful ones would have ensconced the Peruvian product in the niches appropriate to it. One could also imagine that at least a few Peruvian producers would have assumed greater marketing responsibilities in the U.S. and Europe, much in the way that they had done for the previous 40 years in Brazil. However, these are now mere might-have-beens. In fact, the price-cost margins deteriorated and the export business in canned fish came to naught.

An even more cogent example, dating from 1979–80, is recounted by Keesing.[64] At that time, a Peruvian shoe producer made initial contacts with U.S. buyers, who subsequently provided technical assistance

---

[64]Donald Keesing, "Exporting Manufactured Consumer Goods," pp. 8–10.

so that the producer would upgrade his product, enabling it to find acceptance in the U.S. market. The buyers were willing to make such efforts because the original price quotations of the Peruvian exporter were very low, making Peru look like a promising source for future orders. The first buying season went well, but the Peruvian producer raised his price by 30 percent for the second season, and orders diminished so much that the buyers dropped the arrangement. It is not evident from Keesing's account whether the price increase represented a necessity imposed by cost increases or an error in marketing strategy on the part of the Peruvian exporter.

This argument for the primacy of price-cost margins presumes of course a certain responsiveness on the part of exporters, either to price or to the urgings of importer-wholesalers. On the contrary, however, it has often been argued that exporters are unresponsive to price or, for that matter, to anything else. This view, which is integral to the concept of elasticity pessimism, sees exporters as satisfiers rather than maximizers. It finds support in some studies which find low price elasticities in export supply functions and also in methodological criticisms which can be made of studies showing higher elasticities.[65]

However, elasticity estimates are treacherous foundations for erecting arguments about exporter responsiveness. After all, one would expect that response is based on expected future price, not on the current price which is used in export supply functions. Moreover, the relation between current and expected future price is particularly murky in a country which has suffered as much political and economic instability as Peru in recent years.

The actual evolution of the real effective exchange rate has not been tracked with any accuracy. The real exchange rate estimates presented above in Table IV-4 are only approximations and are of very limited use in analyzing the evolution of any given export. Their main shortcoming is that the exchange rate indexes are based on economy-wide price indexes (e.g., the CIP), rather than on the specific prices and costs which apply to a given export sector. It was mentioned, for example, that particular adverse price movements have affected both canned fish and cotton textile exports, viz., the decline of tuna prices and the entry of China into the cotton gray goods export business. These adverse effects are not reflected in any of the various real exchange rate indexes compiled up to the present time. Unfortunately, the relevant sector-specific price and cost indexes are hard to come by, and have not been included in this study.

---

[65]Indeed, the present author has contributed to the Peruvian literature of skepticism regarding supply elasticities. See Shane Hunt, "Peru's Non-Traditional Exports: The Present and the Future," CLADS Discussion Paper no. 75, Boston University, October 1987, pp. 6–22.

Conclusions and Final Remarks

The products chosen for our sample proved to be representative of Peru's nontraditional exports in two respects. First, they showed strong growth in export earnings during the export boom which began in 1975–76 and peaked in 1980–81. Second, after the peak, in the mid-80s, they suffered sharp declines in export earnings. Although for many of these industries earnings recovered somewhat after 1987, none of the industries in our sample enjoyed prosperity during the 1980s.

All the products in the sample either used natural resource inputs or were themselves inputs to natural resource production. Comparative advantage appears much more tightly tied to natural resource use than to labor intensity of production.

The constraints to export expansion given particular emphasis in the study were product quality, marketing know-how, and the more traditional constraint of price-cost margins. Other constraints have been treated in cursory fashion or ignored altogether, even though they might be of substantial importance in certain instances. Among these other factors are the availability of credit, the availability of insurance, diplomatic efforts to remove barriers to imports in other countries, and the reduction of bureaucratic delay associated with the various administrative steps in exporting.

Regarding product quality, the sample was seen to include products which were either standardized or differentiated but relatively simple. In general, the quality was either equal to or, in some cases, slightly inferior to that of the principal competition in foreign markets. However, the competitive pressures of foreign markets did induce exporters to improve product quality in a number of ways. Product quality incorporates subjective as well as objective dimensions. On the subjective side, it was noted that consumer attitudes make the country of origin a liability for many Peruvian exporters, and that some have been tempted to pretend that their Peruvian products come from somewhere else.

Regarding marketing know-how and effort, marked differences were noted within the sample, depending on product and country of destination. The major differences were characterized as stay-at-home and go-abroad marketing. In the former, marketing strategies and decisions are controlled by importers in other countries, whereas in the latter the exporter sets up and manages a system of foreign distributors. Although several cases involving effective management of foreign distribution systems were noted, it was also observed that exporters who began with stay-at-home marketing systems have generally remained tied to them, with little evolution toward the assumption of greater marketing responsibilities. From the standpoint of such exporters, the importer-wholesaler is both facilitator and obstruction. Evidently the export businesses examined have not been sufficiently profitable to induce the exporter to shake loose from importer dominance.

Regarding price-cost margins, a variable which is essentially the same as the real effective exchange rate, the available measures are aggregative, being based on economy-wide price and cost indexes. These measures show (in Table IV-4) that margins improved greatly for exporters in the second half of the 1970s, kept their favorable levels at least till 1981, and then deteriorated during the rest of the 1980s, slowly at first and then quite rapidly. However, the particular experience of some of the products in the sample has apparently been more adverse than what the aggregate indexes show.

Price-cost margins are important for exporting by the conventional reasoning that a higher price brings forth greater quantity. In addition, however, favorable price-cost margins may be expected to elicit greater effort at product improvement and control of marketing channels.

The product quality and marketing variables should be considered only partially dependent on underlying price-cost margins. Other factors which should be expected to influence them are cultural pressures, information flows, and government sanctions. To the extent that product quality and marketing enterprises can be promoted by these other factors, they need not be promoted by increasing price-cost margins. So much the better, for if price-cost margins must be increased, this must be done by real devaluation, a policy which carries a number of political and social liabilities.

Although this study is not primarily oriented toward policy recommendations, such recommendations do emerge from the reasoning just presented. First, price-cost margins have to be kept favorable for exporting. This means maintaining a stable and high (i.e., devalued) real effective exchange rate. Stability is enhanced if the rate depends more on the financial exchange rate and less on Certex, the additional uncertainty of Certex lying in the possibilities of countervailing duties and of cutbacks in moments of fiscal crisis.

Second, it should be remembered that the real effective exchange rate, as calculated, is a highly imperfect measure of actual price-cost margins, and that some policy measures may not affect the former even though they do in fact affect the latter. Such measures should not be overlooked. Two important examples in this respect involve reducing protectionism in other countries and reducing input costs. For example, the Venezuelan CPI may be rising impressively relative to the bolivar-inti exchange rate, but the rise would be meaningless to Peruvian exporters if they were denied access to the Venezuelan market. Also, the price of tinplate may be exceedingly damaging to Peruvian exporters of canned goods, yet have negligible influence in Peruvian price and cost indexes.

Third, regarding the promotion of other factors which influence product quality and marketing effort, the key variable is probably information flows. Much is already done in this respect by Peru's Commercial Attaches and by the Instituto del Comercio Exterior (ICE, formerly FOPEX). Importer-wholesalers visiting Peru have been assisted in making contact with potential exporters. In other countries, go-abroad exporters have been assisted in lining up potential distributors. Interviews revealed a number of cases, particularly in clothing and textile industries, where ICE intermediation had worked very well. Yet while services have improved greatly in the last decade, more could be done. All countries have some type of government agency concerned with export promotion, but such agencies achieve very different degrees of effectiveness. ICE is probably among the better Latin American agencies of this sort, but Latin American agencies are given indifferent ratings when compared to those of East Asia or OECD countries.[66]

Regarding government sanctions against the unacceptably poor quality of some Peruvian exports, again some efforts have been made but more could be done. The government lab which oversees canned fish exports tests to make sure that products are not spoiled. But no means were available for the Colombian supermarket to seek redress against the garlic exporter, nor for the California officials regarding the fruit-fly fiasco. The quality of Peruvian exports could be improved either by self-policing conducted by the exporters themselves or by channels of redress and publicity set up through ICE.

---

[66]Donald Keesing, "Marketing Manufactured Exports from Developing Countries: How to Provide Excellent, Cost-Effective Institutional Support," Washington, The World Bank, processed, April 1988. A sobering comparison is given between the export promotion agencies of Singapore and Brazil, to the detriment of Brazil, on pp. 31–36.

APPENDIX A

Export Successes of Brazil and Mexico

Brazil, along with Argentina, has long exported sizable amounts of resource-based products with limited industrial processing, but other manufactures, reflecting the learning experience of import substitution, also began to be sold abroad in significant quantities as of the late 1960s. As Teitel and Thoumi have written:

> In the period from the mid-1950s and early 1960s to the 1970s, the metallurgical and metalworking industries in both Argentina and Brazil seem to have gone a long way toward closing the efficiency gap. Substantial increases in domestic output provided the opportunity to accumulate operating knowledge and to improve the efficiency of production until domestic costs have become comparable to the international ones. In this way, exports also became possible, albeit sometimes requiring a measure of government promotional support.[1]

The growth of manufacturing exports was high for both countries through the first half of the 1970s, and remained so for Brazil throughout the 1970s and into the 1980s. Alternative definitions of manufacturing exports place the share of manufactures in total exports between 50 and 70 percent by the beginning of the 1980s, and exports of non-resource-based industries were growing more rapidly than the more traditional products. During the 1970s, Brazil had a fairly stable real exchange rate, a highly protected domestic market and a complex system of export subsidies. These represented improvements from the 1960s, when the system did not favor production for export, and, indeed, there was an anti-export bias in most branches of industry at a time when the domestic market was generally buoyant. It is uncertain, considering dynamic fac-

[1]Simón Teitel and Francisco E. Thoumi, "From Import Substitution to Exports: The Manufacturing Exports Experience of Argentina and Brazil," *Economic Development and Cultural Change*, vol. 34, no. 3, April, 1986, p. 466.

tors, whether export incentives contributed to a more efficient composition of exports between the 1960s and the 1970s.[2]

Between 1970 and 1981, the year before the debt crisis, Brazilian
exports of manufactures in constant 1980 cruzeiros increased at a compound annual rate of 23.6 percent.[3] Exports dropped sharply in 1982,
and in 1983 were at a level only slightly above that of 1981. Growth has
been at a compound rate of 8.3 percent during the period 1984–88, but
has been extremely erratic, increasing by as much as 36 percent in 1984,
while declining in two years, once (in 1986) by 20.7 percent. Nonetheless, the level of manufacturing exports, in constant value terms, was
somewhat more than 50 percent higher in 1988 than in 1981.

Transportation equipment accounted for over a fifth of manufacturing exports in 1981, representing the largest share of any industrial
grouping, with machinery, steel, chemicals and petroleum derivatives
the next most important. By 1988, steel was in first place with over a
quarter of manufacturing exports, but transportation equipment still had
nearly a fifth. Chemicals, machinery and footwear followed. Footwear
exports peaked in 1984, however. Similarly, exports of orange juice
were high but not nearly at the level of 1983 in real terms.

Among the Brazilian exports of manufactures with rapid rates of
growth were shoes (labor-intensive), orange juice (natural resource, but
also, to some extent, capital-intensive), and machinery (which is dealt
with in Chapter III). Two major successes were steel and automotive
products, which were clearly capital-intensive.[4] Brazil's exports of steel
products rose sevenfold from 0.2 percent of world totals in the mid-
1970s to 4.0 percent in 1985. Initiated as an import substitution activity,
Brazilian steel has become increasingly export-oriented although the
policies affecting it have had a somewhat higher anti-export bias than
those affecting manufacturing industry on average. The basic reasons
for Brazil's success in steel exports have been a favorable factor endowment (notably iron ore), and the use of a standard international
technology, at least insofar as exports (particularly those to industrially
more advanced countries) have been the simplest and most traditional
flat and non-flat products. Relatively low labor costs have helped make
exporting feasible, but these appear to have been more than offset by
relatively high costs for capital, transport and even coke. The existence
of domestic price controls has provided a stimulus in a number of years.

---

[2]Teitel and Thoumi, *op. cit.*, pp. 482–485.
[3]The calculations in this paragraph and that which follows were derived from the IDB
Country Studies Division Data Bank for Brazil, based on official government publications.
[4]The account of steel and automotive is based on Berhnhard Fischer, Peter Nunnenkamp
et al., *Capital-Intensive Industries in Newly Industrializing Countries. The Case of the
Brazilian Automobile and Steel Industries*. Kieler Studien no. 221 (J.G.B. Moher, Tüb-
ingen, 1988).

So, too, has the slack in domestic demand in years such as 1982–83 and 1987–88. Moreover, the latter has led Brazil to turn increasingly from pig iron, ferro-alloys and traditional steel products to those requiring relatively more input of highly specialized skills (human capital).

Brazilian integrated steel mills are considered to be at the low end of the range of economic viability, with a level of minimum costs approximately 10 percent higher than they would be with the most efficient size facilities. This is likely to be reduced if current expansion plans are realized, and, in any event, it is not so great as to offset the basic advantage in iron ore costs (or the recession year advantage in exporting even human-capital-intensive products at less than full costs). Protectionism in the United States and Europe has been limiting the growth of Brazilian steel exports since 1985. However, insofar as it is aimed primarily at dumping, it has been less of a problem for traditional steel products in which Brazil has a comparative advantage than for the new 1980s exports of more human capital-intensive products in which the country's costs are still high in international terms.

Brazil's exports of automobiles and automobile parts increased most rapidly in the period 1973–78. During that period, the ratio of exports to output was more than three times as high as that for manufacturing as a whole. Early in the 1970s, 90 percent of these exports went to Latin America, but by 1984, the region received only 30.5 percent, with 43.4 percent going to advanced industrial economies. Automobile production in Brazil is not so standardized that the exports can be explained by the product-cycle hypothesis (the contention that after an initial period of technological change and adjustment, production processes become so routinized that minimum cost operations can be achieved even outside the major centers of innovation and industrial development). Automotive bodies and axles are below average in terms of their requirements of human capital, but Brazilian exports have been higher in areas such as motors, in which the labor intensity is high, contrary to what one would expect from the country's human factor endowment. While the industry was favored by prices of steel and labor that often were below international levels (and these appear to have offset higher-than-international costs levels for freight and financing), the major factor underlying the export success was access to export incentives, which, at levels significantly above those for industry as a whole were on balance quite favorable. This was particularly true in the early 1980s.[5]

---

[5]In 1980, Brazil's transport industry enjoyed an export incentives rate amounting to 22.7 percent of sales value, 2.4 times that of manufacturing as a whole, and obtained nearly half of all of total export incentive benefits even though it accounted for only a fifth of all manufacturing exports. At a time when there was a slight anti-export bias for manufacturing industry as a whole, there was a pro-export bias for the transport industry of 34 percent. Fischer, Nunnenkamp et al., esp. pp. 119–126.

Yet the government's restrictions on imports encouraged a proliferation of models which discouraged the specialization that might have enabled producers to take better advantage of economies of scale. In large measure as a consequence, for many years Brazil's gains in economies of scale have trailed not only the industrialized countries but also South Korea, despite that country's smaller volume of automobile production.[6] Automotive export incentives have declined during the course of the 1980s, and the most important such arrangement was scheduled to end in 1989. Even so, automotive exports continued to increase moderately in 1985–86, despite a high level of domestic growth. They increased still more in 1987–88, though in that case because of the domestic recession and the increasing economic uncertainty about the future.

Mexico has provided another major success story. While the growing overvaluation of the peso during 1970–76 discouraged manufacturing exports and helps explain why their value increased at a compound annual rate of only 0.5 percent in constant 1980 dollars, there was a significant turnaround after 1976, when devaluations were more frequent.[7] Between 1976 and 1981, the constant dollar value of manufacturing exports other than assembly industry products increased at a compound rate of 14.2 percent. Focusing on the period since the onset of the debt crisis, when protection with its anti-export bias was sharply reduced, the array of export promotion mechanisms became less important and devaluations took on increased significance (leading to major undervaluation of the peso). The 1980 constant year value of manufacturing exports other than assembly products increased between 1981 and 1988 at a compound annual rate of nearly 19 percent. For the same period, assembly industry exports increased at a compound rate of nearly 17 percent in gross value and approximately 12 percent in value added.

The composition of both categories of manufacturing exports remained similar between 1981 and 1987, except for the doubling of the share of automobile components. This reflected the evolution of an increased number of plants dedicated primarily to export activity, a new development in Mexican industry. Vehicles and components accounted

---

[6]See Fischer, Nunnenkamp *et al.*, esp. pp. 51, 73–79, 263. Independent of this, the foreign producers who dominated local production also may not have been willing to fully integrate Brazilian plants into worldwide sourcing schemes.

[7]Calculations are based on data prepared by José Valero Ríos, drawn from the Working Group of the Instituto Nacional de Estadística, Geografía e Información de la SPP-SHCP-Banco de México, as published in *Comercio Exterior* over the period 1978–1989, and on various compilations of Wharton Econometric Forecasting Associates, based, in turn, on official data (especially CIEMEX-WEFA, *Maquiladora Industry Analysis*, Bala Cynwyd, Pa., May 1988). See also, Rafael Jiménez Ramos, "Promoción de las exportaciones de manufacturas de México, 1970–1986," *Comercio Exterior* vol. 37, no. 8 (August 1987), pp. 666–673.

for 13.5 percent of manufacturing exports other than assembly products in 1981, but they reached 31.5 percent in 1987.[8] The increase in the share of transportation components in the assembly exports rose from 13.0 percent of value added in 1981, to 23.9 percent in 1987. Electrical and electronics products remained the largest category (55.1 percent in 1981, 42.3 percent in 1987), while the leading category of late 1960s-early 1970s, garments, dropped from 10.3 to 6.3 percent of the total.

---

[8]The share of the other leaders were: foodstuffs, 19.8 percent in 1981, 12.4 percent in 1987; petroleum derivatives, 17.8 percent in 1981, 6.0 percent in 1987; metal products, 14 percent in 1981, 12.8 percent in 1987; chemicals 13.3 percent in 1981, 10.3 percent in 1987.

APPENDIX B

Price Elasticity Studies

Among the few efforts to consider the importance of supply as well as demand in explaining the level of manufacturing exports have been those studies which estimate the price elasticity of supply, derived from econometric manipulation of data on realized exports taken from different points in time. For a review of such estimates for Argentina, Brazil, Colombia, as well as these and other estimates for Peru, and comments as to their possible limitations, see Daniel M. Schydlowsky, Shane J. Hunt and Jaime Mezzera, *La promoción de exportaciones no tradicionales en el Perú* (Asociación de Exportadores del Perú, Lima, 1983), Ch. III.

The usefulness of such estimates of price elasticities of supply depends upon the success in adjusting for changes in (1) domestic demand and (2) domestic productive capacity, as well as (3) the degree of disaggregation in the estimates. It further depends upon (4) the degree to which producer decisions to export and thus, in most cases, simply to accept prevailing international prices, reflects the willingness of those enterprises which use a markup pricing strategy in domestic markets to accept a price for sales abroad generally allowing not only for the equivalence of a lower markup than they seek in the domestic market, but for variations in that "markup" as well.

The second factor, domestic productive capacity, is often difficult to estimate. The possible problem of the fourth factor, relating to pricing strategy, is as a rule not even acknowledged. Many firms may decide to export not precisely on the basis of marginal cost and revenue calculations but, rather, after determining whether the international prices that they would have to accept provide as high a margin above out-ofpocket costs as they deem necessary to justify sales abroad at the time in question. This margin—or export market equivalence of the domestic markup strategy—may fluctuate over time, declining, for example, if a country experiences a sharp drop in the level of domestic demand, or if the drop extends beyond a second year, or if the long-term outlook seems more clouded than before, or if the international opportunities seem more limited (or the international competition becomes more severe) than before, or even if the composition of exports shifts towards products which producers have generally exported at prices that reflect markup equivalents different than (usually less than) the average for all products they export (or have exported).

In all of those cases, the data on exports would not reflect points on the same supply curve, even if the year-to-year differences in new productive capacity have been properly gauged; thus, the resulting "price elasticities" reported in studies such as those cited reflect changes not only in prices, but in marketing strategies or in the composition of exports. The same line of reasoning would hold even more strongly for those products in which the Latin American producer was a price maker rather than a price taker.

Implicit in the above is that for many Latin American manufacturers exporting is a residual activity, undertaken only to the degree that there is "surplus" production or capacity. This attitude is fostered in part by (1) macroeconomic policies which often have an anti-export bias, and, at best, provide erratic incentives to export, in part by (2) a kind of inertia due to the fact that many producers only have had experience selling in domestic markets, and, in part by (3) a lack of conviction on the part of firms that have not exported that they can produce at costs low enough to make exporting profitable for a major share of enterprise output. The latter, when true, is based on a variety of factors, and while almost all of them would be overcome in the long run by a more competitive market environment (e.g., with decreased protection), in the short run, auxiliary measures also may be required to avoid an overnight demise of enterprises such as occurred in Chile and Argentina in the 1970s: some of the casualties there might well have attained an internationally competitive position if economic liberalization had been handled differently (accompanied perhaps by special studies on the probable impact of trade liberalization, industrial extension services and reemployment training programs).

APPENDIX C

Selecting Projects for Detailed Appraisal

A first step in selecting projects for detailed appraisal might be to estimate the effective rates of protection—the net incentives—for two points in time, three to five years apart, reflecting comparable points in an economic cycle (each representing a year similar in terms of peak or trough). Though admittedly a major task in itself, this would allow some rough estimation of the responsiveness of different product groups to given levels of incentives.

The second step—the first really essential one—would be to evaluate point-in-time efficiency (e.g., by estimating domestic resource costs) for most of the principal product groups, based on a recent year of a cyclically intermediate character or, if that is impractical, on the most recent year. A second such efficiency analysis should be undertaken for a previous, cyclically comparable year. This would provide some background against which to estimate the impact on future costs of changes in capacity utilization, increased economies of scale, and the other major factors noted in Chapter I, for each of the various product groups, in the context of the particular circumstances—the level of industrial development and economic infrastructure, and the institutions and behavioral responses—of the country in question. But it is likely to be so hard to disentangle the multiple effects that great caution would have to be taken in using the results.

The next—and key—step would be the modification of domestic resource cost rankings by estimating the effects of each of the six categories noted in Chapter I on each product line, thus making possible a new relative ranking.

Increased Capacity Utilization

Increased capacity utilization can be taken into account by estimating
the previous unit costs of, say, the more efficient plants at higher (and
even at lower) levels of capacity utilization, and combining the result
with (1) original cost data provided by equipment manufacturers, and,
perhaps, (2) information (possibly a rough estimation) concerning the
relative changes in unit costs in comparable facilities in the same country
or in other countries which operate at different levels of capacity. The
standard of full capacity utilization might be three shifts, 365 days a
year, minus the time required for other than on-the-job maintenance,
with modification where such operation would require imports of raw
materials that are cost prohibitive because of their low value-to-transport
ratio or their unavailability from any location in the world at certain
times of year. In addition, in view of the difficulty of initiating exports
from recently industrialized countries and the risk inherent in relying
on exports for more than, say, a third of output, note should also be
taken of the (smaller) reduction in unit costs which would accompany
production at levels no more than say 50 to 100 percent greater than
that likely to be demanded by the national market (or the market of
the subregional grouping, if strong preferences apply in the latter).

Improved Operational Efficiency

The potential gains—the gap to be closed—vary greatly from product
to product, and information on the size of the gap (and the cost of
closing it) is often incomplete. Careful estimation would be costly and
the cost not always justified, but rough estimation could probably be
effected much more readily with a team of two or three knowledgeable
engineers and administrators and a coordinating economist. It would be
of greatest relevance for the facility with optimal plant size and technology. In other cases it would be necessary to make a judgment as to
whether the efficiency problem of the product line in question would
be likely to be greater, lesser, or equal in a facility (or facilities) which
were more nearly optimal. An analysis of point-in-time efficiency for
more than one year would be unlikely to be of much use unless there
was then (or once had been) little difference between local standards
and best practices.

Economies of Scale Through Increased Product Specialization

Estimation of this factor could be drawn in part from a number of
published sources, but would probably have to rely on expert opinion

in most cases. The accuracy of the estimates would doubtless fall somewhere between that of the first two factors. However, even very approximate assessments would be quite valuable because of the differences in importance of this factor (and the following one concerning economies of scale) from one product line to another.

Economies of Scale as a Consequence of Larger Plants, Multiplant Operation, and Wider Distribution

Estimation of this factor probably would also have to rely on scattered published sources and, more than anything else, on expert opinion such as that reflected in Appendices E and F.

More Appropriate (i.e., More Efficient) Production Technology

It would be necessary to rely on expert opinion even more than in the above two cases, augmenting the latter with relevant published materials.

The Benefits of Externalities Such as Those Provided by the Learning Curve and the Costs of Others Such as Environmental Pollution

Published sources and expert opinion would be the leading sources of information in this case as well. Given the variation, even under optimal circumstances, of such factors as the contribution of learning, it probably would be best to deal with this factor (and one or two other major externalities appropriate for the products under consideration) by breaking down their favorable or unfavorable effects by range—as, e.g., (a) probably equivalent to less than 3 percent of average production costs; (b) probably equivalent to 3 or more but less than 10 percent of average production costs; (c) probably equivalent to 10 or more but less than 25 percent of costs; and (d) probably equivalent to 25 percent or more of costs.

Interdependencies and Bottlenecks

A first approximation to dealing with interdependencies might be attempted along the following lines. Initial estimates of the potential improvement in the cost of each of the products might be revised for those products whose inputs from the other products analyzed was, say, 20 percent or more of the value of all inputs, where the cost or those inputs was estimated to have a potential for declining by more than, say, 20 percent in optimum size production runs in MOS plants. That would incorporate the effects of the major interdependencies. Similar note should be taken of major bottlenecks, and some estimate should be made of the extent to which, or the time during which, those bottlenecks would impede the realization of the potential for reduced costs.

Final Comments

To provide a test run of this approach to identifying projects that are good candidates for more detailed cost-benefit analysis, one might analyze the impact of the six factors—and the bottlenecks—on a group of perhaps five products in the middle range of the initial point-in-time efficiency ranking, though in that case, given the small group of products taken into consideration, the approach outlined here would cover fewer of the important interdependencies.

Even such rough and ready guidelines should lead to indicators likely to point in the right direction—and likely to provide fewer "false signals" in identifying product lines worth further study than various methodologically more explicit approaches, all of which omit some key variable which may influence potential competitive strength.

APPENDIX D

Ascertaining the Role of Changes in X-Efficiency in Facilitating Industrial Exports

In the case of the Colombian metalworking industries, a study to ascertain the role of changes in x-efficiency in facilitating industrial exports might have focused on, say, five specific products, at least three of which were being exported at significant levels by the late 1970s, and at least one of which was not exported during the decade.

In attempting to estimate changes during the course of the 1970s in the gap between feasible production and distribution costs and the larger costs actually incurred in specific metalworking industries in Colombia (and in ascertaining how this gap was reduced to more nearly approximate the smaller gap between minimum feasible and actual costs in more advanced industrial economies), the following might have been considered insofar as they are deemed important for each of the five products selected:

1. The degree to which the technology incorporated standard, best practice adjustments to local conditions;
2. The adequacy and efficiency of plant layout;
3. The efficiency of work methods and machine utilization, including the degree to which it might have been possible to improve efficiency by utilization of certain additional equipment or raw materials of the same type;
4. The adequacy of worker, machine and process specialization (including subcontracting);
5. The degree to which dies were constructed of materials or in a

manner to have a life consistent with financial advantage, given anticipated demand patterns;

6. The adequacy of materials handling;
7. The adequacy of quality control and the means of dealing with product rejects;
8. Waste control;
9. On-the-job training;
10. Worker supervision;
11. Inventory control;
12. Warehousing of finished products;
13. Marketing efforts;
14. Physical distribution;
15. Repair and maintenance of plant;
16. Repair and maintenance of products (customer service);
17. Cost and certainty of access (or repayment period) of financing; and
18. Adequacy of decision-making guidelines (including sufficient flexibility).

Inquiry on these points would cover a wide scope but might tend to center on issues related to the gathering and processing of information, on the one hand, and motivation on the other. Account might be taken of changes in the access to information, and in the way in which information was transmitted through the firm, changes in the degree to which information was correctly perceived and fully comprehended, and changes in the manner in which the information was processed in arriving at the judgments which underlie decision-making. It is possible that changes in the access to, perception of, and processing of information would prove to be of very great importance to cost.[1] The primary concern in an initial effort such as suggested here would be to ascertain the extent of changes in x-efficiency levels rather than to explain whether the changes took place because of improvements in information processing or changes in motivation, however.

---

[1]Leibenstein, the economist who coined the term x-efficiency, appears to assign relatively little importance to such information and information processing factors, and much more to motivational considerations (and incomplete contracts) to explain low levels of x-efficiency (efficiency in combining resources after the basic allocational decisions have been made). He stresses lack of worker, foreman or middle management motivation, and notes that what might be termed motivational deficiency can exist at the enterprise, industry or national level. He refers to the costs due to lack of competitive pressures within the plant, and, on the other hand, the frequent lack of sufficient cooperative attitudes, both reflecting deviations from any profit maximizing, cost minimizing model. He states that this behavior may reflect the role of incomplete contracts with employees, a lack of competition from domestic producers and a lack of competition (or potential competition) from foreign producers. The last may be accentuated if there is an absence of government pressure with respect to price, product quality (or need to export).

APPENDIX E

Estimates of the Economies of Scale for Industries

Motor Vehicles

The motor vehicles industry is of great importance for developed and developing industrial economies. The industry also has many characteristics common to other second phase export industries which are being developed in Latin America. These characteristics include heavy product development costs, the need for expertise in manufacturing complex products and strict quality-control requirements.

Although a fair amount of research has been done on economies of scale in the industry, hard data on their magnitude is rather limited. Nevertheless, the clear message obtained from writings about the economies of scale for motor vehicles is that they are large, and this conclusion is supported by the structure of the industry and further confirmed by ongoing changes in that structure. The dimensions of scale to which economies of scale relate are set out in Table E.1 (a). The economies of scale are concentrated in:

(a) the development costs of new and improved models which are related to the total output of the models and can be spread over the total amount;

(b) production costs for components, particularly bodies, engines and transmissions; and

(c) research and development costs to keep up with world standards of fuel consumption and emission control.

Table E.1 (a) Motor Vehicles, Cars

Dimension	Cost	Significance of economies of scale	Countering the disadvantages of small scale
Firm			
Firm and size of industry in a country.	Materials	Not the main source of economies	
	Components	Component suppliers can achieve substantial economies of scale up to outputs of at least 1 million units a year.	Importing components for which economies of scale are large. Use of second-hand equipment.
Production:			
Output of models	Labor capital and overhead costs	The spreading of development and tooling costs provide scope for substantial economies of scale to outputs of 1 million units a year.	Collaboration with (or ownership by) an overseas producer, following and copying developments made by world leaders.
Output of factories	Ditto	The optimum size of factories varies for operations; for engines the MOS is a million units a year; for assembly 0.25 million units a year.	Use of second hand machinery, dies, etc.,
Output of firm	Ditto	The main source of economies is spreading design and development costs for models.	As for models.
Firm			
Advertising and promotion	Selling and marketing	Substantial source of economies.	
Salesmen		Not significant.	
Brands		Substantial source of economies	
Distribution network		Ditto; spare parts have to be available throughout a market prior to sales.	
Firm	Research and development	There are substantial economies from spreading research and development expenditure.	
Ditto	Shipping	There are significant economies from using special ships for transporting cars to distant markets.	Collaboration with an overseas producer.
Other determinants of competitiveness:	An important determinant of market success.		
Production efficiency, styling, quality and reliability of products			

Sources:

(1) The author's knowledge of the industry, including *Economies of Scale in Manufacturing Industry.*   (2) K. Bhaskar, *The Future of the U.K. Motor Industry* (London: Nichols Publishing Co., 1979).
(3) Jack Baranson, *Automotive Industries in Developing Countries* (Washington: World Bank, 1969).   (4) *W.D. Rose, Development Options in the New Zealand Motor Car Assembly Industry* (New Zealand: 1971).
(5) L.J. White, *The Automobile Industry Since 1965* (Cambridge Mass.: Harvard University Press, 1971).

Cars

Most of the available quantitative estimates of the economies of scale for cars are now rather out of date. The following sets of estimates were made in 1970. Costs are affected by the range of models made as well as the total number of units produced.

After reviewing the evidence, Dunnett concluded that the MES of production has increased from in excess of 150,000 units a year in 1950 to in excess of one million units in the 1970s. He summarized estimates of firm economies of scale which for research and development and sales continued to a scale of five million units a year.[1] Nicholas Owen suggested larger scale economies for increases in scale between one and two million units a year given a range of four models, with unit costs falling by seven percent over this range of scale.[2] However, a recent estimate gives a lower MOS level for a firm manufacturing cars. Müller *et. al.* estimates the MOS to be 500,000 cars a year with unit costs 10 percent higher at one-third this scale.[3] This MOS output is similar to that of Mercedes and BMW.

The success of General Motors (GM) relative to its smaller domestic rivals in the U.S.A., at least until the 1980s, and the increasing concentration of the European industry, support my estimates that significant economies of scale apply to levels of production up to, and above a million units a year. Ford and the leading Japanese companies which have dented GM during the 1980s have outputs of several million vehicles a year. Superficially, the prosperity of Volvo, Saab, Mercedes Benz and BMW with outputs of 100,000 to 500,000 units a year would seem an anomoly. The explanation is that they have large shares of a segment of the market, namely that for quality cars, and the first three companies can spread some R&D costs to commercial vehicle production.

Components

The manufacture of cars is an 'assembly' industry which uses a wide range of components. Economies of scale for these components are usually analyzed in groups; bodies, engines and transmissions, castings and forgings. This is not a complete list of components. Most automobile producers manufacture bodies, engines and transmissions, and econo-

---

[1]Peter J.S. Dunnett, *The Decline of the British Motor Industry* (London: Croom Helm Ltd. 1980).
[2]Nicholas Owen, *Economies of Scale, Competitiveness, and Trade Patterns Within the European Community* (Oxford: Oxford University Press, 1983).
[3]Jürgen Müller et. al., *Empirische Untersuching von Industriellen Grossenvorteilen* (Berlin, 1985).

Table E.1 (b)   Unit Costs for Automobiles

Annual production	Relative unit cost
50,000 units	120
100,000 units	110–115
200,000 units	103–105
400,000 units	100
800,000 units & up	99 +

Sources: L.S. White, *The Automobile Industry Since 1945* (Cambridge, Mass: Harvard University Press, 1971), and this author's estimates.

Table E.1 (c)   Illustrative Estimates of Costs and Scale for the Production of One Basic Model and its Variants[a] 1970

Output (thousands per year)	100	250	500	1,000
Initial costs for model £ million	15	20	28	38
		Costs per Vehicle £		
Initial costs	38	20	14	10
Materials and components bought out[b]	265	250	240	235
Labor (direct and indirect)	102	90	86	83
Capital charges for fixed and working capital	60	53	50	48
Total ex-works costs	465	413	390	376
Index	100	89	84	81

[a]A production run of 4 years is assumed, and the basic model is assumed to be in the range—1,000–1,200 ccs.
[b]The estimates of economies for material and component purchases which we obtained from firms varied. Some estimates suggested that these economies would be smaller than those shown and others that the economies would be greater. It is assumed that the total output of suppliers is not affected by the purchases of the firm considered.
Source: Pratten, *Economies of Scale in Manufacturing Industry*,Table 14.3.

Table E.1 (d)   Illustrative Estimates of Costs and Scale for a Range of Models (Consisting of three basic bodies with variants, and five basic engines)[a] 1970.

Output (thousands per year)	100	250	500	1,000	2,000
Initial costs for model £ million	40	50	60	80	110
		Costs per vehicle £			
Initial costs	100	50	30	20	14
Materials and components bought out	290	270	255	247	240
Labor (direct and indirect)	120	100	92	87	84
Capital charges for fixed and working capital	75	65	58	53	48
Total ex-works costs	585	485	435	407	386
Index of average costs	100	83	74	70	66
Index of marginal costs		72	65	66	62

[a]Costs have been standardized to be comparable with those in Table E.1 (c). If the range of models included large and sophisticated models this would, of course, raise average costs per unit, but we have ignored this factor.
Source: Pratten, *op. cit.*, Table 14.4.

Table E.1 (e) Body Shells*

| Annual Output ('000) | Index of Body Costs | | | Unit Material Costs | Unit Operating Labor Costs |
| | | | Expected Life of Basic Model | | |
	2 years	5 years	10 years	(2-year life)	(2-year life)
25	100	78	70	100	100
50	86	70	66	100	97
250	64	58	57	97	90
500	57	56	55	96.5	80
1000	56	55	54	96	80

*The costs include tooling, materials, labor, depreciation and other works overheads, and are for the production of body shells; i.e. they include the cost of assembling panels. For the purpose of making these estimates, it is assumed that the total output of the factory at which the body is made is not affected by the output of this model. No allowance is made for interest on capital.
Source: Pratten, *op. cit.*, Table 14.2.

Table E.1 (f) Lines to Machine Engine Blocks

Annual capacity (thousands)	25	100	250	500	1,000
	Index Numbers of Costs per Engine				
Capital charges	173	100	60	60	60
Operating costs	129	100	80	80	80
Operating costs and capital charges	155	100	64	64	64

Source: Pratten, *op. cit.*, p. 138.

Table E.1 (g) Economies of Scale for Tractor Production

Annual output	20,000	60,000	90,000
Cost per unit US$[a]	3,875	3,412	3,121
(index)	100	88	80.5

[a]The 'cost' covers all factory costs, including a 7 1/2 percent return on invested capital and all administrative costs at factory level. It does not cover the costs of developing and designing a line of tractors.
Source: Canadian Royal Commission on Farm Machinery, *Special Report on Prices of Farm Tractors and Combines in Canada and Other Countries* (Ottawa, 1969).

mies for these components are included in the earlier estimates of economies of scale for cars production. The scale economies are pronounced for these components and extend to high rates of production. Tables E.1 (e) and (f) show my estimates of economies of scale for body shells and engines and transmissions made circa 1970. It is not only these components for which economies of scale apply. One source of GM's success is the economies of scale it achieves for the vast range of components it uses. In the future, economies of scale for the complex electronics which will be installed in cars will be of increasing importance.

Table E.1(e) illustrates an important feature of initial costs. These can be spread either by making many units during a short period, or by extending a model run over a longer period of time. The figures indicate that an output of a million units is required to achieve the main economies of scale for body production costs, but this can be spread over two years (500,000 per annum) or five years (200,000 per annum).

Risks

White emphasized GM's advantages for absorbing risks, particularly in designing and marketing a range of models.[4] A company tied to one model is likely to meet unfavorable market reaction in some rounds of model changes and have difficulty surviving the set back. Volvo has shown one strategy for circumventing this problem, it has been able to market an unchanged basic body shell. Also the introduction of robots facilitates the production of a range of models and reduces the disadvantages of producing a range of models in low volume.

Other Motor Vehicles

With respect to light commercial vehicles, for which many components are shared with cars, economies of scale are very similar to those for cars and the industry is realistically viewed as a part of the car industry.

The structure of heavy commercial vehicle production has been more fragmented than that of cars, although in recent years there has been a rapid movement towards global concentration. The main explanation for the greater fragmentation is the diversity of market requirements: many commercial vehicles are specials. For standard trucks, chasis, engines and components, economies of scale are at least as significant as for cars. Output is much lower so costs fall steeply with increases in scale but material costs are a larger element of costs because of the size of products—a factor reducing the economies of scale.

Rhys estimated the difference in costs of UK manufacturers with outputs of 1–3000 and 30–50,000 units as 25 percent; there was a reduction in costs of 25 percent between the two rates of production for the manufacture of similar products. The diagram drawn by Rhys to illustrate these estimates suggests that economies of scale are not exhausted at the higher rate of production.[5] A study by Müller and Owen indicates economies continuing to an output of 250,000 trucks a year with costs 12 percent higher at one-third of this scale.[6]

Nicholas Owen has emphasized the advantage of the larger scale producer to be able to produce a greater range of products and to offer

[4]L.J. White, *op. cit.*, p.44.
[5]D.G. Rhys, "Heavy Commercial Vehicles: The Survival of the Small Firm." *Journal of Industrial Economics* vol. 20(3), July, 1972, pp. 230–52.
[6]Jürgen Müller and Nicholas Owen, *Economic Effects of Free Trade in Manufactured Products Within the EC: A Pilot Study of Some German Industries.* Report of a Study for the Commission of the European Communities (Berlin, November 1983).

quick and reliable delivery dates. Developments in information technology have eased the problems of controlling large manufacturing operations and have reduced the potential disadvantages for managing and controlling large scale operations. He estimates that unit costs fall by 16 percent between scales of 20 and 100,000 units a year.

In Britain the manufacturers with output of a few thousand units a year brought out more components than their competitors with larger scale. They concentrated on segments of the market. During the 1970s they were squeezed by the leading European producers.

Economies of scale for tractors are similar to those for trucks. The following estimates were published in 1969 and are based upon North American costs.

The study by Müller and Owen estimated the MOS for the production of combine harvesters at 20,000 units a year. Costs were 8 percent higher at half the MOS.[7]

Latin American Countries

So far the evidence relates to developed countries. Production scales for many vehicle producers in Latin America are below 100,000 cars a year at which the estimates made by White and myself begin. It is generally agreed that unit costs rise sharply below this rate of production. Perhaps the main correction to the estimates required to adapt them to Latin American conditions is to allow for a more restricted supply of components from specialist manufacturers; that effectively increases the economies of scale and lowers wage costs, which dampens the advantages of scale compared to those enjoyed by large producers in developed countries.

Economies of scale are one source of competitiveness in export markets. In the case of motor vehicles, efficiency and the quality of products are also very important. The estimates suggest that the economies of scale with respect to production are not an impenetrable barrier to exports from the larger Latin American countries. Economies of scale with respect to marketing and distribution in export markets are important. A comprehensive spare parts and servicing network is required in each new market. Initial costs are incurred in establishing such a network and economies of scale apply to its operation.

The focus has been on economies of scale relevant to standard products, cars and trucks. There are numerous niches in the motor vehicles market; luxury cars, sports cars, cross-country vehicles, special trucks, etc. The Japanese industry broke into world markets for standard products first and then tackled the special markets. This may not be the

---

[7]*Ibid.*

only approach for Latin American countries. In some respects developing countries have greater advantages for the labor intensive specialized products because of their low labor costs. Their disadvantage lies in the lack of skills and knowledge. The development of vehicles for special market segments should not be ignored, however.

Home Appliances

The home appliance industry developed simultaneously with motor vehicles, and it has a number of features in common with that industry. It is an assembly industry, and economies of scale play an important role in the production of components.

The dimensions of scale to which economies of scale relate in refrigerator production are listed in Table E.2 (a). Assembly is not the main area in which to pursue economies of scale; these relate to the production of motors and other components and to press work. Both the output of models and the total output of a factory affect costs of production. Nicholas Owen has obtained evidence that economies of scale extend to higher rates of output for washing machines than for refrigerators. As for the motor vehicle industry, increasing concentration in the European industry supports the conclusion that considerable economies of scale are at work.

Machinery

Machinery leads the list of exports from the developed industrial countries and accounts for a small share of LDC exports. The importance of the industry is brought out in the following: "Within manufacturing the chief difference between the developed and developing countries is that the former concentrate on the engineering industries."[8] The manufacture of machinery is an important part of the engineering industries.

Characteristics of machinery production are the relatively small number of each product manufactured and wide range of specifications covering diverse applications. The quality of products and their reliability are also very important. Breakdowns in use can be expensive in relation to the capital cost of machinery. A consequence of these characteristics of machinery manufacture is the critical role of skilled and experienced design and manufacturing staff. One key to German success in this industry is excellent apprenticeship training. Since the 1970s the industry has also been marked by the introduction of electronics. Pioneering the use of electronics has enabled new firms to enter some

---

[8]R.A. Batchelor et. al.; *Industrialization and the Basis for Trade* Economic and Social Studies no. 32 (London: Cambridge University Press 1980), p 97.

Table E.2 (a) Domestic Appliances

Dimension	Cost	Significance of economies of scale	Countering the disadvantages of small scale
Firm	Materials and components	Up to ¼ million units a year, moderate economies, with potential economies up to 1 million units a year.	The availability of good quality, price competitive components would be an important determinant of the economies of scale and competitiveness of production in an LDC.
Plant-batch size or length of production runs	Labor capital and overhead costs	Tooling costs are substantial. (1) (3) A significant source of economies for long runs is that rejects are reduced. (1)	As for cars there is scope for dampening the disadvantages of small scale by importing components, collaboration with or ownership by an overseas producer and by the use of second hand equipment.
Capacity of factory	Ditto	For a factory making two types of refrigerators the MOS would be 1–2 million units a year. For a factory making two models of washing machines it would be 800,000 units a year. (3) (4)	
Firm	Selling and marketing		Exporters to the UK can sell to multiple retailers. Some multiple chains provide or arrange for servicing.
Advertising		Moderate. (1) (2)	
Salesmen		Slight because there is a limited range of outlets in the UK. (2)	
Brands		Moderate; brands can add 1–8% to wholesale prices. (2)	
Servicing facilities		A source of significant economies for other white goods. (2)	
Range of models		Distributors handle a limited range of models and it is difficult to break into the market.	
Firm	Research and development	Slight to moderate. (1)	
Other determinants of competitiveness: Prompt delivery Styling		Not very important in the past, but of increasing importance.	

Sources:
(1) F. M. Scherer et al., *The Economies of Multi-Plant Operation: An International Comparison Study* (Cambridge, Mass: Harvard University Press, 1975).
(2) The author's knowledge of the industry.
(3) J. H. Hatch, *Competition in the British White Goods Industry, 1954–64*, (4) Jürgen Müller and Nicholas Owen, *Economic Effects Free Trade in Manufactural Products Within the EEC* (Berlin, 1983).

segments of the market, and is a source of competitive advantage of Japanese machinery manufacturers.

The main dimensions of scale to which economies relate are shown in Tables E.3 (a), (b) and (c) for those groups of machinery, turbo generators, machine tools and printing presses.

Although the machinery industry characteristically manufactures products in relatively small numbers, there are substantial differences. For example, certain Japanese firms produce 300 units of a standard model of a machine tool a month, while many machine tool firms make only two or three units of a specialized model each month. At the high rates of production, manufacture can be automated and different techniques of production used; these result in substantial cost savings provided the capacity of plant and machinery can be utilized.

The main point about economies of scale as they apply to machinery is that they are not exhausted for most types of machinery at the scales achieved. Each doubling in the production of a model will bring cost reductions. For manufacturers in advanced countries innovation is required to enter and maintain a place in these industries. This is generally more difficult for manufacturers in LDCs. The card for LDC producers to play, is lower costs, particularly lower labor costs, but it is less likely to win in those industries where the competition can respond with complex products made in advanced industrial countries.

Economies of scale and a shortage of technical know-how will generally keep the machinery industries in the third wave of export industries for LDCs to enter, though there will be many exceptions. Low costs may give a competitive edge for products which are not evolving rapidly—mature products—and for applications for which advanced or complex products do not give an advantage.

Engineering Components

Bearings

This section concerns itself with the components used by three groups of industries described previously. Like other components, bearings are made in a wide range of sizes and types. The output of different types of bearings generally varies in inverse proportion to size. The industry is dominated by multinational companies and both SKF and Timken operate in Latin America.

The dimensions of scale are listed in Table E.4. The main economies relate to the rate of output of types and sizes of bearings. Estimates of the economies of scale for the industry made by the companies in it suggest that these economies are substantial and persistent, so that Eu-

Table E.3 (a) Turbo Generators

Dimension	Cost	Significance for economies of scale	Countering the disadvantages of small scale
Firm	Materials and components	The main economies for material and component costs relate to the output of each design.	For purposes of manufacturing for domestic markets, licensing agreements reducing the cost of R&D, and purchasing of some components from the licensor would further reduce the diseconomies of a small output. This strategy would preclude or limit entry to export markets. The markets for generators are limited by national utility companies which favor local suppliers.
Plant-output of a design and rate of output of a design (the output of a design may be spread over a short or long period).	Labor, capital and overhead	The two main sources of economies of scale for large outputs of a design are the spreading of initial costs and learning. These economies also apply to the rate of output. An important source of economies related to the total output of a factory is the use of special purpose machinery. For the production of 1,000 MW generators the MOS scale is about 10,000 MW a year.	
Firm	Selling and marketing	Many home markets are restricted to domestic suppliers. In import markets which are open to competition, there are substantial costs for establishing a position to tender and preparing tenders.	
Firm	Research and development	All the companies operating in the industry in developed countries are diversified electrical companies. This enables the companies to withstand the sharp fluctuations in demand and carry heavy R&D costs.	

Sources:
(1) A. J. Survey and J. H. Cheshire. *The World Market for Electric Power Equipment* (Sussex, 1972).
(2) The author's knowledge of the industry.

Table E.3 (b) Machine Tools

Dimension	Cost	Significance for economies of scale	Countering the disadvantages of small scale
Firm Plant-batch size or length of production run.	Materials Labor, capital and overhead costs	Slight For many types of machine tools there are large economies of scale obtained by spreading the initial costs of design and development. Different techniques for larger output also make economies of scale possible in machining large batches of components.	The range of machine tools is immense. The economies of scale for simple machine tools are less, especially because they are not subject to rapid development.
-size of factory	Ditto	The MOS size of factory depends on the type of products, but for many types it is less than 500 employees.	
Firm	Selling and marketing	Promotion costs significant for some sectors of the industry.	Exporters to the U.K. can sell via distributors.
Advertising and promotion including trade fairs Salesmen Brands Firms	Research and development	Not significant. Slight source of advantage. Development important for many types of machine tools.	
Other determinants of competitiveness Reliability, Design		The quality of designs and their reliability are important sources of competitiveness.	

Source:
1. The author's knowledge of the industry.

Table E.3 (c) Printing Presses

Dimension	Cost	Significance for economies of scale	Countering the disadvantages of small scale
Firm	Materials	Small or negligible in developed countries.	In LDCs, steel of satisfactory quality may not be readily available.
Plant-batch size and length of production runs	Labor, capital and overhead costs	In machining large batches, substantial economies are derived by spreading set up time and using different techniques.	
output of model	Ditto	Spreading development and tooling costs are a substantial source of economies, as is learning.	
-size of factory	Ditto	The total output of presses at a factory determines the scope for using specialized machinery.	
Firm advertising and promotion salesmen brands	Selling and marketing	Not important. Slight.	
Firm	Research and development	Development is an important source of economies for large outputs of a model and range of models. The reliability of presses is of great importance.	The possibilities of licensing apply to printing presses as well as generators with similar effects and consequences.
Other determinants of competitiveness: Reliability			

Sources:
(1) Author's knowledge of the industry.

Table E.4 Bearings

Dimension	Cost	Significance for economies of scale	Countering the disadvantages of small scale
Firm	Materials	Slight at most.(1)	International companies-SKF and Timken are very active in this industry and the former operates plants in many countries.
Plant-batch size or length of production run	Labor, capital and overhead costs	Large economies of scale obtained by spreading set up costs and by using different techniques at progressively higher levels of output.(1) (2)	
-size of factory		Equivalent of 800 employees. Rise in costs at one third MOS, 8.0 percent.(1)	
Firm	Selling and marketing	Brand line preferences.(1)	
Advertising and promotion		Sales force and technical support significant.(1)	
Salesmen			
Brands		Moderate source of advantage.(1)	
Firm	Research and development		Moderate source of economies.(1)

Sources:
(1) F. M. Scherer, *The Economies of Multi-Plant Operation.*
(2) The author's knowledge of the industry.

ropean producers find significant advantage concentrating production of given types at different factories in Europe to serve the European market.

Springs and Fasteners

These industries have not been as closely studied for economies of scale as bearings. However it is unlikely that economies of scale are nearly as important. The scope for mechanizing is less because the range of operations is smaller than for bearings. The number of units produced is larger, especially for fasteners, but there are applications where special sizes and specifications are required. That provides an opening for small firms and factories to specialize. Such firms may have less than 100 employees.

Manufactured Materials

In this section we consider the manufacture of materials, steel, paper and chemicals. The processes used in these industries have some similarities. We start with the steel industry, in which economies of scale have undergone fairly extensive research.

Crude Steel

The introduction of faster production techniques and plants with larger dimensions have, with certain qualifications, greatly increased the economies of scale in the crude steel industry since 1950. Important economies of scale have also been achieved in the handling of materials.[9]

The dimensions of scale are listed in Table E.5. Economies of scale relate to the total output of plants. Again it is the size of markets which limit the economies of scale. For crude steel made via blast furnaces and oxygen converters, economies of scale would extend to at least four million tons and perhaps ten million tons. In part, the extent of the economies of scale depends on the source of materials and the siting of plants. In most countries new plants with this capacity are not practicable. Also for mini-mills converting scrap, the economies of scale are less and the MOS scale much lower.

---

[9]Bela Gold, *Productivity, Technology and Capital* (Lexington, Mass: Lexington Books, 1979) p. 130.

Table E.5 Steel*

Dimension	Cost	Significance for economies of scale	Countering the disadvantages of small scale
Firms	Materials	Significant economies for bulk deliveries of iron ore and coal. Coastal location important.	The economies of scale are smaller for steel made in mini-mills (not from iron ore in blast furnaces).
Plant-production runs	Labor capital and overhead costs	Significant for some finishing operations	
Steelworks	Ditto	MOS 4 million short tons per year. Increase in costs at one-third MOS, 11 percent.(1) For new steelworks to produce hot rolled strip, 10 million tons with costs 25 percent higher at one-third MOS.(3) MOS for integrated steel works 2.6–12 million tons a year. Costs more than 10 percent higher at one-third MOS.(4)	The competitiveness of this process depends on the price of scrap.
Firm -advertising and promotion salesmen brands	Selling and marketing	Customer ties are important.(1) Negligible significance(1)	In the UK steel stock-holders control a significant share of the market and provide opportunities for exporters to the UK to break into the market without heavy preparatory marketing costs.
Firm	Research and development	Slight (although smaller companies have been responsible for some of the most important development in the industry, R&D is the source of advantage for the largest companies).	
Other determinants of competitiveness		Customers require a wide range of sizes and specifications and prompt delivery is important.	
Prompt delivery			

Sources:
(1) F.M. Scherer, The Economies of Multi-Plant Operation.
(2) The author's knowledge of the industry.
(3) T.A.J. Cockerell (in collaboration with A. Silberston), The Steel Industry. Comparisons of Industrial Structure and Performance. Occasional Papers Ser. no. 42 (Cambridge: Cambridge University Press: 1974).
(4) Müller et al. Empirische Untersuchung von Industriellan Grossenvorteilen (Berlin, 1985).
*ingot output. The MOS for a semi-integrated plant making bars only would be much less. The decline in costs between 1 million and 2.5 million tons is only 1 per cent.

Steel Products

The extent of economies for rolling operations varies for different products. Economies are very great for wide strip rolling mills, less for narrow strip and less again for light section, bar and wire mills.[10]

Special Steels

Traditionally, special steels have been made in much smaller quantities than crude steel, and the industry has been fragmented. The economies of scale are considerable; this is not surprising because the processes are of the same type as for crude steel. A factor reducing the economies of scale in relation to total costs is the high value of ingredients for which the economies of scale are low. The rapid movement towards concentration in the European special steels industry supports the view that considerable economies of scale are possible in the industry.

The Paper Industry

The processes used in the paper industry can be likened to those in steel. The availability and movement of materials is important, and processes are carried out in large vessels or tanks and rolling operations. Estimates of costs show economies of scale for newsprint mills falling at 200,000 tons a year, with unit costs falling by about 15 per cent between 100,000 and 200,000 tons. Guthrie has used the survivor technique to estimate the economies of scale for the pulp and paper industry. His analysis does not conflict with estimates that economies of scale continue to scales above 200,000 tons a year.[11]

As in the steel industry, markets limit the scale of plants producing special papers but, in principle, economies of scale apply to large outputs of types of special paper.

Chemicals

Chemicals, too, can be divided between bulk chemicals, sulfuric acid, ethylene, pvc, etc., and speciality chemicals. The division can be compared to that for steel between carbon and special steels, and that of paper into newsprint and special papers. The pattern of economies of

---

[10]A. Cockerill, *The Steel Industry, International Comparison of Industrial Structure and Peformance*, p. 73.

[11]J.A. Guthrie, *An Economic Analysis of the Pulp and Paper Industry* (Washington, 1972).

Table E.6 (a) Fabric Weaving

Dimension	Cost	Significance for economies of scale	Countering the disadvantages of small scale
Firm	Materials	Small or negligible.(1) (2)	
Plant-batch size or length of production run	Labor, capital and overhead costs	Slight to moderate.	
Plant capacity	Ditto	The MOS is 37.5m yds per year. Equivalent to 600 employees in a modern integrated plant. Rise in costs at one-third MOS, 7.6 percent	Economies of scale not a problem
		Slight in UK. Moderate in the USA. (1) (2)	
Firm	Selling and marketing		
Advertising and promotion		Not very important.(2)	
Salesmen		Slight to moderate.(1)	
Brands		Very slight in many sectors of the industry.	Exporters to the U.K. can avoid these economies of scale by selling to multiple stores and mail order houses as well as to converters.*
Firm	Research and development	Slight.	
Firm	Shipping	Important in parts of the market. Rapid response to market demand is important.	Economies of scale not a problem.
Other determinants of competitiveness	Styling		
	Prompt delivery		

Sources:

(1) F.M. Scherer, *The Economies of Multi-Plant Operation.*

(2) The author's knowledge of the industry.

(3) G.F. Rainie, *The Woolen and Worsted Industry,* (Oxford: Clarendon Press 1965).

*The quality end of the market is more subject to brands, so LDC exporters have more difficulty penetrating these segments of the market.

Table E.6 (b) Shoes

Dimension	Cost	Significance for economies of scale	Countering the disadvantages of small scale
Firm			
Plant-batch size or length of production run	Materials	Small or negligible.(2)	Economies of scale not a problem.
Plant: capacity of factory	Labor, capital and overhead costs	Slight to moderate economies depending on the construction of the shoe.(2)	
	Labor, capital and overhead costs	MOS 1 million pairs per year about 250 employees on single shift operation. Rise in costs at 1/3 MOS-1.5%(1)	
Firm-			
Advertising and promotion	Selling and marketing	Moderate.(1)(2)	Exporters to the UK can avoid these economies of scale by selling to multiple stores. But this means exclusion from some segments of the market, e.g. for quality footwear.(1) There are also risks: retailers may switch to other manufacturers and it is difficult to replace a large customer quickly.(2)
Salesmen		Significant.(1)	
Brands		Important in some segments of the market.(1)	
Firm	Research and development	Very slight.(1)	
Other determinants of competitiveness			
Prompt delivery		For fashion shoes, prompt response to buying patterns is required.	
Styling		Important for a large part of the market.(2)	Possible for exporter to use distributors designs.(2)

Sources:
(1) F. M. Scherer, *The Economies of Multi-Plant Operation.*
(2) The author's knowledge of the industry.

scale is also similar, with substantial ones for large plants producing bulk chemicals and potential ones in the field of special chemicals.[12]

Textiles, Clothing and Shoes

This final section deals with industries in which LDCs have taken a large and increasing share of world trade. These industries, textiles and clothing, are ones in which economies of scale do not predominate. Typically, small efficiently operated factories can compete. It is tempting to conclude that, if LDCs can compete successfully in these industries, economies of scale must be the barrier to their doing equally well in the other sectors covered in this survey. This sweeping conclusion is not warranted because textiles and clothing are industries in which technical progress is not so important. The advanced countries have less scope for competing by developing new and improved textile and clothing products.

The two trades taken as examples of the textile and clothing industries are fabric weaving and shoes. The dimensions of scale for these trades are listed in Tables E.6 (a) and (b). Although the economies for batch sizes and production runs are shown to be slight to moderate, the scope for these economies should not be ignored. Where production runs for a fabric or style of shoe can be greatly increased, significant economies can be obtained from learning and using special jigs.

---

[12]The economies of scale for ethylene, sulphuric acid and dyes are described in Pratten, *Economies of Scale in Manufacturing Industry*, Chapter 5.

APPENDIX F

Exports of Latin American Countries and Economies of Scale[1]

This appendix outlines Latin American exports in the period just before the debt crisis, and considers the implications for achieving economies of scale. Salient features of the structure of Latin American exports are brought out by comparing Latin American and EEC exports, and the exports of Latin America and East Asia in the first 3 sections. The implications of the comparisons are outlined in the fourth section.

The EEC and LAFTA

Table F.1 shows the flows of trade between and within LAFTA (the Latin American Free Trade Association—now ALADI) and the EEC. Latin America's exports to the EEC are concentrated in the food, raw materials and "other manufacturing" sectors. Two-thirds of the EEC exports to LAFTA are from the chemicals, machinery and transport equipment sectors. These are sectors which leap to mind as ones en-

---

[1]*Editor's Footnote*: This appendix has the limited purpose of considering the importance of economies of scale in explaining differences between the recent growth of manufacturing exports from Latin America and that from East Asia. For a fuller and differently oriented analysis of Latin American manufacturing exports which uses broader-based definitions of manufacturing exports, see Simón Teitel and Francisco Thoumi, "From Import Substitution to Exports: The Manufacturing Exports Experience of Argentina and Brazil," *Economic Development and Cultural Change*, vol. 34, no. 3 (April 1986), pp. 455–490. For a recent comparison between Latin American and East Asian trade and growth experiences, see Ching-Yuan Lin, "East Asia and Latin America as Contrasting Models," *Economic Development and Cultural Change*, vol. 36, no. 3 supplement (April 1988), pp. S153–S198, and the references cited there.

Table F.1 Trade between LAFTA and the EEC in 1979

	To the EEC $ million	Percentage of total	To LAFTA $ million	Percentage of total	To LAFTA $ million	Percentage of total	To the EEC $ million	Percentage of total
Total trade	*12,460*	*(100)*	*8,794*	*(100)*	*12,859*	*(100)*	*307,729*	*(100)*
Food and beverages	5,251	(42)	1,686	(19)	637	(5)	39,991	(13)
Textile fibers	418	(3)	226	(3)	28		2,104	(1)
Metaliferous ores	1,123	(9)	311	(4)	11		2,865	(1)
Animal and veg. oils and fats	300	(2.5)	209	(2)	19		1,701	(1)
Mineral fuels	1,056	(8)	1,224	(14)	138	(1)	25,052	(8)
Fertilizers	39		67	(1)	19		1,400	(0)
Chemicals	245	(2)	611	(7)	2,115	(16)	36,646	(12)
Machinery and transport equipment	486	(4)	1,607	(18)	6,734	(52)	88,619	(29)
(Passenger cars)					(362)	(3)	19,746	(6)
Other manufactured goods	2,476	(20)	2,525	(29)	2,452	(19)	99,177	(32)
(Textile yarn and fabric)	(311)	(2.5)	(215)	(2)	(131)	(1)	13,811	(4)
(Iron and Steel)	(195)	(1.5)	(363)	(4)	(805)	(6)	15,716	(5)
(Clothing)	(140)	(1)	(143)	(2)	(46)		8,621	(3)

Source: United Nations, *Yearbook of International Trade Statistics,* 1980, vol. 1.

Table F.2   Summary of the Minimum Optimum Scale for Industries

	MOS as percentage of U. S. market		Brazil's Production as percentage of U.S. production	
	No. of observa- tions	Average	No. of observa- tions	Average
1. Consumer goods industries other than those shown below	10	2	6	11
2. Textiles, clothing & footwear	3	0.4	2	23
3. Synthetic fibers	2	9	1	9
4. Raw material processing industries	6	3	4	11
5. Industrial materials & component industries	4	2.5	2	5
6. Products of machinery building industries:				
Consumer goods	3	9	3	18
Capital goods	7	13	2	2

Source: F.M. Scherer, *Industrial Market Structure and Economic Performance*, and William R. Cline, ''Latin America's Stake in Economic Integration,'' in Eduardo Conesa, ed., *Terms of Trade and The Optimum Tariff in Latin America* (Washington: Institute for Latin American Integration and the Inter-American Development Bank, 1984), 195–212.

joying substantial economies of scale. They are also research and development intensive sectors.

The analysis in Table F.2 supports this conclusion. The MOS forms a large percentage of the output for the machine-building capital-goods industries in the United States. Brazil's production of these groups of products is only a fraction of that of the USA, and most other Latin American countries' production, if any, is even smaller. This author's studies pertaining to the production of dyes and special steels suggest that similar relationships apply to many special chemicals and steels.[2]

Latin America and East Asian Countries

The second comparison, shown in Table F.3, is with East Asian developing countries. These countries have been selected for comparison because their export record in recent years has been very good. There is likely to be more to learn about the causes of differences in export performance from comparisons with them, although other international comparisons would be more favorable to Latin American countries.

There are four main points which emerge from this table:

(a) The East Asian countries (apart from Hong Kong) had lower average per capita GNP than the Latin American countries. Since

[2]Pratten, *op. cit.*

Table F.3 Latin American and East Asian Countries Income and Trade 1979

	(1) GNP per capita $	(2) Exports per capita $	(3) Manufacturing exports per capita $	(4) Exports of manufactures as percentage of total* (3) as percentage of (2)	(5) Total exports as percentage of GNP (2) as percentage of (1)[a]
Korea	700	415.3	370.1	89.1	59.3
Taiwan	1050	n.a.	432.6	n.a.	n.a.
(Hong Kong)[b]	(2930)	(2790)	(2684)	(96.2)	(95.2)
Brazil	1300	139	53	38.2	4.1
Argentina	1580	264	65	26.4	4.1
Colombia	650	102	19	18.8	2.9

Source: See Table F.1
[a]The world average was 12 percent.
[b]Data for Hong Kong is shown in brackets as it is a city rather than a nation state.

*If all products which enter into the manufacturing component of national accounts are included as manufacturing exports, this greatly increases the proportion of Latin American exports that are manufactures. See UNIDO, *World Industry in 1980* (New York, 1981), p. 69 and Inter-American Development Bank, *Economic and Social Progress in Latin America 1982: The Export Sector* (Washington, 1982), Ch. 5. Such a definition overstates the relative share of manufacturing exports just as the elimination of all processed foodstuffs and other raw materials in SITC 0–4 understates the relative share of "manufacturing" exports. Some foodstuffs and processed minerals with as much as 50–60 percent manufacturing value added are among the products eliminated from the narrow definition of manufacturing exports. The broader definition of manufacturing exports has not been used because of incomplete data availability and because the manufacturing value added of foodstuffs and processed raw materials is, on average, lower than that of the other manufactures in SITC 5–8. In any event, economies of scale are not as important for foodstuffs and some of the other excluded processed raw materials as for the industries in SITC 5–8. In particular, the economies of scale relating to product development are less important. Processing many products in large plants yields major economies of scale, but even these are not always pronounced in relation to total manufacturing costs. Important economies of scale apply to marketing, selling and distribution in parts of the food industry.

the population of these countries is smaller, the aggregate level of GNP is significantly less than in the Latin American countries shown. (b) Exports per capita of the East Asian countries are over five times as great as those of the Latin American countries. (c) Manufactures represent a far larger proportion of East Asian total exports. (d) Total exports form a larger percentage of GNP for the East Asian developing countries than for the Latin American countries. While only three Latin American countries have been shown, similar conclusions would be drawn were the rest included (see David Morawetz, *Why the Emperor's New Clothes Are Not Made in Colombia*, Oxford: Oxford University Press, 1981).[3] Differences in the

---

[3]Between 1964 and 1974, exports of manufactures from Latin American countries increased by 18 percent per annum. In the latter year they represented 1 percent of world exports. Barend A. de Vries, *Export Promotion Policies*. World Bank Staff Working Paper no. 313, (Washington: The World Bank, 1979), p. 2. Latin American countries increased their share of total developing countries exports of manufactures from 14 to 17 percent (1965–1976). In the same period the East Asian countries increased their share from 38 to 60 percent. Donald Keesing, *World Trade and Output of Manufactures: Structural Trends and Developing Countries' Exports*. World Bank Staff Working Paper no. 316 (Washington: The World Bank, 1979), p. 16.

Table F.4   Manufacturing Exports from Selected Latin American and Asian Countries, CIRCA 1979

Export category	Colombia	Argentina	Brazil	Korea	(Hong Kong)	Japan
			Composition of total exports (in percentages)			
SITC* (0+2)	(76.1)	(66.0)	(53.5)	(9.6)	(2.7)	(2.2)
5	2.1	3.5	2.8	3.3	0.8	5.8
6	8.7	11.1	14.8	32.2	11.6	25.4
7	2.6	8.0	16.0	21.2	16.7	56.8
8	5.4	3.8	4.6	32.4	67.1	8.1
Exports of manufactures as a percentage of total exports of which:	18.8	26.4	38.2	89.1	96.2	96.1
SITC 5	11.2	13.3	7.3	3.7	0.8	6.0
6	46.3	42.0	38.7	36.1	12.1	26.4
7	13.8	30.3	41.9	23.8	17.4	59.1
8	28.7	14.4	12.0	36.4	69.8	8.4
Percentage of exports of manufactures exported to developed countries	40.5	42.1	51.0	72.6	81.9	50.0

Source: Table F.1.
*Standard International Trade Classification. 5: Chemicals. 6: Textiles yarns, iron ore, etc. 7: Machinery and transport equipment. 8: Clothing and other manufactures.

importance of trade and the structure of trade would be expected between the resource-rich Latin American countries and the resource-poor East Asian countries. Nevertheless the scale of the differences is striking.

Analysis of Exports by Selected Countries

This section looks behind these statistics by considering the exports of three Latin American countries in more detail. The aim is to discern major export lines and the major markets for each country's products. The three Latin American countries selected are Colombia, Brazil and Argentina. Korea and Hong Kong from the East Asian developing bloc and Japan are also included for comparative purposes. The comparisons are summarized in Table F.4.

Latin American Countries

Colombia has as its main export coffee, which accounted for 62.5 percent of all its visible exports in 1977.[4] More than 90 percent of coffee exports

---

[4]The years cited are the latest years for which such data were available at the time the initial draft of the chapter was prepared and have been kept as representative of the period prior to the debt crisis.

went to developed markets (with the U.S. and West Germany taking 30 percent each). Only 18.8 percent of total exports were manufactures, with textile yarn (3.4 percent of total exports) and clothing (1.7 percent) being the main lines. Of these manufactures, 41 percent went to markets in developed countries; the main market for manufactures was LAFTA (44.4 percent), and Venezuela alone imported 23.9 percent of Colombian manufactured exports.[5]

Brazil's main commodity export is also coffee—but in 1979 coffee comprised only 15.3 percent of total exports. All foodstuffs accounted for 39.4 percent of total exports. As with Colombia, the vast majority of coffee exports (88 percent) went to developed countries. Iron ore (8 percent of total exports) was also a major export.

Manufactures accounted for 38.2 percent of total exports, and the main market was again the LAFTA bloc (33 percent). Sixty-four percent of Brazil's total exports and 51 percent of its manufactured exports went to developed markets. Non-electric machinery (7.1 percent of total exports) was the largest class of manufactured exports, with textile yarn and iron and steel also large. The latter two exports were mainly sold to markets in developed countries, while the main market for machinery and car exports consisted of the LAFTA countries (44 percent in both cases). Thus the natural resource-based exports went to the developed countries and the more advanced engineering products were sold in the developing countries. This generalization held reasonably well for the exports of most Latin American countries, although Brazil did increase the proportion of its manufactured exports which it sold to the developed countries during the 1970s, and again, dramatically, in 1984. A number of the smaller countries of the Caribbean Basin also have increased the share of their manufacturing exports sold to developed countries, this being attributable to the rise in assembly industry exports.

Argentina sold a smaller percentage of total exports to the developed countries: 58 percent (1978), with the US accounting for only 8.6 percent of total exports (compared to 19 percent for Brazil and 29 percent for Colombia). *LAFTA* countries took 23.7 percent of Argentina's total exports, but 43.4 percent of its manufactures. Europe accounted for 44.1 percent of total exports, but only 23 percent of manufactures. Within total exports, meat and cereal exports were the main lines. They were sold to Europe and the centrally planned economies. The USSR took 21 percent of cereal exports, and a growing proportion of all exports.

While recognizing the special conditions of booming world trade in 1973, it is worth noting that manufactures accounted for a *smaller* pro-

---

[5]*Editor's note*: Most of the exports to LAFTA countries did not benefit from preferential trading agreements, however.

portion of total Argentine exports in 1978 (26.4 percent) than in 1973. Of the 1978 exports, 42.1 percent went to developed countries and 43.4 percent to the LAFTA countries. Only 17.4 percent of Argentina's exports of machinery and transport equipment (SITC 7) went to developed markets.

Asian countries

Korea's export structure has changed dramatically in the postwar period. In 1979, 89.9 percent of total exports were manufactures. Clothing accounted for 19.1 percent of total exports and textile yarn 12 percent, sold mainly to Japan and the US. The Middle East was a growing market.

In contrast to the South American countries, 21 percent of Korean exports were in Division 7 of the SITC—the technically most complex division, including such products as telecommunication equipment, cars and capital goods (equivalent percentages for Latin American countries were Brazil, 16 percent, Argentina, 8 percent and Colombia, 3 percent). Indeed, radios and television sets—skilled-labor-intensive products— were 7 percent of total Korean exports and sold in *developed* markets (44 percent in the US and 27 percent in Europe). In total, 73 percent of manufactures went to developed markets, with Japan taking 18 percent. The Middle East took 10 percent and was a growing market.

Hong Kong exported 82 percent of its goods to developed markets. Of these, 96 percent were manufactures. Clothing (36 percent of total exports) was the main line, but photographic equipment (9.2 percent), toys (9.3 percent) and telecommunication equipment (7.3 percent) were also major exports; all went chiefly to developed markets.

Japanese manufactures form a percentage of total exports similar to those of Hong Kong—96.1 percent—but fewer of Japan's exports go to developed countries. In Japan's case, road vehicles (21 percent) were the main line, with the U.S. as their main market (47 percent). Asia is the market for 39 percent of total Japanese exports compared to 26 percent to the U.S. and 16.8 percent to Europe.

Implications of the Comparisons

Latin American countries depend for up to three-quarters of their export earnings on natural-resource-based exports, which are sold in the developed countries. Manufactures, other than those based on natural resources, typically account for about 25 percent of total exports; approximately 40 percent of these went to other LAFTA countries circa 1978–80. This share has been declining since, particularly in the case of those countries in the region which have experienced the most rapid rates of increase in exports of manufactures during the 1980s. Even Brazil, with its large home market and relatively large share of exports of manufactures, depends on *basic* manufactures (textile yarn, iron and steel). Although there are other important outlets, many of Brazil's capital goods exports are sold mainly to LAFTA countries. Colombia has exported proportionally fewer products based on intermediate and advanced technology and has been more dependent on sales to LAFTA countries (though not always under preferential trade arrangements). Argentine exports of intermediate and higher technology manufactures increased significantly in the 1970s, but most of these declined or stagnated thereafter. In contrast, exports from East Asia have a heavy bias towards manufacturing, compete successfully in developed markets and include sophisticated products, e.g., telecommunication and photographic equipment.

Why is it a matter for concern that, compared to less developed East Asian countries, Latin American countries export a lower proportion of their total GNP, that a lower proportion of their exports is in manufactures, and that a smaller proportion of these manufactures go to the developed countries? Plainly, the fact that Latin America is a resource rich area and East Asia is not accounts for a part of these differences, but we believe, although we cannot prove, that this is only a partial explanation. There are three reasons for concern about the structure of Latin American exports. Each of the three points is considered separately below.

Low level of exports

Simple trade theory says that a country can make substantial gains from trade through specialization in products in which it has a comparative advantage, i.e., those which it can produce more cheaply than its competitors. As well as improving resource allocation in line with comparative advantage, exports increase capacity utilization, exploit economies of scale and lead to faster output growth.[6] Furthermore, the increase in foreign exchange earnings and resultant reduction of bottlenecks in importing intermediate and capital goods brings development advantages.

The corollary of Latin America's low exports has been a high level of import substitution. The latter can be efficient and, indeed, many of Asia's as well as Latin America's export activities began as import-substitution industries. However, much import-substitution investment

---

[6]See Bela Balassa, *Structural Change in Trade in Manufactured Goods Between Industrial and Developing Countries*. World Bank Staff Working Paper no. 396 (Washington: The World Bank, 1980). p. 23.

in Latin America has been undertaken with high and seemingly unending protection, and has led to high costs which have constrained development. Balassa concludes that ". . . trade orientation (towards exports) has been an important factor contributing to the intra-country differences in the growth of GDP; i.e., those with export-oriented policies have grown faster."[7]

Low proportion of manufactures

Suppose that Colombian exports per capita were as high as Hong Kong's. Would there still be concern about trade if 63 percent of the former's exports were coffee (although this would not be a practical possibility, it can be used to illustrate the issues)? An economist's instinctive answer would be no. Patterns of exports reflect different sources of comparative advantage, and Colombia has advantages in the production of coffee. But there would be qualifications. Firstly, the world price for coffee fluctuates wildly, engendering insecurity and providing an unstable base of foreign exchange earnings with which to finance development. In comparison, prices of manufactured goods have been relatively stable — or at least their movement has been predictable. To some extent this problem could be and is being dealt with by diversifying to a range of resource-based industries.

There are other advantages in producing manufactures. The technical know-how, training of qualified and skilled labor and economic integration with more prosperous countries which arise from trading in manufactures brings externalities. This experience opens the possibility of competing with countries producing advanced products with a higher percentage of value added relative to material costs.

Low export share to developed countries

Of the three phenomena noticed in South American export structure, this is least obvious as a problem. Surely a dollar earned exporting to Venezuela has the same value as one earned exporting to Japan (assuming no conversion problems); but we concentrate again on externalities. Exporting to developed markets requires tighter quality control, design awareness, marketing skills, punctuality, etc.; in general, a far stricter attention to production and marketing performance. The necessity for this filters down from the "front line" of exporters and permeates every section of the economy engaged in export supply, including ancillary services, port and customs efficiency, etc. Such things may not

---

[7]Balassa, *op. cit.*, p. 23.

be required to export to other protected developing country markets (see, for instance, *Morawetz, op. cit*). Thus only exports to developed countries may force domestic industries to achieve rigorous quality standards. The recent increase in Latin American exports to developed countries and the reduced protection of many Latin American markets will provide a test of these effects.

Conclusions

Marked contrasts between the product and market structures of the exports of Latin American, EEC and East Asian countries are described in this appendix. The composition of Latin American exports of manufactures, especially to developed countries, has been concentrated on the products of resource-linked manufacturing industries and industries such as textiles, clothing and footwear, for which the economies of scale are generally less important, and away from the industries where the technical economies of scale and costs of development relative to output are large—chemicals, machinery, electronics and vehicles. (We do not intend to imply that the economies of scale are negligible in industries such as food processing, clothing and footwear, just that they are generally smaller and less pervasive than in industries such as chemicals and vehicles. The economies of scale possible in industries such as textiles and clothing are considered in the main text). In contrast, EEC exports are concentrated in products of industries where economies of scale are captured on a permanent basis. Furthermore, Japan and other Asian countries are increasing their exports of these products. Although simple trade theory can account for such differences in the structure of exports, there are reasons for suspecting that these differences operate to the disadvantage of Latin American countries.

APPENDIX G

A Summary of Endogenous Firm Spin-Offs

CONFAB: Equipment division

Learning or spin-off

There is a natural progression in the design and manufacture of increasingly complex but related items of equipment such as varieties of tanks: floating roof tanks, simple pressure vessels, spheres, etc. (for a similar pattern, see Pescarmona).

Mechanisms

(i) Similarity of equipment.
(ii) Accumulation of manufacturing capabilities: manufacturing methods, welding, metallurgical knowledge, etc.
(iii) Development of mechanical design capability, e.g., calculation of thickness relative to stress in tanks; selection of materials.
(iv) Development of a process design capability for certain types of equipment and industries (tanks, fire heaters, and cellulose processing plants).

Remarks

Association with foreign companies is required; the typical sequence is: first, learning how to manufacture; then adapting to local conditions; finally, the company adapts or improves without the licensor's help.

Each type of knowledge or capacity represents a stage in mastering the technology. Mastery of the third stage (design capability), which may be very important for exports, requires the promise of a strong market.

CONFAB: Pipe division

Learning or spin-off

Contribution of early types of pipe and operation of early plants to:

(i) Planning and execution of new investment.
  –Layout
  –Speeding up plant installations (time was cut by half)
  –Designing or specifying new machinery
  –Reducing errors in predicting the cost of investment programs
(ii) Producing and selling pipes with more exacting specifications.

Mechanisms

(i) Operating experience with early plants (A1, A2).
(ii) Experience in planning and executing investment programs (A1, A2).
(iii) Firm reputation effects critical for prequalification (A2).

Remarks

The firm installed 11 pipe plants, starting in 1961. The first two were designed and installed by the firm (including all the machinery) and produced water and petroleum pipes respectively. The third plant produced pipes from steel coil (rather than steel plate) and was based on imported machinery. The modifications introduced in this plant made it possible to produce pipe casings for the expanding oil well market and led to a completely new plant also based on steel coil. In the meantime, another huge plant using steel plate was set up, for which the company planned the layout and designed and constructed most of the machinery. This plant led the firm to develop special steels to reduce the thickness of pipe walls. Later plants produce pipes with more exacting specifications (e.g., coated for low temperatures, off-shore drilling, of X-60 or higher grade steel). This required new steels and new technology.

DEDINI

Learning or spin-off

(i) Diversification from the company's original lines (equipment for the production of sugar and alcohol) to new types of equipment: calcination plants (for the cement industry); basic oxygen furnaces and heat-recovery systems (steel industry); equipment for the paper and pulp, chemical, and petrochemical industries.

(ii) Adaptation of boilers, turbines, and other equipment to other uses and markets, e.g., coal-fired boilers, turbines for the petrochemical industry.

(iii) In the original lines, learning made possible maximum exploitation of market growth after 1973, both at home and in other Latin American countries.

Mechanisms

(i) Accumulation of manufacturing capabilities (A1, A2, A3).

(ii) Similarity of equipment: heat recovery systems for steel plants are similar to boilers; speed reducers for calcination ovens (cement industry) are similar to those used in sugar plants (A1, A2, A3).

(iii) Development of design capability: especially important for sales to non-sophisticated users both at home and abroad (A3).

Remarks

The motive for diversification was market trends. The decision to produce steel equipment was based on manufacturing capabilities (e.g., the firm decided not to produce blast furnaces). In both steel and cement equipment, the company acquired a design capability that enabled it to offer complete plants (in association with a Japanese firm) (A1).

There was no special difficulty in adapting boilers and turbines associated with sugar and alcohol. Coal-fired boilers, in which the company is quite successful, use foreign technology. The company has also made know-how agreements in the area of turbines (A2).

MEITAR APARATOS

The company was established in 1962. Its first product was stainless steel plate heat exchangers for the food industry. It diversified into equipment for processing citrus fruit, milk, tomatoes, etc. In 1973 it exported its first turnkey plant.

Learning or spin-off

(i) Adaptation of basic components for processing of a wide range of goods.

(ii) Adaptation and diversification of equipment. Supply of equipment and plants to a growing range of markets. The firm supplies around 50–60 different types of equipment.

(iii) The first exported turnkey plant paved the way for subsequent ones.

Mechanisms

(i) Similarity of equipment (A1).
(ii) Creation of a network of suppliers of the components needed by the firm—"one learns how to buy" (A2).
(iii) Better knowledge of markets (A2).
(iv) Development of a total project capability, including a design capability (A3).
(v) Firm reputation (A3).

Remarks

The firm created a process engineering department in order to supply its first turnkey plant abroad. This and the reputation acquired helped it to export other turnkey plants (Costa Rica, Colombia, etc.) (A3, B4, B5). The spin-offs were not so great owing to overvaluation of the currency (which severely cut down sales): the engineering team was drastically reduced.

METAL LEVE

The firm was established in 1950. Its first activity was import substitution (automobile pistons). Today it is a major producer of pistons for motor vehicles, aircraft pistons, piston pins, plain bearings, and bushings.

Learning or spin-off

(i) Domestic supply of aircraft pistons made exports possible.
(ii) Exports of aircraft pistons raised overall productivity.

Mechanisms

(i) Access to foreign know-how: the company's success in developing and supplying aircraft pistons to the local market enabled it to obtain a license from a foreign company, which helped in its initial export efforts. Foreign firms were unwilling to provide the technology before the firm succeeded in the local market.
(ii) The introduction of quality control: obtaining FAA approval for sales in the United States involved the introduction of formal quality control procedures, which made it possible to mass produce high-quality bearings and pistons (A2).

(iii) Emergence of a design capability: this probably benefited from quality control. The recently established R&D center was originally staffed largely by personnel from quality control (A2).

(iv) Firm reputation (A1).

Remarks

The value of the spin-off is high since there is a trend to stricter specifications in response to the energy crisis, even though significant complementary investments in physical capital are required.

The technological base, including the capability acquired, enabled the firm to participate in a joint development effort in pistons for alcohol-burning engines (such pistons require tougher materials and a different design, but are not exceptionally difficult to produce).

An important factor in the firm's development was its forecast that market trends would favor heavy duty pistons, which are more difficult to produce (they are larger and require iron-nickel inserts and more precise work because the engines work closer to their theoretical limits).

PESCARMONA

In 1967 the firm began producing a wide range of capital goods: for process industries (tanks, etc.); overhead cranes (from 1969): steel equipment (1971); equipment for nuclear-power stations (1975/76).

Learning or spin-off

(i) The production of heavier and more sophisticated components (e.g., nuclear components) benefited from the prior production of lighter and simpler products.

(ii) Experience with particular processes, such as welding, enabled the firm to produce to more exacting specifications (e.g., the welding required for overhead cranes is simpler than that required for nuclear components).

(iii) Experience with particular lines makes it possible to adapt products to the needs of a variety of users. The original service crane produced by the company in 1969 had a lift capacity of 25 metric tons; the crane supplied in 1977 had a capacity of 380 metric tons. The cranes were supplied to hydroelectric stations, ports, the steel industry, nuclear power stations, etc.

Mechanisms

(i) Accumulation of production experience, e.g., in machining and welding (A1, A2).

(ii) Quality control procedures were very important for the firm's entry into the nuclear components field (A1, A2).

(iii) Firm reputation effects enabled the firm to participate in international tenders for the supply of heavier components and gave it better access to the requisite foreign know-how (A1, A2).

(iv) Similarity of equipment (A3).

(v) Development of a design capability (A3).

Remarks

The firm's decision to produce bigger and more sophisticated products (e.g., nuclear components and water turbines) required an investment of $150 million (A1).

Association with a foreign licensor (Cleveland Crane) was an essential first step in acquiring a manufacturing and later a design capability (A3, B5).

PROMON ENGENHARIA

An engineering consultancy firm founded in 1960. Its initial area of activity was in the process industries (e.g., petroleum refining). Since then it has diversified into aluminum, hydroelectric power, transport, and telecommunications. In 1975 the firm started exporting its services and set up an independent R&D facility.

Learning or spin-off

Learning occurred

(i) Within a particular area, such as the civil engineering aspects of hydroelectric power, where increasingly complex projects were undertaken.

(ii) Across different areas: early activity in process industry projects helped in other engineering projects such as dams.

Mechanisms

(i) Accumulation of a design capability (A1, A2).

(ii) Development of a capability for total project management (A2).

(iii) Firm reputation.

Remarks

The firm always entered a new area in association with a foreign partner from which it acquired a design capability that helped it in subsequent projects (A2); in particular, its ability to offer turnkey plants enabled it to export (B2). Exports also benefited from the firm reputation effect (B3). The firm started exporting hydroelectric projects in 1981 (to Chile, Costa Rica and Nigeria).

TREU

The firm started in 1943, supplying the pharmaceutical industry; in 1968/69 it began to supply the emerging petroleum and petrochemical markets, and since 1979, the nuclear power industry.

Learning or spin-off

(i) Supply of mixers and other equipment to the petrochemical and nuclear power industries benefited from the firm's prior experience in supplying the pharmaceutical industry with similar products.

(ii) Supply of equipment of various types to the petrochemical industry helped the firm to sell equipment to other industries (e.g., mixers to the paper and cellulose industry; small mills to the ink, cocoa, and food industries).

Mechanisms

(i) Manufacturing experience (A1).

(ii) Similarity of equipment: the only difference between different mixers was their size (3 hp for the pharmaceutical industry; 3 to 300 hp for petrochemicals; 3,000 hp for the nuclear power industry). Methods of manufacture and quality control were similar, for example, in machining, casting and welding. Experience with smaller equipment reduces the risk in manufacturing bigger equipment (A1).

(iii) Firm reputation was critical for entering the nuclear components market (A1).

(iv) Accumulation of a design capability: this evolved at a later stage and helped in the adaptation of equipment to other industries (A2).

Remarks

The first trained engineers to be hired (i.e., other than the owners) were engaged in 1970, and quality control and process engineering were developed (B4). The firm predicted that the new nuclear market was coming and prepared itself by investing in a large new tank for full-size mixer testing. The new market reduced excess capacity (i.e., the economic value of the spin-off from past activity is likely to be high) (A1).

AUTHOR INDEX

SUBJECT INDEX